D1554083

DOWNWARDLY

MOBILE

for
CONSCIENCE
SAKE

Edited by

Dorothy N. Andersen

ISBN: 0-931803-03-9 (perfectbound)
Printed in the United States

Book Design:
Vesta Publishing Services
P.O. Box 5474
Eugene, Oregon 97405

Published by Tom Paine Institute, 1993
3120 North Romero Rd. #39, Tucson, AZ 87505

CONTENTS

ACKNOWLEDGEMENTS

I want first to express my gratitude to all of the authors, whose responsiveness and friendliness have made it so enjoyable to be the coordinator of this cooperative effort.

Several readers of an earlier draft of the book made thoughtful, helpful suggestions. This group includes Jim Best, Jack and Felice Cohen-Joppa, Nikki Gray, Elizabeth McLaughlin, Oliver Loud, Mildred Stroop Luschinsky, Paul Hugh Smith, Naomi Stucky, and others. My thanks to them, and to those who simply gave encouragement.

Gwen Rhoads of Eugene, Oregon, designed the cover and advised on formatting.

Thanks to Al -- husband, co-worker, companion -- for essential assistance with the computer and for help in ways too numerous and multifaceted to adequately express. Without him, there would have been no book. I would not have experienced downward mobility a second time; I would not have known most of these authors; I would not be the person I now am.

Dorothy Norvell Andersen, editor

PROLOGUE

My hope in writing this prologue is to turn a casual browser into a reader. So here are the reasons why I collected these stories and why I hope you will want to read them.

There are many warnings -- global warming, the hole in the ozone layer, and growing deserts, to mention only a few -- that we human beings in the industrialized countries are endangering life on the planet by our life styles. Less frequently heard now are the warnings of nuclear war, but such warnings are still relevant as long as nuclear weapons exist and the disposal of nuclear waste remains an unsolved problem. The on-going "conventional" wars and "low intensity conflicts" are as tragic for their victims as war has ever been. Biological and chemical weapons are a present and growing menace. Still less frequently heard are the pleas for justice for the poor, the starving, the oppressed, but these may well be the most urgent reasons of all for changing one's life style; even as I write this, about 35,000 children under the age of five are dying from starvation and its related illnesses every day. Sometimes this tragedy is called "structural violence" because their deaths are an integral part of the way our society is now structured.

The stories in this book were written by people who have changed their life styles in response to these ecological warnings, the evils of war, and the cries for justice. We realize that we are only a few members of the vast family of people who have done so, and we lay no claim to being the most worthy of attention. I did not search for the most dramatic stories; these writers are people in my circle of friends. It was Dorothy Granada who started me thinking about putting together this book when she said in an interview about her life at the time of the Fast for Life, "I seem to be downwardly mobile."

I gave very few guidelines to my friends when I asked them to write, which is one reason why the chapters are so varied. We have common concerns for the environment, for justice, and for peace, but we give them different weights and we respond in different ways to the same concerns.

Even our common response, being "downwardly mobile for conscience sake", is expressed differently by each of us. Here are a few glimpses into each of these responses.

Anne Near, looking back on a long, full life, tells us that she knew, even as a very young child surrounded by wealth and privilege, that that life was not fair and that it would not be the most satisfying to her. Because she has led such an "examined" life and been so aware of the society around her, her chapter also might be called "A Thinking Woman's Journey through (most of) the Twentieth Century."

Kathy Epling, Peg and Ken Champney, and Barbara Terry all share their experiences of simple living in family life. Ken and Peg Champney speak from the perspective of a grown family and stress the great help they have had from a supportive community. They raised a family of five children and two foster children while keeping their income below taxable level by giving away all their earnings above that amount. More than most of the chapters, theirs gives practical advice on simple living.

Kathy Epling, a sensitive poet, writes as a mother presently in the midst of raising young children with all their needs, demands, and questions. "Are we poor?" her little girl asks -- and then answers her own question with "Poor people don't have enough and we have enough, so I guess we aren't poor." Reading Kathy's chapter we see where the child's sweet, enlightened attitude comes from.

The life style Barbara Terry was born into wasn't as luxurious as Anne Near's, but it was definitely well-to-do, and it's mobility was decidedly upward! Her story reminds us that the search for right livelihood isn't always clear. It may require, as it did for her and Warren, many new starts, moves, and job changes.

Jo-ann Jaeckel lets us know we're not alone when we find ourselves inwardly torn by moral dilemmas and in disagreements with our partners as we try to be ecologically and socially responsible. She shares with us some of the ways that she and Sage have worked things out in their rammed-earth home in Northern California.

Juanita Nelson sees so clearly and feels so keenly the connections between her own life and the evils of economic injustice and war that she tries to disassociate herself from the whole "violent U.S. economy". She writes, "I was in pursuit of a life that holds up to the light practically every breath that one breathes in terms of nonviolence, in terms of how the practice meets the preachment." In informal, lively journal entries she shares her life and thought with us.

Charles Gray, deeply concerned about tragic extremes of wealth and poverty, decided in middle age that he should live on the amount of money each person would have if the world's income were equally distributed. He recounts his experiences of living for sixteen years in response to that challenging belief.

Judi Buchman and Richa, like Juanita and Charles, work hard to make their everyday lives consistent with their moral and political values. In addition to offering shelter and companionship to those in great need -- a difficult, but widely approved, task -- they have taken on the very controversial witness of refusing to pay property taxes in order to show us all the connection between our local prosperous economies and poverty in poor countries. They give us a detailed account of their resulting life style.

Alfred Andersen, writing from a philosopher's perspective, searches for ways to assure that power will be used humanely. He is especially concerned with the role major universities play in fostering injustice and the part they could play in developing solutions. Like all the authors, he writes of the effects of his beliefs on his life, but rather than emphasize the personal aspects of solutions he proposes some radical structural remedies. The one I see as most basic is a suggested method for sharing the income from our common heritage -- which includes land, resources, and the contributions of previous generations -- among all the earth's inhabitants.

My own story is included mainly so that you, the readers, can understand the editor's background.

We, the authors, give different names to our respective experiences: simple living, right living, being centered, downward mobility. For each of us the search has been, and is, for a life of social responsibility, moral integrity, and spiritual depth.

My purpose in asking my friends to write about their experiences can be simply stated. I presumed that many people want to be more just to other people and more harmonious with the planet. I thought that if they could read the life stories of personal friends of mine who have been living out these concerns for many years, they wouldn't be so fearful of changing their life-styles to help accomplish these ends. Instead of being fearful -- or maybe in addition to feeling fearful -- they might be excited and happy as one is when anticipating a new adventure..

In addition to those who *want* to change their life-styles for ecological and justice reasons, there are many people who face lower income due to factors completely beyond their control, such as the export of industrial jobs to countries with lower wage rates. We would be happy if our book could also be helpful to them.

We do have one worry. It is that wealthy people, who make decisions about the incomes of others, might point to these writings and say, in effect, "You employees, you homeless people, you welfare recipients don't need any more money. Look at these people. They like being poor." As Juanita Nelson says so pointedly in her chapter, "People who coo about how the poor are so often more content than `we' are don't seem anxious to become poor and happy." We're hoping this book helps each person who reads it in her or his own personal search for a good life; it is not to be used as a weapon with which to lower the incomes of others.

The other authors and I hope this book will play a role, however small, in the great drama of making the changes we as a society need to make. We are glad to be in touch with you through the pages of this book. We hope that you will find us to be friendly companions on a journey we are all making together.

Dorothy Andersen

THE WISDOM

OF A CHILD

A LONG JOURNEY

FROM ONE CLASS TO ANOTHER

Anne Near

The title language, *downwardly mobile*, floats upstream against the dreams of a nation of immigrants. It offends our inculcated shape of mind. Our literature is rich in testimonial stories about parents who worked sacrificially so that their children could go to college or in some other way qualify for lives that would not be burdened by labor for someone better off, so that their offspring, or they themselves, could be that more affluent person. Without denigrating the generous and spiritual aspects of those hopes, we must recognize that educational goals have been associated with the goal of economic access and an upward change of class. Not so for me.

This is not to forget that bare survival was the primary struggle -- often lost -- for thousands who came to this land in chains or fleeing persecution or to challenge a poverty preordained by birth. I do not presume to plumb the pre-invasion consciousness of the aboriginal Americans whose culture expresses an awesome comfort within creation, but one can infer that *upward mobility* was not their concern. It was the European man who tried to get ahead. He did not worry much about depleting the apparently boundless resources "discovered" in the "new world". His idea of frugality seems to have been a moral one, deriving not from an awareness of planetary finitude so much as from fear of envy for wanting more than others. Horrendous dumpsites attest to the fact that his disapproval of waste did not modify his behavior appreciably. Having the habit of taking all he wanted from Mother Earth, the descendant of Europeans had to find his way to the moon and then look back, before he could comprehend what the Indians had told him all along. When I was invited by the editor of this volume -- because of our friendship and my known junket across life's choices -- to share my experience of downward mobility, another friend directed me to an article by Rita Mae Brown. It was entitled *The Last Straw,* and was excerpted from her book, *Plain Brown Rapper.* In it the author addresses the concept of downward mobility, calling it the greatest insult yet devised by middle class people against the working class. She acknowledged that "for some middle class women, downward mobility had been a first attempt to start changing their ways that were hurtful to others," but she found "the attempt fatally flawed exactly because these women could afford to reject materialism."

> If you have money, sister, don't deny it, share it. If you have advanced skills, don't make pottery in your loft, teach us your skills. If you have good clothes, don't walk around in rags, give us some of your clothes. Downward mobility is a way to deny your material privileges to prove how `right on' you are. We know that anytime you get tired of poverty you can go right back to them . . . .

With this fortuitous warning -- once again, books find me out -- I begin my story. As long as I can remember, I wanted to be downwardly mobile, although I had never run into those particular words; they were not on every corner seventy-two years ago. I did not want to live on a hill with a commanding view, but rather to stand in a fertile valley and be proud of a working relationship with dirt, mud, soil, earth and the people tilling it. When I was driven with my parents through the countryside of France in a chauffeured limousine with our trunks strapped on the roof, golf clubs, tennis rackets, bathing equipment, I would shyly glance with profound wistfulness at the peasants in the fields who stopped their work to stare at rich Americans in flight. Our native driver wore his uniform, a white duster, black glasses, a little visor cap; no one would mistake him for us. He sped through the narrow streets of charming towns, blowing his outrageous horn. Who was he! Did he really think we were so important that chickens should scurry out of the way? Was he deriding us, displaying his catch, so that he could return to his people with some of the wealth we scattered around? Mortified, my sister and I sometimes hid below the window.

When we stopped for the night, my parents would ask for the best rooms in the hotel; my mother loved a balcony with a view and my father felt insulted if he was offered less than all. My mother used her Baedekers to guide us to the loveliest towns; one cannot fault her taste. Our luggage would arrive in our quarters. My mother would rush to scrub the already gleaming bathroom facilities. This was the only time she performed these chores, but she knew how. She did not want us catching diseases. Whose diseases? Those of the tourists who occupied the rooms before us? Foreign people? Local populations? I never asked and never helped. I was young. I did not worry about diseases.

When the rituals had been accomplished, my sister and I would escape while my mother rested and my father touched base with "the people" in his way, at the tennis courts or golf course. We would seek out the cobbled streets and little stores in search of something to bring home, or a pastry shop where we could try out the language with someone real. Our adventures were limited by who we appeared to be, and in fact were: girl children of Americans; we received courteous attention which we tried to deserve by sensitive behavior. This was a time before the seemingly endless years when the United States would sorely tax the natural affection of our mother countries. At that time people liked Americans, and we tried to be in harmony with that perception, but for me a duality had been developing for years. I do not refer to my use of the plural pronouns "we" and "us", appropriate to these early days fully lived as identical twins; I had the joyous privilege and peculiar security of a constant companion my own exact age, neither solicited nor won. This given had the disadvantage of a self-actualizing mirror ever in my view; it doubled the shame, as it were, as well as the rapture. Rather, the duality I speak of had to do with the sense that I was not leading my own life. Only temporarily was I enjoying my parents' life and world style; my own had already started elsewhere, it would seem, in early childhood.

I travelled through my parents' ways in the manner that Americans used to travel abroad -- even to the moon -- the better to see themselves, and I enjoyed their homes immensely. My first memory is of a two story wooden country house in Connecticut. The shades are pulled down because my brother has just hit my sister in the eye with a golf ball. He is coming in for some criticism along with the general dismay, but I know it was not his fault; his aim is not that accurate! I sympathize with him, the accused. Then I remember a house near Lexington Avenue in New York City; it shared a garden with two facing blocks of similar houses. I doubt such a garden survives in New York City today. Memories become clearer after the family moved to an apartment home three stories above the pavement. The whole floor was ours. There were large windows from which we could toss pennies to the costumed ragamuffins who roamed the streets on Hallowe'en: it was clear to me, those kids had the best of it. This could not be verified, for we were never allowed to walk their neighborhood.

Though high off the ground, our Park Avenue home was spacious and, with the help of roller skates, Central Park was our back yard. There was a bar installed across a hall so that we would go with a swing and stretch our backs. A full-size pool table easily found room in the entrance way. There was a study and a living room with a grand piano and a massive record player that tried to shuffle a stack of brittle discs of classical music, often disastrously. My brother had a room of his own when he was not away at boarding school in Aiken, South Carolina -- a burden laid upon him since the age of ten because he had to be groomed to take his place among the leaders of men. If I had known the words at that time, I might have figured this would take considerable upward mobility on his part. We wept with him as he was shipped away in his grey flannel shorts, little jacket and cap to grow up in the care of masters. We loved him; we were rivals in his service; only he could divide our twinship.

While our brother was away, his room became the province of a seamstress who "did the sewing". I cannot remember what this sewing was, for my mother had clothes sent home from Saks Fifth Avenue and Bonwit Teller and special little shops opened by two of her friends whose husbands' wealth-making faltered during The Depression; my father's suits were tailored at Brooks Brothers. Still, Mrs. Hubner stitched away, her knuckles gnarled by arthritis.

My parents had a room with windows on both street and avenue. They retired here everyday from five o'clock until cocktails at eight. There was a large dining-room, a pantry, a kitchen and, on a smaller scale, rooms for the use of *the help*, a butler, a parlor maid, a cook and kitchen maid, a maid who took care of my mother's clothes. A certain hierarchy was to be sensed. The butler was English, the cook French or Swedish, the maid French or Scandinavian or Scotch/Irish. The Middle European countries were never represented, nor were people of Jewish or Black African descent. Our governess was English or French. To borrow words from a beloved television drama, she belonged neither "upstairs" nor "downstairs". To me, the women who played this role were a politely tolerated presence, barely. I loved no one of them. Do others take this job today? I do not know, being excluded from such information by my downward mobility.

All of these people accompanied our family to a summer home on Long Island where their accommodations were sunnier but in the same size ratio as in the city. They were not invited to play tennis or use the swimming pool or go with us to country clubs where these amenities were duplicated in unique ways that included the shores of Long Island Sound. Our grounds were tended by a German gardener and a Swedish second-man. Their wives did the care-taking, jam making, canning and laundry.

There were horses, presumably taken care of by my sister and myself, but in retrospect this is unrealistic. We did well when it was the season for jumping our elegant hunters over rail fences or driving our little Welsh pony in a jaunting cart around the lanes between estates; for the rest of the year, someone else was bringing them in and out of the classic red barn and feeding them hay and a rasher of grain. They prospered. Playing with horses proved to be of unimagined value. Years later, horses carried me to elucidating experiences of downward mobility.

My parents entertained a lot, hosting or going out for dinner many days of each week. Delicious meals were served on time, a contract between those who knew how to prepare the best and those who expected it. When I observe the style of young families today, I see a wholly different timing incompatible with yesteryear -- more spontaneous, less commitment to pattern, and, of course, no "help". My parents dressed for dinner; they put the day away. When the children were too young to participate in dinner they were served separately and early, requiring double cooking -- or rather triple cooking, for the staff had its own menu. I remember my mother, still in bed with a silky coverlet while the cook stood, pad in hand. Together they would plan the meals, complicated because "the servants" ate first. If they had dined second, they could have carved from the family roast . . . but *we* could not be presented with a half-eaten dish. This seemed all right, a matter of schedule, but it followed from a deep misconception. It was a matter of class.

Our closets and drawers were always filled with freshly laundered clothes, sweet-smelling, starched and ironed in a time before perma-press. We wore school uniforms because our excellent institution, deprived only in its exclusivity, and admitting all grades, kindergarten through twelve, did not want apparel rivalry between the daughters of the rich and a little less rich. We were all girls. During The Depression, uniforms saved a lot of face.

In recounting little memories that rise when bidden from my childhood in New York City and Long Island -- our place sweet with the blossoms of apple trees and pears and locusts in the spring, surrounded in the fall by aromatic fields of purple cabbages tended by Polish women whose names we never thought to ask -- I do not mean to suggest that this was all we "had". As a reprieve, there was a rustic camp on a blue lake fathoms deep in the Adirondack Mountains, preserved and, of course, reserved. Once a summer, an Indian appeared in a canoe at our dock to sell trinkets now made by a people who had thought this land had been given to their use by God. I thought so too. Now, as I write, the spruce trees which gave the skyline a cathedral grandeur, have withered under the airborne onslaught of some polluting particulates from beyond the mountains. Because I am not a creative dreamer, that is, I do not remember my dreams the way my daughter Timothy does who regales us with a hilarious nocturnal life, I was deeply impressed by a dream played against this backdrop. I arose at dawn and went down to the edge of the lake where a tall Indian was standing. He told me, "Bend down, drink of this water, and then you will know all you need to know."

Every few years in summer my parents rented state-rooms on an ocean liner bound for Calais or Bremerhaven or Marseille, and when winter palled in Manhattan, they also retreated to enchanting sunny places in the U.S.A. They joined a club at Boca Raton on the east coast of Florida, a place of Moorish splendour and tropical planting. Visiting them there, I took one lesson from the famous golfer, Tommy Armour, and drove the ball so well that I thought I had found my way out. By the second lesson I had lost my natural swing and had to continue my search for a life I could believe in without the help of any compelling talent therefor.

My father in his last years, suffering from heart trouble, bought a house on Sanibel Island in the Gulf of Mexico. My parents loved the blue-tiled roof, terrazzo floors, bougainvillea vines with orange and magenta leaves, and the clean white beach where gentle waves did not break the shells. My mother took her art materials to the little public schools -- one for blacks and one for whites; her joy in all children was genuine and attainable here. And my father spent a lot of time on a fishing boat, at ease in the company -- hired -- of the skippers, drifting in the Gulf, hoping -- not passionately -- for a school or was it a run of tuna. I visited my parents on Sanibel Island. They loved their house so much, they gave it a name, *techado azul*, and these were the first Spanish words I had ever learned although I had grown up in New York City! We studied French and German. Assessing such incredible provincialism allows me to believe in the walls that exist between people, but also to know that they can be brought down. I did not dare stay long with my parents on Sanibel Island. It never occurred to me to look for real people there; this paradise belonged to my parents. I would not pursue my Holy Grail at their gate.

When I was not militantly engaged in defining my own truths, I felt very comfortable with my mother. She was frail with a brittle-bone disease since childhood, attributed to a surely very expensive infant-feeding fad. We were frequently warned, "Don't bump into your mother!" and this worked so well that it lingered on as, "Don't worry your mother!" which is more political. She was indomitable in a helpless sort of way. She expected herself to give orders. She rang for things. She wanted me to and I refused, it now seems, gracelessly. After all, bad manners is not a useful way of changing the social structure of society. I loved talking with her . . . about myself. (She was not at liberty to talk about herself; she was married.) When I was sick, I wanted only her and raged against my father's decree that a trained nurse be hired to relieve her. (Many times I have thought of her, a parent without the backup of antibiotics which came upon the market just in time to lower my own children's scary fevers -- although such life-supporting drugs are still not available to all the mothers of the world. Of course, one must not approach child health by this road. I mean, all powers of the world must place potable water highest on the priority list. Assuring pure drinking water is the best way to start saving children -- and food. The next would be to ban war.) My mother was my witness; I tested my vocabulary within her mothering pride, but I did not want to be like her. She was not a useful role model for someone like me who had a journey to make. I did not want to ring for things!

I trusted her with little rejoicings that I would not confess to others; many years later, I would share my pride in my children and my surprise about the directions in which they chose to go. Together, my mother and I learned from the children.

The journey I wanted to make is one of life's longest, encompassing the road from one class to another. The route is seldom direct and never to be trusted. My mother was inordinately generous and I had to defend the integrity of my choices from her boundless enthusiasm exactly for the work-related aspects she admired; she was an artist. She was strongly fascinated by the sight of people working. During World War II she loved that I "made airplanes". She was entranced when my husband decided to undertake a cattle ranch in Northern California. She sent him a fine leather coat from Abercrombie & Fitch; with a happy flourish of her pen she could have written a check worth all the calves he would raise in a year of early risings, long days in the saddle, fence-building, spring development, cowboy camaraderie. She never understood how she endangered my intent. My mother's daughter, it took me some years to comprehend an important distinction. Being a hard working rancher did not make my husband a *farm worker* with all the connotations that cling to that honorable labor. Many years later, on stage, a daughter, Holly Near, who grew up on the ranch but wandered far afield, would introduce a song with these words, "I have just come from where a group of mighty organizers have some endless spirit and the ability to see their future very clearly. They are called the United Farm Workers. I was taking part in an event a while ago when they arrived, one hundred and fifty strong, all standing on stage singing together -- men, women and children, they had faces like maps of the earth. These are the people who feed us and meanwhile are starving." We were not *farm workers*. We owned 1800 acres.

Where did our money come from? My mother's mother had come East from an affluent Pittsburgh society to marry George Campbell Smith, second generation scion of the Street & Smith publishing company that produced the pulp magazines, reaching out to newly immigrant readers with simple stories of romance and sports and adventure and mystery -- *Love Story, Western Story, Detective Story, Nick Carter* and many others. In his book, *Fiction Factory*, Quentin Reynolds says it was the largest publishing company in the world, though I did not know this in my time. Reynolds tells the story of two young men, Street and Smith, ". . . who knew what the masses wanted to read. They wanted to read of girls pursued (but never quite caught) by villains, of poor boys who managed to overcome all obstacles to achieve success . . . and stories in the virtue-must-triumph school that held out hope to the over worked, underpaid shop girls that Prince Charming would come along." I thank Quentin Reynolds for publishing this poem by my great, great uncle, Francis Smith, written in the 1880's.[1] His "muse may be rude" but I am glad to find this theme in my background.

If I can any pleasure give

---

1. *The Fiction Factory*, by Quentin Reynolds, Random House, 1955.

To those who daily labor

If I can send one ray of joy

To any lowly neighbor

'Tis all the recompense I ask -

I labor for no other -

In any man, however poor,

I recognize a brother.

If I can cheer an aching heart

However poor and lonely

Though rude my muse and plain my verse

My mission still is holy.

And I care nothing for the sneers

Of pompous schools and classes

So that I reach the hearts and win

The plaudits of the masses.

But my mother, seeking her own mode as I myself, was determined to be an *upwardly mobile* reader. She did not read the pulps. She read classical and current novels, especially historical best sellers like *Mont St. Michel.* Slender volumes of poetry rested on her bedside table -- Edna St. Vincent Millay and Eleanor Wylie and Robert Frost. She did not notice the many writers who were being paid -- underpaid, but paid -- for written words, downtown at Street and Smith, including Theodore Dreiser.

When I was a student at Bennington in Vermont, I came to New York City to interview Daisy Bacon, editor of the enormously successful *Love Story.* She looked the part. Daisy Bacon apologized to no one for the calibre of her writers -- and especially not to a literature major who attended a private, experimental college on money produced by her editorial acumen. I was impressed by Daisy Bacon. She respected and was one with her readers.

At this same period of my life I studied in the library of my mother's brother, George C. Smith, Jr. Although he had a desk at Street and Smith, I think of him primarily as a serious collector of rare books and first editions including works of Mark Twain and William Blake. He designed and had set into the wall of his library a little scene showing Samuel Clemens piloting a river boat. I remember his reproduction of a

Blake drawing, "I want . . ." was the title, and this in no way expressed a desire for more worldly goods; he already had all that. George suffered the same bone infirmity as my mother; he walked with a slight limp. George and little Dorothy had been child artists together, doing meticulous copies of any pictures that came their way when they were unable to go play. To this companionship I attribute my mother's later gift for "getting a likeness" in her portraits, to the delight of parents and the envy of other more creative painters. Uncle George wore beautiful clothes. He owned a small yacht to cruise on Long Island Sound and to dock at ports on Manhattan's East River. For this activity he wore white flannels, a nautical serge blue jacket and a captain's hat. I had rides on his boat but I never found my way beneath his family smile to his lonely eccentricity. George C. Smith, Jr. died in his early forties; I was twelve. A few more years and we would have known each other.

My paternal grandmother had a more substantive disability. My mother faithfully took the twins to see Grandmother Holmes. I remember the twisted paralyzed and delicate hands with which she managed to paint a lovely self-portrait in which she wore a flowered taffeta dress. So fine was the work that someone suggested the picture had been painted by her loyal care-giver. In my recollection, Lillian Holmes bends attentively toward us, offering a cookie and inviting us to talk with her parrot. Her husband had been a New York lawyer who bought and lived in one of the Villard homes (now historical landmarks) east of St. Patrick's cathedral on 5th Avenue. Health can be a major factor in downward mobility, though not of the spirit.

My father had been nick-named "Judge" as a child because his face did not seem to smile, but he was unfailingly good-natured and popular with many sorts of people. His given name was Artemas. In his youth he was a minor tennis champion. He played the courts of Europe, a "tennis bum". There is a story that when some people were stumbling over protocol among Swedish royalty, Judge said, "The King and I'll take on you two," and settled the problem. His behavior was untrammeled by pretense. He made people comfortable. He insisted on playing to win, but he was never out of control, never angry at his partner's gaffs or his own, always courteous, always amusing. His tennis game was cerebral, compensating for a rather stiff musculature; it drove my brother crazy, plunging from side to side, to the net and back, in pursuit of Judge's ball. My father was not an intellectual. I cannot recall a single political or philosophical opinion he espoused, even while his friends were vitriolic about President Roosevelt. He liked to boast about his one book-of-the-year. My mother loved him more than books, even more than her considerable talent in art, more than her children; she had promised him always to have child-care in place so that she could go with him. When I observe the struggling young parents today, I think Judge had a good clue for a strong marriage -- child care in place. My parents were friends, lovers, and bridge partners. My father's skills were with people, organizing and enabling in a peaceable way. His attitude toward my going to the fledgling Bennington College, one year old, for which he would be paying handsomely, times two for twins, was "All right, but don't take anything seriously." At the time I did not appreciate this attitude and today, at seventy-two, I still cannot . . . but maybe I will tomorrow.

Sundays throughout the winter in New York City my father went off to his club for a game of squash racquets or a rubber of contract bridge -- occasionally he played with Eli Culbertson -- which paved the way for my mother to take us to church. First we attended St. John's Episcopal Church, a few blocks to the south. I enjoyed the pageantry as priests in gorgeous vestments carried the golden cross down the aisle toward the altar, followed by choir boys with angels' voices, then tenors, baritones, basses -- the whole tonal spectrum of male sound approaching where I stood, passing, disappearing into the sanctuary. Later, my mother changed her allegiance to the Madison Avenue Presbyterian Church, a few blocks north. It was here that a young Scotch preacher interpreted the New Testament in a way that profoundly affected my life. The parish ran east from Central Park and cut across the socio-economic boundaries. Sunday morning George Buttrick preached The New Testament to the rich, making manifest the message of Jesus lest anyone dare to misunder-stand, just because the hymns were sweet and the stained glass windows filtered the harsh light. During the week he ministered to the poor through visitation and to the many neighborhood organizations supported by his wife as well. A few years ago I sat in such a church in El Salvador listening to just such a preacher. My glance fell on the earnest, solemn faces of the young people. "Be ye sheep, but also the shepherd. Care about the world!" It was a dangerous message in El Salvador and would have been dangerous on Madison Avenue, if it had been heard as literal rather than poetic truth.

It was Dorothy Holmes who took me to church and to art galleries, to plays and to concerts for the best of reasons -- she loved to go herself. This was her enormous contribution to the development of a radical mind in my young head. But in childhood I was closer to another, and had to learn that these two women had the possibility -- the probability -- of hurting each other, given their worlds, living in the same household, next to each other, divided by class.

My Earth Mother was Kate Mannix. She was our Irish nurse. Kate was one of the adventurous or desperate young women who left their homes in Ireland and, with their courage in their pockets, maybe little else, walked up the gangplank of a ship bound for New York. Now, with adventurous children of my own, I think of Kate. I look back at her, where once I looked ahead into her red-cheeked face and laughing eyes. I hear her singing. Did she leave her cottage in the spring with the *wild Irish rose a-bloomin'* that she loved to sing about? Did her new shoes scuff along a dusty road or her skirts billow in a country cart? Was it as hard for her as it was for Danny-Boy who heard the *pipes a-callin'*? Did her father tell her that it would *not be her beauty alone* that would make people love her, but the *truth in her eyes ever shining*? Did a homesick boy in New York promise, *"I'll take you home again, Kathleen, across the ocean wild and wide."* Did a friend plead, *"Come back to Erin, Mavourneen, Mavourneen!"*?

Kate allowed us to feel that we were her whole life, but I wonder now. Did she have a mother in "the ould country" who walked a piece of the way with her and then turned back to the cottage weeping -- but knowing there was one less mouth to feed? Did Kate arrive at Ellis Island all alone, or was the substantial Irish community ready to receive her? I believe she had uncles "on the force". I know she was friends with the member of "New York's finest" who directed traffic at the intersection below our windows. Kate had one day off a week "when possible". I am under the impression -- or the hope -- that she was well-paid; my parents would have thought so -- they did not cut corners, but the current estimate of what "green labor" was worth probably was not "union". Domestic workers have a hard time organizing because they seem to be part of other peoples' families. Kate bought into that idea. After she had to leave us, with a similar sense of belonging she raised the little boy who became Congressman Hamilton Fish.

Kate exchanged letters with me and with my sister for many years. Her handwriting was florid and, as years went by, looped up inextricably into the letters of the line above. I know she continued to scan the society pages and compared notes with other nurses as they sat in Central Park, rocking perambulators. Why not! She knew more than I about life on and off those pages. It was a fair exchange. I did not want to grow up to be, like her, a "child care worker," but I imagined life in her ethnic community had more meaning than in my own.

I remember the day when Kate was fired. I can almost see the richly appointed room in a hotel off the Champs Elysées near the Arche de Triomphe. I can feel the red velvet on a chair. It was raining in Paris, a summer rain. We were told that Kate would be leaving us here; kindly, we had brought her this far on the way to her home; she would be rejoining her people across the English Channel; an English governess would take her place, a woman more able to school us in the ways we would need now. Kate was for childhood, Miss Potter was for young ladies. I knew Kate was sad to be going. *Her people* were us, or others in New York! I knew it was not her choice. I could have fought for her, no matter to what avail, but I already had some inkling of where my life was slated to go. I cried tears into the red velvet cushions. That was sixty years ago.

At 72, autobiography is not a linear vision -- the line would be too long, it would get tangled as when a fisherman casts too boldly into a rough pool. Fisher-person! At 72, biography is magically entertained, concentric for the most part, a multidimensional blend of landscape, portraiture, film clip, stage dialogue pulsating in and out of hearing, a moving figure reflected in a store window, a bunch of dates scrawled upon United Nations Children's Calendar or simply recalled with a special person who, for me, would be my twin. Tonight my twin lies in an oncology hospital. I read that if we live so long, we'll all have cancer. Is this "normal" then for being on the earth, a natural diversity from perfection that is ultimately lethal? Or have we human beings polluted a prior perfection? If the earth was made perfect, why were we not also made perfect instead of designed to spoil it all!

Where was I! Where did I first engender ideas for improving my economic status -- my economic class -- downward? Out of respect for the modern wisdom that everything significant happens in the early years of life before one is in any position to do anything about it, I have indulged my early memories for whatever symbolism they may offer. Now I must rely on facts. I attended a private girls' school that placed its buildings not among its likely customers but on cheap land near tenements inhabited by the poor. The drive across town provided a daily lesson for children in the family limousine, piloted by a uniformed chauffeur. The lesson was not titled. It was in this school that I wrote a composition about a hungry man watching the cooking of roasts through the street level window of a brasserie. ". . . The lights blinked on and off like an eye red with weeping." I was rewarded with an A from the literature teacher, a grand woman with cigarette stains on her fingers, undecipherable layers of clothes, and an affirming smile that was worth working for. There were ashes in the pages of my homework, and authentic writer's margin notes.

At college I first met people from other states who did not think the world revolved around New York City, especially not Park Avenue. This was liberating news. I was friends with the daughter of a Jewish clothing factory worker, of a Philadelphia lawyer, of a Vermont co-educational school founder, and I met many people with brilliant literary minds and memories for the written word. I almost drowned in humility but was repeatedly rescued by New England farmscapes, snowscapes, and a little undying love from afar. My beloved was with the ambassador to Japan.

In spaces between semesters of study, I went to the Frontier Nursing Service in the Kentucky mountains. Here I had the opportunity to meet British nurses, working class women who were representatives of a distinguished tradition -- missionary or colonialist -- of health care pioneers who went forth to help people of other lands, especially those within the British Empire. Mary Breckinridge, daughter of a well-known Kentucky family, grieving for the loss of her two children, had chosen an area of the Appalachian mountains in which to develop a midwifery and nursing model that could be adapted to similar conditions the world over. Her model had been the work of the Queen's nurses in London. Mary Breckinridge had added a unique enabling idea. The nurses, who would of necessity reach the cabins of their patients by horseback, would be supported by the idealistic daughters of rich people who had had horses to play with throughout their childhood. They were called couriers. These young women could be counted on to lose their hearts in Kentucky, though not their senses. Only a few would become midwives, but the great majority would return home to be the fund-raisers for the Frontier Nursing Service among their parents' friends.

It was here that I had the opportunity to use my riding play, to observe rural poverty. I did not become a midwife but the experience deepened my conviction that there were conditions in our country demanding more profound change than the most imaginative and touching charity could bring. Bending over the feet of our horses cut by the iced-over streams we had to ford, riding out on nights so dark one could not see the horses' ears, making tea for the nurses to British specifications -- these roles and many more felt downwardly mobile, except that, as Rita Mae Brown says, there would come a time when I could go home.

Years later a daughter, Holly Near, wrote a song, "Kentucky

Woman", which has been sung all over the world. It tells of a country woman who refused to move when the oil companies came to drill on her land. "Of course, she was carried off, but I want you to know, she did not go willingly!" There were no political issues raised at the Frontier Nursing Service; if there had been, support would have plummetted. At that time health care -- hands on -- was urgent, kind, and safe. It did not ask, why are these people poor?

Another adventure away from my idyllic college campus in Vermont was a visit to The Catholic Worker on Mott Street in downtown New York City. I had been introduced to Catholicism by a beloved professor of French literature, Wallace Fowlie. I had learned to revere the name of Jacques Maritain. The cathedral-like structure of Catholicism elicited my deepest admiration as distinct from the historical activities, both good and evil, which it had been called upon to bless. Following a tendency to seek synthesis, I attended lectures on the Catholic trade union movement. I have always been moved by religion coming down to earth. I spent time at Dorothy Day's Hospitality House doing menial tasks reverently, but I was not yet ready to engage her in conversation about the world. I was still watching. I did meet a dynamic character by the name of Peter Maurin who was developing ideas he brought together as the *green thumb revolution*. It sounded good to me.

After college I wanted to find a job. I wanted to be paid for work; it would be a talisman. Without teaching credentials, I was hired at the Professional Children's School on Broadway while pursuing a Masters Degree at Columbia University. I taught Fifth Grade. I can only hope in retrospect that my energy and good humor made up for all I lacked in pedagogical practice. The school principal was supportive but even she had misgivings when she entered my classroom during an enactment of Vachel Lindsay's poem, *The Congo*. Oral reading was being assayed. It had gotten somewhat out of hand -- uproariously.

My students were actors and models -- or their parents hoped them to be. After two years I felt deprived. I went to my professor at Columbia. "Direct me to a job where I can learn more about the world; my students know more than I do, they all carry union cards." He smiled enigmatically and said, "Why don't you go to Commonwealth College?" Why not! With very little research I was soon on my way to Arkansas. The goal of the school was to offer useful skills to rural southern organizers. I arrived with the idea that after all my costly education I might have something I could teach, but quickly I changed roles. I took classes in labor history and the use of theatre arts to disseminate political truths. In other words, people were learning how to use little skits to make a point that had something to do with life and death -- if one was organizing in Arkansas in 1939. I learned to milk a cow and make brown gravy by burning the flour slightly in the pan. I learned what it was like not to have enough food, to live where representatives of the government came and put a padlock on the library door. I went home, cashed out my savings account and returned to Commonwealth College. The money helped for a short while. I cannot remember why I had to make the trip; it must have been because we did not trust the local post office. The school stood accused. Soon there was to be a trial. I cannot remember what the charges were but I remember the brooding quiet with a patina of violence in the court room on a hot summer day. I was not privy to the central councils of the school leadership but I was disappointed when it was decided that we would ask for a change of venue. I wanted to confront evil with innocence in a testimonial setting. Wiser southerners recognized a lynch mood. Sometime ago, a black colleague had stayed overnight at the school; there was no use having a school if this could not happen again. Commonwealth College was teaching democracy and change. The fervent administration did not want to be outmaneuvered in a southern court room, expensively. They called retreat.

I rode north with members of the New Theatre of Philadelphia who had presented the writing/acting courses. For some years, the New Theatre had been producing plays that were both creative and of social purpose. Clifford Odet's *Waiting for Lefty* had been one of their hits, and Marc Blitzstein's musicals, *No for an Answer* and *Cradle Will Rock*. I strolled hand in hand through the Jewish ghetto of Philadelphia with a young man who knew every melody and word. He confided to me that his parents would be angry if they knew he was out with a goy. Stunned, I learned from his language. I had thought prejudice was a one-way street: something only I had to get over.

World War II was upon us -- upon the world. It took me awhile to set aside my life-long commitment to pacifism. I did not believe in war as a way of settling disputes. I think I drew a parallel from my childhood with a twin, a friend and rival, living so close. I saw the countries of the world as similarly close and at risk. We had to work it out or perish. I felt "the allies" had each at some time participated in creating Hitler, hoping his armies would contain what they saw as threatening about the Russian revolution. I turned away. I said, "Thou shalt not kill." And then I knew I must take part in defeating the monster. This explanation is not offered as political analysis; it is simply the way I felt at the time. I could not imagine joining the army, but with the encouragement of a friend I began to take courses at a machine shop. And then -- coincidentally, for reasons of an impossible love -- I took a train to the farthest place in the land the tracks would go. Every car was filled with wartime travellers, mostly soldiers. For three days and nights I perched on my suitcase in the aisles, tears streaming down my cheeks, unnoticed in the crush. I did not have a Pullman berth this time, and never did again.

The aircraft companies of the West Coast were hiring everybody. With the skilled workers leaving for the services, their jobs were broken down wherever possible into simpler tasks for which women, blacks, older people eagerly applied where once they had been excluded. I refused jobs in management; I wanted manual work. Suspicion of me arose because of my education but was lost in the paper work; they hired me. What an astonishing scene was the huge hangar at dawn with people in so many costumes pouring through the gates to take their places by the great silver skeletons of airships. My first job was Electrician One. I crawled up in the plane, tidied the bunches of electrical wires lying along the hull, and secured them with a cord and a dab of red lacquer. I was proud.

I lived in a single room right on the beach. The sand strewn with gobs of oil from the tankers was at my door, and so were magnificent sunsets over the Pacific. I climbed a steep little street to catch a bus to my job which was clocked at ten hours a day, six days a week. The company kept workers on hand in anticipation of new orders and sometimes it was not possible to keep so many people busy. I cannot describe the boredom of being idle with nine and a half hours to go. "Go hide!" "Hide?" "Just pick up a piece of paper and carry it around!" There were other days when I earned my pay and felt satisfied to be part of an extraordinary effort to put wings under the defense of democracy. It is hard to remember, now, that there were times when it was not a foregone conclusion that we would win.

I recall a deep excitement in realizing that I was now a worker in the social order, at risk. I expressed this realization by timidly entering the union hall. Local 887 UAW (United Auto and Aircraft Workers) was organizing from a small building across the highway from the plant. It was uphill work for many reasons. An unsuccessful strike before the war years had left disillusionment in its wake. In the workforce there were many newcomers, especially women who did not plan to be there once their men came home. Job descriptions were changing so rapidly that it was hard for a shop steward to argue a pay grievance. Patriotism seemed to require that all difficulties be endured and yet my definition of patriotism rested upon a trust in those who, to get ahead, must bring all others with them -- working people and the poor . . . and their associations.

I became a union member, attended meetings and was appointed women's representative on a labor-management committee dedicated to maximizing the war effort at the plant. If it had not been for the special circumstances, I would not have taken part in a labor-management committee, because I see the union movement as essentially adversarial in its finest moments. I would not bargain with inequality as a maxim, as a given.

I first saw Russell Near from the window of a B-27. He was driving a little train of carts that delivered parts to the different areas of the factory. It was a good job for a union organizer; he got around. Later, we were both members of the contract committee, meeting with management. My assigned concern was to be the conditions and pay levels of women. I had to learn about them, myself.

One day within this period, Russell Near and I were married. His schedule included union work in another plant across the city and also membership in the CIO (Congress of Industrial Organizations) Council, so a wedding could not be a grand scene; come to think of it, I had no one to invite. My family and old friends lived on the East Coast. IS THIS TRIP REALLY NECESSARY? NO, IT IS NOT! Still, married we were in Russell's parents' little living room -- I remember his brother in a navy blue suit -- and it became significant to have a document when, a year or so later, our first child was born. She was both welcome and legitimate! We called her Timothy after the grasses that blew on the plains of her father's native North Dakota. I still remember waking up one morning and seeing Russ' beat-up work boots by the bed. Downwardly mobile!

When the war ended, Russell was fired from his union job. "The reds", who had been such staunch leaders in the wartime factory, were no longer welcome in Walter Reuther's plan. The McCarthy era with all its folly and damage was on its way. We used some of my money to buy a little house to live in with Russell's parents. Teaming up with an equally dislodged friend, Russell built a toy train a child could ride on along a silver track assembled from surplus airplane parts. It was a beauty -- as was his partnership with Preston Tuttle -- but after the costs were figured and doubled for the distributor and doubled for the toy store, it became apparent that only the wealthiest children would get to ride this train. We closed up shop. Preston went back to more cerebral pursuits. We bought a pick-up truck and started off in search of good work. We found a hill-land ranch in Potter Valley, northern California. Growing fruits and vegetables might have been better but we did not come upon an orchard or a farm. Nor were we then aware of the political and ecological implications of meat production -- so much soil, water, forest land and grain are used to create a pound of burger. We paid for the cattle ranch with some of my money and our War Bonds. We set about to learn to-gether the multiple skills of animal husbandry, mechanics and agriculture, but it was not long -- with all the blossoming and birthing around about, dehorning, branding and castrating -- that Russ became the rancher among men and I became the rancher's wife among a brood of children with all outdoors as our play yard.

I think of the next fifteen years as the body of my life. We both had to work hard on a place euphemistically known as a one-man ranch. While the cultural richness of our days was greatly enhanced by contributions from my mother, the substance of our working day did not change. From what we earned as cattle raisers we could not have sent our children to the many inspiring experiences and family assemblies for which my mother bought airline tickets. Without the nature of our work, our children would not have been who they were then perceived to be and are today. They were raised on a ranch.

Gradually Russell's back weakened, chancy from a childhood bout with polio that left one leg crippled. It was true but it is hard to write, for he was the best dancer I have ever followed. It became hard for him to walk the steep hills; he had to do most of his work on horseback. It was also becoming apparent that one could no longer make a living on 1800 acres of Mendocino hill-land, meadow, brush, and forest. Russell was pragmatic. He had learned the rancher's trade and relished it and plied it well, but he would not work for scenery or romance. We put the ranch up for sale. There were no buyers. And then one appeared. The ranch was sold -- a few years before the extraordinary rise in property values.

With a pocketful of money that was perhaps no more than the money we had come with, transposing for inflation, Russell chose a sweet place in a canyon near town; a swimming pool allowed three giant redwood trees to scatter their seeds in the aqua-blue water. It was not my idea of *moving to town*; I had imagined a noisy, busy working class street where I could achieve another stage in downward mobility. I think Russell imagined being a gracious host to the young men and women who would be friends of our children, now almost grown -- but this was not to be.

Alcohol and drugs were warping the possibility of a generous hospitality. A carload of youngsters had left a pleasant party and died minutes later speeding on the highway. Our children did not want to lay on us the sorry guilt for the behavior of their peers or of themselves. Other families must have felt the same. Parties moved to the anonymity of orchards and vineyards. My son told me, "We'll do the best we can, but we will be with our friends -- and on our own." They lived. We left Doolin Canyon after a few years. I think of it as a party which took lots of work to get ready and never quite came off.

Since this story is about downward mobility, I must not forget to keep noticing where "my fortune" went. The question was never integral to my decisions but it is to this tale. The simplest explanation is one everyone should know: if you don't use money to make money, it disappears. There were other factors. My mother was trapped for many years in a situation that used up a lot of the money she had so looked forward to leaving for her children -- her children to whom she had given so much during her lifetime that it was a habit and a self-image. She was imprisoned in her bed in a darling little house on a cobble street in Philadelphia.   She required nursing care around the clock, and the complementary services of a housekeeper, cook, laundress, book-keeper. All her children were glad that she could have this help. It was her way. She could not imagine any other way. She would have been welcome to live with either one of us -- but in our way. None of us believed in having "servants". We thought it might even be better for her; she would not be spending her last days with hired help as her friends. But they were good friends, the black women who worked for her, doing their jobs well. With us, my mother would not have been so well taken care of. She would not be the center of the world. She would not be able to ring for things. We asked ourselves, "What on earth do poor people do?" They take care of each other within a bond mixed of duty, anguish and love -- maybe chaos. I loved the talk I had with my mother though it was hard to have mother/daughter communion with so many listening in that little house and hard, too, to have her ring for someone to bring me a cup of coffee.

What happened to my fortune? I spent it along the way. It was Russell's instinct to save and store (away) for the future, for the children. I believed in investing in skills: I wanted to support every opportunity the children had the heart and energy to take. *Provide experience and they will make their own money,* later. This is not a story about my children, but I can say that they inherited a tendency to think more about making a life than about making money. When they did -- and they did -- they never used money to make more money. They live creative lives, a few dollars away from impoverishment . . . at least so far.

I am happy with what my children chose to do with talents drawn from the genetic pool and a spacious country childhood. Timothy has had a self-sustaining career in the performing arts and is presently director of a metropolitan community theatre. Holly has used the gift of a natural singing voice to carry the songs of peace and justice between people, across the world. Fred? I often heard my husband say that to build a house was an elemental task that every man should know. I would not have put it that way, but perhaps a little boy heard and signed on. In any case, it is he and not his sisters who is a carpenter. Laurel's life illustrates the decade. It is highly representational. She is a single mom, seeking the outlines of a benign separation, trying to learn the art of dancing, to teach dance for a living, and to give her two small sons the love which is as essential to the world as food. Meanwhile, high quality childcare, in absentia, has become a controversial women's issue -- unaffordable, underpaid, undervalued and in short supply.

I am getting ahead of myself. After selling our ranch and moving to town, Russell turned to real estate; he sold ranches. He said it was the only thing he knew how to do. I looked another way and began to write a book. In response to a feeling of deprivation, I wrote down everything I could remember of life in Potter Valley. It was a long book. It has since been pared down but it has not found a publisher. I am only now realizing what the book is about. It's about race and who owns the land. Now that I know, I could take it up again -- but there are other more current metaphors for these two fundamental areas of conscience.

When the children had grown and moved on, we did live down town a year or so but it did not work out well for me. I shyly but hungrily observed the proliferation of women's groups but there was no similar means of association and communication for men -- unless one was a lion or an elk. Men's way was to share a drink. While Russell had demonstrated energetic versatility as a broker, teaching himself the rigorous rules being developed around property exchange, he wearied of the endless specifications. I came to believe we should go *back to the country*. We found a little ranch on an old-fashioned winding lane -- a sheep ranch. As many years before, I watched Russell teach himself his way around new animals and new acres. Sheep were not like cows; North Dakota farmers had despised sheep because they cropped the grasses down to the mud and then jerked out the roots. But this was California, 1979. Russell found them to be amusingly personable -- not at all *alike as sheep*. Indeed the lambs did gambol as the poets promised. Russ learned to shear their wool, trim their hooves, doctor their runny noses instead of being repelled. He practiced liking them. It was a pretty good time, tinged with an irreparable sadness. Then Russell died. I do not know if there is a cause of death, hidden in the pages of life, shielded by medical names.

I stayed on for some time, following the paths we had stepped out. But I had not learned to plow and disc and sow and mow and rake and arrange the hay in windrows for the baler. One night while I was in San Francisco for a concert, somebody's pet dog got loose and killed or maimed most of my sheep. It was a devastation caused by ignorance; new people had been allowed to buy small pieces of the neighboring 5000 acre ranch; they do not know what the family dog can do and no one stopped to acknowledge what he had done. I felt profoundly guilty that I had not protected the animals in my care, nor could I again. One day a woman came from Petaluma. She had goats and thought mine was the place of their dreams and of hers. Perhaps it was. I told her my story. At least, I thought, she knows as much about the trade as I. She had a partner who said he knew everything. I was free to go.

Presently I live in a little house on a broad street in a small town such as I have seen so many times from train windows in my youth. In my abode, there is no insulation, the porch is sagging, the wallpaper is peeling, everything needs paint -- tomorrow. The heater is broken and it is cold enough to wear four sweaters. Being poor is often wasteful -- of human and material resources. At the moment, one daughter and her family share the space. This is characteristic of our times, this doubling up -- and a foretelling. I have arrived; in regard to the subject of this essay, I am at peace.

Tonight in my eighth decade, I have come to my house after a day spent with a host of people who gathered in the town of Mendocino in behalf of the Pacific Coast. They are organizing to protect a resource of great beauty from the degradation of oil rigs and drilling platforms and tankers that can run aground. They declare that the coasts belong to all people -- to a child in Iowa, to a child as yet unborn. The sun shone over the blue water as high officials took turns with poets, painters, environmentalists, businessmen, fishermen and owners of a piece of the loveliest real estate in the world, to say, "The ocean coast is not for sale!" Children arriving in yellow buses were given time to sing their thoughts.

They will win their case . . . for now, but what lasting effect will their brilliant environmental alert achieve? Will we use less oil? Will we park our cars? Will we play at home with our kids instead of strapping them into car-seats for a drive along a road? Will we learn to tap the sun? In the meantime, will we study peaceable trading skills -- for it is said that trading is good for the world? Noel Brown, a director of the United Nation's Environmental Program, sees "an open moment in history where a new ecological alliance in the service of the Earth is possible. Ecological conflict must be put in balance as we redefine security, not just in military terms." For example, Brown suggests modifying trade debt in exchange for massive reforestation programs. A fresh sense of the commensurate!

I end with this parable -- the North Coast defense day -- because it illumines my thesis that the lifestyle of my childhood should not prevail nor be aspired to. If many should live as we did, the planet would not do well. I am proud to have found my way to those souls who recognize this flaw in the aspirations of Western Civilization, a spiritual flaw at the heart of our extraordinary know-how and unique mode of ambition. I did not see this when I was five or ten or even fifteen, but early I did sense that something was wrong, some privilege I did not appreciate. A childhood uneasiness became the cornerstone of my wisdom.

COMMUNITY

MADE IT POSSIBLE

Peg and Ken Champney

Downwardly mobile? Perhaps so, but upwardly rewarding!

-- A healthy diet, lower on the food chain, centered around garden vegetables.

-- No TV in the house, resulting in more time for self-initiated creative projects.

-- Better winter health after turning down the thermostat.

-- Learning how to repair cars, washing machines, lawn mowers, house wiring and plumbing, you name it.

-- Increased use of bicycles or feet for short trips: fun and good exercise.

-- Whole wheat bread, made at home.

-- Chores which have real meaning and importance for the children.

-- Homemade Christmas and birthday gifts.

-- Strengthened community ties through sharing of skills and tools. We rototill the neighbor's garden and give piano lessons to their six year old. Later their auto mechanic dad helps us with car repairs.

The list could go on.

Our family adventure in simple, "downwardly mobile" living began in 1965. We were: Ken and Peg Champney and children - Carl, 11; Becky, 9; Wendy, 7; and Heidi, 5 - plus a 12 year old foster son, Glen. During the next year this tribe was joined by Glen's younger sister, Beth, and an adopted black baby, Jack. Beth later lost her life in an auto accident, at age 18.

Ken was (and is) printer and co-owner/publisher of the local weekly newspaper, the Yellow Springs News; the job is very demanding and satisfying. Peg was equally busy bringing up the family and teaching in our neighborhood alternative school. Our home was, and still is, The Vale, an intentional community with five member families (in 1965). While each family owns its own home, The Vale's 40 acres of woods, a garden area, commons and home sites are held in a land trust. Ken had been a non-registrant during the Korean war and, as a result, served 20 months of a five year prison sentence in federal prison. Peg, likewise, came from a pacifist background -- she grew up in a Quaker family which took the peace testimony seriously. When we launched our simple living adventure, our primary motivation was to live on an income that resulted in owing no federal income "war" tax.

By 1965, we had been concerned for some time about paying our federal income tax, more than 50% of which was spent to finance past, present and future wars. We had tried including a note of protest along with our tax form, and, later, paying only the "peaceful" portion of the tax; the government's response to this was to take the unpaid portion plus interest from our bank account.

We remember a conversation about that time in our lives which went something like this:

Peg: "Perhaps we could live on an income low enough that we wouldn't owe a tax."

Ken (after some figuring, with his nose in the tax-payer's manual): "That means we'd have to live on about $5000 a year, and give the rest to charitable organizations." He thought that would obviously end the conversation.

Peg: "I think we could do it."

And so we have done it -- ever since. The dollar amounts have changed of course, along with inflation, but the basic plan has remained the same: we've spent for our living expenses the amount allowed tax-free by the Internal Revenue Service. Ken has carefully studied the tax manuals and taken advantage of whatever tax credits and deductions are available; and we've given substantial contributions to charitable organizations, often about 20-25% of our annual income.

As we carried out our simple living venture over the past 25 years we were helped along by a number of factors: determination, Ken's thorough study of the tax laws from year to year, our own upbringing as children born during our country's Great Depression -- cutting budget corners came naturally. But living in The Vale community has to be put at the top of the list, when we look for the enabling support system that made -- and continues to make -- our venture possible. From time to time we are asked to share about our life style, at Quaker gatherings and simple living workshops. During these occasions someone in the audience will invariably respond, "It's great what you're doing, but, then, you have The Vale community to support you. We could never make it work in our living situation." And it's true. As we describe in the following pages various aspects of how we have carried out our lives at a no-federal-income-tax level, the positive role of The Vale will be mentioned repeatedly.

Gardening -- Growing our own vegetables had always been part of our life. Our simple living experiment only served to increase the scale, time- and space-wise. Our original goal had been to produce all our own fruits and vegetables. Over the years we have gone beyond that goal to the place where we've stopped buying meat and the garden is the mainstay of a vegetarian diet. We eat like kings and queens -- so we are convinced; perhaps the conviction is strengthened by our exposure to all the information in the mass media about the harmful effects of commercially grown food -- exposed as it is to pesticides, preservatives, what-have-you.

The Vale provides land sufficient to the gardening needs of the people living here -- for us about 1/4 acre. An interest in the land, in protecting it and increasing its fertility, and in growing food is a binding element among Vale members. Gardening has rarely been done as a group cooperative venture, but there is much mutual support through shared interest and exchange of tools and know-how.

The routines and rhythms of the gardening year set a background -- indeed a spiritual grounding -- to our lives. In January and February seeds are ordered, an act of faith when the ground is frozen and the temperatures frigid. Some time in March the soil can first be worked. Early greens, onion sets, radishes and 7 or 8 pounds of pea seeds are planted, the peas in rows a yard apart over a large proportion of the entire garden. In the meantime cabbage and broccoli and later tomato and pepper seeds are sown in an indoor seedbed under fluorescent lights. When their first two sets of leaves appear, they will be potted, hardened off gradually to sun and cold, and, at the proper time, planted in the garden. Tomato and pepper plants and corn seeds are planted midway between the pea rows in May, so that in June, just when the peas are harvested, eaten or stowed in the freezer, and their vines wither, the second crop of tomatoes, peppers and corn takes over the same garden area. Later yet, a third crop will occupy the same area - fall turnips which are sown between the rows just after the peak production of the second crops. Popcorn, green, lima and soy beans, summer squash and a large planting of winter butternut squash (which will be stored and eaten right through winter and early spring) are other major crops.

Tomato canning -- we aim to put up 100 to 200 quarts -- is an August chore, as are corn and bean freezing. Further harvesting goes on during September and October. It's always a challenge to guess which night will be the first killing frost, and to harvest remaining tomatoes, peppers and the butternut squash the day before.

Late fall is a time to revel in fall greens - which means our November standby, green soup: blended cooked turnip or mustard greens combined with a thin white sauce. Kale is usually the latest crop to be harvested; it is still edible and quite delicious even after the mercury drops as low as 10 degrees.

As gardeners we make our share of mistakes and continue to learn, and of course we're always somewhat at the mercy of the weather. Ken studies the garden books and learns the important things like how high a **ph** count is ideal for which crops and what to do about it. When some friends donated old windows to us, we added a cold frame to the south side of our house, and learned how to extend the season for greens and tomatoes.

The Champney children growing up had mixed feelings about gardening and our diet. They definitely shared their parents' enthusiasm and excitement for the first fresh peas in June, for biting into tomatoes warm from the sun, for corn on the cob in August and homemade tomato soup in January. They weren't however, always thrilled about garden chores. (Even so, some of Peg's fondest memories are of gardening projects such as planting or hoeing involving the entire family.) Carl missed meat during his high school years and bought his own steaks. Jack preferred meat and potatoes to a vegetarian diet all his growing years. However, we judge the long-range effects on the children as positive: both in terms of their good health and of their enthusiasm for "our kind" of food. Eating our home-cooked garden meals is one of the high points for them when they visit over the holidays. Carl, Becky and Heidi have all done some gardening as adults. Becky called me long distance from Wisconsin last summer -- she was in the middle of canning tomatoes from their garden and had some questions about the process.

Even Jack, now in his mid-20's, says he's learned to like salad greens. And grandson Max (Carl's 3-year-old) is already keen about vegetables.

Raising chickens -- A perfect companion to gardening is raising chickens. In addition to the obvious advantage - the addition of protein-, vitamin-, and mineral-rich eggs to our diet -- there is the extra bonus of chicken manure for the garden. Our chicken yard is a compost heap in action. All of the garbage is thrown over the fence to the chickens. What they eat is an enriching addition to the feed we buy for them at the grain elevator. What they don't eat mixes with their droppings, with earth (chickens are great scratchers and mixers), and with the Champney straw substitute -- what else from a family of printers but newsprint strips, the by-product of our folding machine. The mixture decomposes into a rich compost, which we spread on the garden each spring.

All you need to get started raising chickens is a chicken house well enough constructed to keep out varmints and a small fenced-in yard attached. Carl built our chicken house during a college vacation when he needed to earn a little spending money.

Some questions for which chicken raisers need to find answers:

-- What will you do with the chickens after their egg production is no longer sufficient to be worth the money to put into feed? The advice in the poultry raisers' manuals is not to keep them past the first year. We've usually stretched that to 2 years. Are you willing at this point to kill and dress your chickens and eat their meat? We are; we compromise on our vegetarian scruples when the alternative seems so wasteful. And, let's face it, we enjoy chicken soup and chicken pie. The actual killing and dressing is not a favorite job, but Peg's country upbringing provided her with the necessary know-how.

-- Do you want to raise your hens from baby chicks, or buy them as laying pullets? We have followed the latter option until just this past year. The main difficulty is the need for a second house and yard space for the baby chicks if you have an already established laying flock; the old hens would attack the young intruders if they share the same space. Advantages of starting with chicks are that they can be procured by mail-order, while it is getting more difficult, at least in our area, to find places to buy laying pullets; and that watching chicks grow is great fun. It's been a pleasure we've shared with our grandson Max who lives nearby.

Living space -- One of the first things to be dropped when we opted for living on less was the plan to make an addition to our smallish home, a 3-bedroom, 1 story, 768 square feet prefabricated house. Interestingly enough, while the children grumbled about some aspects of the simple life, they never complained about our limited living space. Four girls and a baby brother shared one bedroom for many years, while two older brothers occupied the adjoining bedroom. We shoehorned them in with the help of double and triple decker bunk beds.

Living in The Vale community was a great help and served as a safety valve. If our own walls seemed too confining, we could step out the door into the 40 acres including woods and fields, a commons area with play equipment and picnic tables, and six houses of congenial neighbors.

Growing up in The Vale our children felt welcomed and at home with all the neighbors. This meant that some rainy Saturdays Peg might find herself in charge of 7 or 8 children in a pretty small space; the next day or week our house might be empty because the children congregated elsewhere. Adult companionship for Ken or Peg was always within walking distance, whether it took place as a few words exchanged while borrowing a teaspoon of baking powder, or at a potluck get-together.

With very few exceptions, the now grown Vale children look back on growing up in this community as a pretty ideal situation.

There were, of course, challenges in living in a small house. At one period five of the seven children were taking music lessons. Finding a place to practice wasn't always easy. We can remember when the bedrooms, the living room and even the bathroom were utilized simultaneously as practice rooms in our Champney conservatory. Ken found space by pursuing hobbies which took place at home after the rest of the family was in bed. Since he was another amateur musician, the children learned early to sleep through noises like piano practicing. We like to think, in fact, that our entire family learned many valuable skills about relating to other people, simply by being so many in such a small space.

Of course, by world standards our "small space" was a mansion.

No TV -- When our old TV broke down, early in the days of our simple living experiment, we decided not to fix or replace it. We feel that was just about the wisest decision we ever made. Of course, sometimes our kids--Jack more than the others--watched TV with friends at their homes. We're glad that, for the most part, our children were spared from TV violence and materialism. Perhaps we're even gladder that they and we were not caught up in the passive nature of TV watching. We were freed to pursue self-initiated, more creative pursuits. Ken has learned all kinds of do-it-yourself repairs, created a contract bridge bidding system and composed music in the after hours of a demanding job. Peg has had time to can and freeze and to use creatively our garden produce, to sew, and has also taught in our Vale alternative school, and founded a summer Quaker music camp.

Glen pursued his natural inclination toward taking everything apart and putting them back together to become something of a mechanical wizard. All of our grown children are creative cooks; the girls are good at sewing - Becky sometimes even designs her own patterns. And -- being able to take lessons and practice music as children, without the competing time demand of TV watching, seems to have paid off: music remains an important part of their adult lives. Wendy and her Swiss husband Matthias are professional string players; their string quartet gives concerts all over the world. Heidi is a gifted violin teacher and plays in professional orchestras. Carl is an old-time fiddler in demand by local square dance groups. Becky sings beautiful lullabies to her 18 month old Suzie.

Turning down the thermostat -- Learning to be comfortable in a 60 degree house -- or even at 55 or 50 degrees -- is one of our simple living accomplishments. Ken and I are cool house enthusiasts: it's comfortable, we feel it's cut down on the occurrence and duration of winter colds, and it saves a huge chunk on fuel bills as well as on energy. However, this is one area of our life where we've been unable to convince children, other relatives, friends, neighbors. There is something about a warm house in winter which apparently strikes deep-down feelings of nurturing and care in most people; or perhaps it's simply that folks have allowed themselves to become accustomed to a warmer-than-necessary environment and it becomes a habit difficult to change. We turn up the heat when guests are expected.

In the meantime, we still recommend that others give it a try. If you're used to 75 degrees, try 72; if 72 is what you like, try 70 or 68 -- and so on. There are all kinds of tricks involved in learning to be comfortable in a cooler house. One obvious one is wearing more clothes -- layering is helpful, as is wool. Not every one is aware how important a warm cap is in keeping the entire body warm.

Exercise also makes a big difference. A brisk morning walk outdoors with the dog makes Peg's internal heater go to work. Ken has the perfect exercise contraption, a hand-operated grain grinder. Turning wheat berries into whole wheat flour is hard, aerobic exercise, and Ken ends up peeling off several layers of sweaters and shirts as he grinds away. When Peg turns that freshly-ground whole wheat flour into bread, the result is one of the most delectable luxuries of the simple life.

Still another method to get the body's own internal heating mechanisms grinding out warmth is a cold bath. Ken says it works. Peg refuses to try this method.

We challenge our readers to give a try at adjusting to temperatures a few degrees lower. Even Jack, who was our most vociferous objector to a colder house, now claims his upbringing with us toughened him so he's more willing to do outdoor work in cold weather than his buddies.

The Vale School -- The founding of our school in The Vale predates our simple living experiment by quite a few years, but the way we carried out the school fits in so well with simple living that it bears reporting.

The Vale Friends School was our alternative neighborhood school for children pre-school through 3rd grade. Although it was intended originally chiefly for the children living in The Vale, throughout its 35 years' existence it attracted a steady stream of children from the surrounding area -- often but not always children with special needs which were not being met by other schools.

Teaching was always done by Vale parents. It might be described as cooperative home-schooling, always on a volunteer basis. In this way we were spared one big hassle which often plagues small alternative schools -- how to afford a paid teacher. We feel that our children had the privilege of an excellent education in their early years, without the usual high costs of private schooling, which would have been beyond our simple living budget.

One early motivation for starting our own school in The Vale was that we lived two miles from town, and the normal school day plus bus trips at either end of it seemed too long for small children. Our purpose soon grew beyond that. We came to envision an early school experience where community living was an integral part of each day's experience. Thus the children helped make their lunches with the help of various adults among the participating families; they baked bread, made applesauce and cider; and other such projects. They became involved with neighborhood repair projects such as fixing bicycles and automobiles; made Christmas presents--woodcraft with one parent, sewing with another; and they planned and carried out parties, plays and picnics for the entire Vale community.

Besides offering this community experience and the chance to relate to several adults in the neighborhood (the beginning of friendships which have lasted into adulthood), our school was small enough that it could truly individualize each child's learning experience. The academics -- the 3 R's -- were handled much as is done in a one-room schoolhouse, each child progressing at his or her own pace. Particular interests and talents were also encouraged and given a chance to grow and develop. Those Vale School children have grown into artists, engineers, computer programmers, skilled mechanics, musicians. In most cases, the budding interest and talent which later developed into these adult callings was noticed and encouraged in those early years of our school. Time was set aside in the school day for those mechanically inclined to take apart and reassemble old appliances, cars . . . the would-be musicians practiced their instruments during the school day . . . the future artists were encouraged to experiment with paints and clay.

Because our family didn't wish to earn more money due to not wanting to pay a war tax, the volunteer teaching suited Peg's needs. She viewed the teaching as an exciting challenge, and a way of relating to a wider group of people than might have otherwise been possible.

When the Vale Friends School was laid down after 35 years, Peg received as a retirement gift a totally unexpected but wonderful present from many of the parents who had sent their children to the school over the years -- the cost of a trip to Switzerland to visit daughter Wendy and her husband Matthias who live in Zurich.

Vacations -- We learned to vacation on a shoestring budget: exchanging visits with relatives and friends; camping at state parks; attending Quaker happenings such as conferences, Yearly Meeting get-togethers and family camps.

We have fond memories of packing our VW bus with camping gear, foodstuffs and our kids plus one or two of their friends, and heading off for a weekend, or perhaps a 10-day summer vacation.

We swam and hiked the dunes around Lake Michigan, climbed mountains in New York state and New England, rented canoes and rowboats in Ohio parks. Our camping gear was of the simplest sort: two old-fashioned umbrella tents which we inherited from relatives when they went on to something more useful to them, a camp cook kit, sleeping bags. Much of our food we prepared at home and took along, such as pancake and cocoa mixes, and the makings for sandwiches and soups.

I do sometimes wonder in retrospect how we fit all of us and our camping gear into one vehicle. Sometimes the gear even included a diaper pail and potty chair! But fit in we did. If tensions rose or tempers flared as we drove to our destination, we found a place along the road where kids could run off some steam before continuing on our way.

Perhaps one reason our shoestring budget vacations and outings worked so well is that such simple activities -- visiting friends, camping, participating in Quaker gatherings -- are actually the most enjoyable type of recreation.

At this point in our lives, we look forward to camping weekends with the grandchildren, as well as holiday visits from them and their families.

Charitable contributions -- In order to keep our income tax-free we've contributed a sizable chunk of our earnings to tax-deductible charitable organizations. Making the decisions about how much to give, and to which of the many, many worth-while undertakings in this world needing financial support has become an end-of-the-year ritual for us. We get a good deal of pleasure out of this annual event in our lives. Our goal is to divide our contributions among the organizations working toward the various goals we share with them: peace, environmental concerns, social justice, aid to the suffering, education, community, and so on. Knowing someone personally involved in such activities often influences us to make a contribution to that particular organization. We also lean in the direction of fewer but larger contributions, rather than a large number of smaller ones. That's our pattern -- others would do it differently. Whatever the method of doing it, we're convinced that contributing financially to such undertakings is an important part of bringing about the kind of world we all want.

The Yellow Springs News -- Ken's job as publisher-administrator-printer of the Yellow Springs News is extremely demanding -- but at the same time very satisfying. The weekly newspaper has played a real and positive role in making the town of Yellow Springs the unique and dynamic community it is. Readership is high and there are many letters to the editor, where a lively exchange of opinion occurs. For economic reasons, many weekly newspapers have gone out of business, or been purchased by large publishing chains, over the past few decades. Ken has considerable pride in keeping the Yellow Springs News afloat and modestly flourishing through these times.

The Yellow Springs News also played a prominent role in our family's simple living adventure. Although the pay is relatively low, Ken has pioneered an outstanding health insurance plan for Yellow Springs News employees and their families. For our children, the family business also provided after-school and summer employment. They learned responsibilities and skills. All of the kids held jobs at the News, as janitors, typesetters, bookkeepers, press and folder operators, darkroom workers, secretaries in the office. The jobs also provided them with spending money for items which our family's tight budget would have otherwise denied them -- food treats and clothing, and sometimes activities such as summer camps.

****

What began as merely living in a way to avoid war taxes has expanded for us into a way of life that is not only enjoyable, but which makes sense in many ways. We believe that simple living is healthy, psychologically beneficial, and perhaps -- for ecological reasons -- necessary on a large scale if the human race is to survive.

SIMPLE LIVING

IT'S EASIER
THAN WONDERING
WHOSE DEATH
MY DOLLARS BOUGHT

Kathy Epling

Some years ago I became aware that although I was living well below the so-called poverty line, nonetheless about $150 of my wages per year were being held by the government and used, I was certain, for deadly purposes. This knowledge haunted me and obsessed me as I sought for alternatives to passively allowing my money to pay for the killing of people or the jailing of my friends or the destruction of the planet. My imagination is vivid; so were my many images of what that money was doing. And while certainly it might have made me feel slightly more moral to zip off a note or two to the IRS or the Congress or the President saying "well, when you kill a young mother in Nicaragua with my tax money remember I really didn't think that was nice" -- what I really felt was essential was that no more of my dollars went to this government whose aims and purposes are so far from my own values. Outright refusal, so far as I could gather from cases reported in this newsletter[1] and elsewhere, coupled with passionately indignant notes, seemed in most cases to result in eventual payment to the government plus payment of fines. In other words I might be lucky enough to discover after much righteous rhetoric and sense of self-sacrifice, that now the government would have enough of my cash to kill that young mother and two of her neighbors, too. It did not seem a good solution somehow. So I looked into declaring myself self-employed. Though I work for hourly wages at a bookstore I am also a writer; possibly I could declare poet rather than bookseller my prime occupation. I considered quitting work entirely -- but I enjoy my work and did not relish the thought of going on welfare to feed my son and myself.

I was lucky; fate, in the shape of the birth of my daughter and my subsequent desire to work fewer hours to be able to have time at home with my children (as well as a faltering economy which made my employer pleased to hear I could do as much work in less time for less money) successfully dropped my income (and raised my deductions) so that there is no withholding whatsoever from my weekly wages.

So how do we live now? I am always interested in the concrete details of other folks lives, and think it may be important to share the prosaic details of ours. Certainly, there are other ways to avoid taxes, but this is how it is when one (or in our case a family of four) tries to live simply.

I earn these days about $80 a week; come summer, when business is fast, I may work a few more hours and earn a little more; I expect my yearly earnings to be between 5 and 6 thousand as they were last year. Paul, running his used book store, brings in about 3 or 4 thousand a year; thus we figure we probably live on about 9 thousand or so a year. Additional income, though usually not much, comes from sale of my poems and essays and from occasional gifts from relatives. (To Paul's dismay I usually count such money as a frivolity fund and am prone to spend it on rosebushes, fruit trees, and nonessentials for the children. The year I was pregnant with Laurel this sort of money paid for my prenatal visits to our local clinic.)

Our work on the *Peacemaker* is done on a volunteer basis; we don't take payment for it. We pay no rent, living in a small (12' X 20' plus upper sleeping room) handmade cabin on our 20 acres of woods. The land is paid for; we have yearly land taxes (about $200). We have no electricity nor plumbing; our "utility" bills come in the form of our pur-

---

1. *The Peacemaker*, March 11, 1988, Box 627, Garberville, CA 95440

chase of candles and kerosene and propane for our small cookstove. The cabin is heated by a woodstove; wood is gathered from fallen trees and branches on our land and is thus free to us. Paul does most of the laundry in cold water in tubs under the fir trees. Dishwater (and drinking water) is hauled in and out of the house in buckets, carefully dispensed to my trees and gardens. Our clothes are not cleaner than clean, but they feel soft and smell fresh, and we aren't pouring strong detergents onto the land.

Our clothes are not bought new: indeed they are rarely purchased at all. It amazes me what an adequate wardrobe one can gather from the local dump and freebox. Our loose network of friends here often pass on a find or two and there is the occasional spontaneous act of sweet kindness. Recently a woman at the health food store next to the bookstore I work at noticed my rather worse for the wear 6 year old work boots. "What size shoe do you wear" she asked after commenting that I looked due for new boots and hearing my response that I figured on at least another year from the ones I wore. She brought in a fine pair of her own boots the next day saying she'd just bought herself new ones. They fit. Warm feet. How nice!

Shoes and clothes for my 10 year old son take more searching or finer budgeting; I usually buy him new shoes a few times a year -- children of his age and activity seem to really use up their shoes. He earns some money himself babysitting for Laurel during some of my working hours and recycling aluminum; he knows and accepts that most of his special desires will have to be bought by himself. Recently he scraped together enough to buy a much coveted bicycle, used, in good condition.

Our major expenses are food and transportation. We have a faithful 1971 Chevy, given to us by a dear friend (given her upon her mother's death). Thus far it has kept running in amazing condition, but it does require attention a few times a year. A run of bad luck with our car can nearly wipe out a month's wages (as happened last autumn) -- but we are finding friends who understand cars, and our town mechanic, a sympathetic soul, has gone out of his way to save us money. We buy food in bulk, cooperatively, in a buying club which orders it from a coop about 60 miles north; it is delivered to Paul's store and sorted out there. As vegetarians we stock and use lots of grain and beans, fresh fruit and vegies, flour, etc. Buying organic food in bulk we avoid poisons and plastic -- but we still shop at local markets and, alas, still use, I think, too much processed, prewrapped food. The amount of plastic we gather in a week dismays me: wrappers from cheese, bread, tortillas. I do bake bread and make tortillas but on our workdays it is far too easy, still, for us to grab up some prewrapped package and my 10 year old considers that "real" food comes sliced and wrapped and, if possible, sugared. I also have a small vegetable garden and many young fruit trees but neither garden nor trees contribute yet a large percentage of our food. It has been interesting to us that as the economy worsens we have been attracting more and more people of all sorts of backgrounds to our buying club -- and I feel that cooperation is an essential in so-called simple living. (Paul keeps reminding me that simple living isn't easy. Friends and support make it much more possible and pleasant.)

Living on the edge as we do we have little room for the unexpected expense or emergency. Thus far we have, however, coped well. Necessity has led me to a study of homeopathic medicine and with that, some herbal knowledge and a lot of luck, fresh air, and good food, my family has been thriving. We did have cause to take Laurel to our local clinic with an infected toe when she was about a year and a half old. The clinic charges on a sliding scale (we were off the scale). The doctor ended up giving us the requisite antibiotics free: "You've spent too much already," he said.

We are a family of book addicts and here Paul's store is of great worth to us all -- all those boxes of books traded for; all those hours of delight and education. Since we are homeschoolers the bookstores (his and the one I work at) are wonderful sources of material.

When we visit more affluent friends and relatives I am often amazed at the great range of material goods we don't need or desire (or in many cases even know about beforehand). With Thoreau we can say that we are fortunate in having few wants -- this has been and continues to be a great source of wealth for us. Which is not to say that occasionally I do not feel the pinch of living on little -- when I lust for some frivolity like a new rosebush, or suddenly all Garth's socks are worn out, or Laurel tells me she really needs a tricycle. Usually then, if I am lucky -- and I am often lucky -- I sell a poem or two, or a friend drops by with a cutting, or an unexpected gift comes to us.

Recently I watched a slide show of photos of Nicaraguan villages. The little shacks seemed inexplicably familiar to me until I recognized that they looked a lot like my tiny house. I'd much rather live at a third world level than contribute to destruction and agony. It is much easier to live on little and breathe freely than to earn lots, pay taxes and give my children all the mass produced toys in the world. I'd rather walk with them on our dirt road and think of some other mother somewhere walking with her children, still alive because my money won't pay for the weapons to kill her. Finally, simple living is easy -- a lot easier than waking at night wondering whose death my dollars bought.

*   *   *   *   *   *   *   *   *

There is a cool fog in from the coast this May morning. I am up before my household to start breakfast and to have some clear time before the demands of the day engulf me.

On the way back from the outhouse I notice the beautiful white rugosa rose, Blanc Double de Coubert, is in bloom. I love this time of year here -- there is always such lushness and promise. It feels like every flower will bloom, every tree set much fruit, and each infant tomato or squash bear bumper crops.

It is almost two years exactly since I wrote that Simple Living essay, and our life here has changed a little, and my sense of -- shall we call it planetary emergency? -- has grown stronger.

Changes: a year ago in April the universe brought us a new bright soul, my third child, Gabriel Merlin. He was born here in the same sleeping room his sister Laurel was born in, attended by two of my dearest midwife friends, and in the loving presence of his father Paul and sister and brother. It was an ambivalent and difficult pregnancy, in part because I wondered deeply about the morality of having a third child. I was 41, Paul 51. I did a great deal of soul searching and praying, and finally thought, "I may not have planned this child, but this child was planned." It seemed churlish not to say yes to a gift, so I did sort of gather myself together, reach out my hands, and say, yes, I will love this new one too. My prenatal care during this pregnancy was all conducted very informally by my dear midwife friend. We shared a lot of lunches and a lot of hugs and intense conversations and I stayed out of the clinic. My primary labor support for most of the unexpectedly short labor was my eldest son, then 11 and 1/2, who showed himself to be a tender and competent labor coach while Paul and Laurel went in search of the midwives.

Now it was a family of five living simply! And the 12 by 20 cabin was feeling a little crowded. When Laurel was born I had hopefully bought some marked down wood -- enough for a floor for a new room. For four years it sat and weathered and provided homes for ants and mice outside. With Gabriel's birth it seemed we really could use a little more space. So last summer we called a Peacemaker work/rap, inviting friends from all over to come camp out on the land for a week or so and help build a new room, meet baby Gabriel, and share hours and hours of intense conversation.   Paul's sister Elaine had salvaged eighteen big windows from the local dump. These helped dictate the design of the new room, which is 16 by 12 and has one wall with nine, count 'em, **nine** windows facing the woods to the south. The lumber we needed we got from a small local family owned business. These folks carefully harvest and tend their woods and use an old mill to make full dimension, rough cut lumber. It is very sturdy and very lovely. Our Peacemaker friends, as well as local folks, worked hard, fueled by pots of plain vegetarian fare, and when the session ended we had a floor and one and a half walls. One of my brothers decided to stay with us through much of the summer and he and Paul completed the room by August. It is very pleasant to sit in a light filled room built with so much love. Every morning when I come downstairs I am filled again with gratitude and wonder. To us, our cabin seems quite palatial, with room for the children to play. To most of our city visitors it is still awfully spartan: beds that are really blankets on the floor, candles for light, water hauled in and out, outhouse from which we compost all our excrement. (My roses and fruit trees love the sweet dark compost cooked up from our wastes and leafmold and rotting, powdery old wood, mixed with some wood ash. There is a sort of magic in this process that I love. Visitors find it much less romantic. Laurel, at 5, wishes we had a nice flush toilet like her town friends.

And more changes. Shortly after I wrote that original Simple Living article, to which some folks responded with 'How on earth can you stand to live that way?" and others with "Well, we know someone who lives on much less," we were in fact called on to live on less at the same time that, paradoxically, some extra money came through to my eldest child. Now, it has never been my goal to prove I could live on less and less and less, or to enter into some sort of Holy Lifestyle competition. For me it has been a question of living simply, living responsibly, living with joy. For us there has seemed room for indulgences on a below taxable income. But I have had cause to be grateful to the people who assured me they knew folks living on much less. It gave me faith that I could do it too, as my work hours were cut drastically (last year I earned 2,000 in wages) while Paul's store brought in less income as well. As to that paradoxical money for my eldest son -- his father turned 65 the year Garth was eleven, and decided to allot a portion of his social security check to his son. This was most unexpected. Since I had been providing Garth's food, clothing, and so forth for all these years it didn't seem as if I should or could use that money. It was/is Garth's. An education fund? Travel money? I don't know. I don't know, either, if in not using it I have done the correct thing, but it feels right.   Is this good for Garth, now an independently wealthy child in a voluntarily poor family? (wealthy by our standards, in that I have allowed him to use his funds for some things he much desired that I could not stretch my budget to include -- some fancy new jeans, shoes, a skateboard).   I have realized that friends and Garth's father expected me to simply spend all this money (a bit under 300 a month) rather than letting/encouraging Garth to save it.   This has been interesting to me, casting light on my attitude towards money and my attitude towards children and money.

When my hours at the local bookstore were cut to an extent that I didn't seem to be able to support my family I decided to take another leap of faith (or craziness) and quit and start my own mail order book business.   I had been managing a mail order book business for the store I worked at for 12 years and figured I might as well do it for myself.   Small business is probably a surefire way to stay way below taxable income. That I nearly called mine Lilies of the Field Books says something about my business philosophy, which is not a philosophy recommended much by business experts.   Paul groaned and vetoed Lilies of the Field.   I call my business Tiger Lily Books and specialize in books for children and families.   It is fun, exciting, anxiety producing.   You need not be rich to place Mammon before God, and I struggle often with my tendency to worry overmuch about business.   Because we are adept at living on very little we seem to make it from week to week.

A few stacks of whole wheat pancakes later.   There is a deermouse trying to live in our cookstove.   Each morning I lift the burners and remove her little nest before lighting the flame.   She is a pretty creature, white footed and sleek.   Our cats spend a lot of time staring at the stove these days.

Our life is far from perfected and always subject to change.   There are, I think, still major contradictions.   Our use of a car is probably the largest and the one we have as yet not seen how to change.   Paul is currently working on ideas for local cooperative transportation and we shall see what comes of this.   For now we travel back and forth to town, 11 miles away, four times a week.   This is an expensive and ecologically bad thing to do, but I am grateful for the continued life of our rusting 1971 Chevy.

I think, too, that we need to provide more of our own food.   Our fruit trees are bearing well now, except the apples.   Living as we do in the forest, and being unwilling to cut trees, we find large scale vegetable growing difficult -- yet somehow I sure do grow lots of flowers!   This year I'm trying container grown vegies, to thwart gophers and conserve water, placed in sun spots in the rose garden -- as well as my usual hopeful vegetables grown in the sea of daisies that is the Vegetable Garden 300 yards from the cabin. Bucketing water by hand to that garden is hard in August.

I consider too, cutting down our dependence on milk and eggs, but worry about balancing the diets of our growing children -- and also, to be honest, much like butter and cheese myself. Probably this keeps me a little humble when I get impatient at the reluctance of friends who think they can't live without meat. It was very easy for me to stop eating meat some 20 years ago -- but to give up cheese! My appetite protests vigorously.

I think sometimes that folks speaking or writing or thinking of living simply are too apt to emphasize the Saintly Deprivation. I think if one comes to this with a sense of Doing Good (or Living Virtuously) Though It Is Painful one will find it very hard indeed. Always at the back of one's mind there lurks then the sense of doing without. I think therefore it is important to live simply with a sense of joy and wealth. Not to count what one doesn't have but what one has abundantly. We have peace of mind in living without paying taxes, and more peace each time we do not buy something that has caused suffering or destruction. When one is blessed with a vivid imagination and a tender conscience it is good not to buy into death and ruin.

A break to change diapers and water the roses and tomatoes and play a while with Gabriel. Just as well; I was getting pretty rhetorical. Paul and I just had a discussion as to whether we can still be said to be voluntarily poor. He is worried today. Where will the money for food come from? Will he be able to continue to pay the store rent? Before I left my waged job we could count on my wages. I say yes, we are still voluntarily poor. We continue to choose our way of life and the consequences of living this close to the edge. The consequences (to go back to living with joy! Paul tells me were I in hell I'd chirp "what interesting people -- and how nice and warm it is") include time. Time to be with our children, who are the great delights of our lives. Time to play and venture. Paul, Garth, and I all have radio shows on the local station this spring. Garth does a fine Old Time Radio show, Paul a political talk show, and Paul and I and a friend a weekly poetry show. In a subtle way perhaps the consequences include love. We must cooperate with our friends in our food buying club. And how richly we have benefitted from the work of so many friends, given in love. I suspect if we lived standard middle-class lives we might not have so much sharing.

Trust is a curious other consequence. I try to live my life in trust. Certainly I don't always succeed. So far, though, I don't seem to have been led to venture farther than I can manage.

I am writing in the garden, in the bright sunlight. Another of the scented white roses (this one is Madame Alfred Carriere) is blooming in the top of the greengage plum I planted to celebrate Laurel's birth. Her placenta is buried beneath it. A little further on a Satsuma plum, bearing its first fruit, marks the spot where Gabriel's placenta was buried last year. The first butterflies -- swallowtails, cabbage whites and Admirals -- are drifting all around.

Another morning. I have just taken the poppyseed apple leftover-cereal muffins from the oven. In our household this seems to be the year of the muffin; great for making odds and ends tasty. I've stirred the starter for the Amish friendship cake passed on to me last week by Garth's dad.

And did I really write yesterday that living simply gave one TIME? Some days, in my household, I wonder that I get anything done. Yesterday, what with hauling and heating water the dishes took a few hours to get done, and then it was dinnertime. But let's be honest -- I did a lot of other things in between dish rinsings. Usually, thank heaven, Paul does the dishes late at night while he listens to our taped together old radio pulling in some classical station and our children sleep and I, if not sound asleep too, get some reading or writing done. Dishes. How does this fit in with NOBLE RIGHT LIVELIHOOD? I always seem to find myself talking and writing of the most mundane reality. Somehow, though, it seems important. I guess I'd rather have some one tell me who does the dishes and how in their household than say "We must all strive for Peace or Revolution". (I might add that in the interests of simplicity and less work Paul keeps trying to get us to a one bowl system. Thus far without success.)

I hear Gabriel babbling to Laurel upstairs -- may have to stop for awhile.

Ravens calling to each other from the big tanoak. They are such impressive birds, huge and glossy, with so many different calls. Laurel and Garth have both learned to make some of the raven words and sometimes go out and talk with them.

I just took time to figure out our current financial standing. My checking account has a bit under one hundred dollars in it (I don't have a savings account). I have 13.11 in cash. Paul has squirreled away almost enough to pay this month's store rent (it is 350 a month). We have a bill of 180 due this week for food for the month from the buying club and I have about 600 due in the next two months to publishers who have sent me books to sell. I ought to be putting out a new catalog right now, but the money is obviously not on hand -- not this week anyway! Well, something will turn up -- it always does (until it doesn't, remarks Paul). The *Peacemaker* account is fine (it goes for printing and mailing the paper only). There should be good crops of raspberries and strawberries and plums and roses; summer is a time of sweet abundance, no matter if our pockets are full of pretty rocks, pieces of rosemary, and little toys instead of money.

Paul and I seem to take turns worrying. While I am blithely talking of the birds of the air and the lilies of the field and tenderly watering the gardens, he sometimes figures we really went under last week and I didn't notice it. But then when I am sleepless with anxiety and allowing business to cloud my thoughts too much, he will steadily insist we can do impossible things, and remind me there is a world of folks living on much less than we do.

Last night we gathered with about twenty friends and neighbors in town in a converted garage for yet another Empire Cabaret -- sort of a cross between a neighborhood talent show and a party. Paul started organizing these events about four years ago when Laurel was tiny and he was facing a prison sentence for climbing the fence at a naval base north of here on Hiroshima Day. We figured we needed some way to meet legal costs. The first Cabarets were held in relative luxury in a real theatre. Red plush seats, great acoustics. But after a couple of years the school district, who owned the place, decided insurance problems made it impossible to let these events go on. The current location is pretty down home but what fun!

Last night a dear friend sang and another played the accordian and we had poetry and some of Paul's KCIA newsbriefs. Laughter, and Gabriel bouncing to the music. It is these moments of sharing that seem so essential somehow. My friend the singer had just heard that she will be a grandmother early next January. My own sort of grandson (child of Garth's dad's daughter -- these confusing blended families!) is due any day now. It keeps coming to me that these children need song a whole lot more than lots of money. And clean air, clear water, some wildness, some wilderness . . .

Children. Mine are, as I have written, the great delights of my life and my greatest self indulgence. We wonder sometimes about how our lifestyle will affect them -- especially as we are not sheltered from the influences of the world, try as we may, with our homeschooling and lack of TV. Our children have many friends who live lives of middleclass splendor, who go to school, who have those flush toilets my Laurel thinks are so great. Garth currently wants to be a ball player: "They make lots of money!" Gabriel, with his almond eyes and his sweet laugh is today 13 months old and not yet crawling, though he sings well and charms us completely. Perhaps his gentle nature is such that he will continue to love the roses and the cats and this life of ours in the woods that he doesn't yet question. Will these children, raised in voluntary poverty, come to think they were simply raised in poverty? I don't know. But I can't impoverish the earth, or someone else's children to give my own more luxury. Love and care and lots of silly times (Laurel's term for those times of giggles and fun) will have to fill our lives. Maybe not having lots of material things leaves more room for them. I like to think so.

Laurel asked me the other day "Are we poor?" As I readied my answer, she answered herself. "No, we have a house and flowers and food and toys and books. I have lots of clothes. Poor people don't have enough and we have enough so I guess we aren't poor." She went off to play with her papa. And maybe that's it. We have enough: may all beings on this earth have enough. May we know when we do have enough, and be joyful.

A WORLD FAR REMOVED FROM MY FAMILY OF ORIGIN

Barbara Terry

By the time I came along, my father had increased his apple farm at the edge of a small town in upstate New York from 20 acres to 200 acres. The house we lived in had been enlarged also. What was once a two bedroom, two story old Dutch farm house was now a seven bedroom, four and a half bathroom home. Two of the bedrooms were over the two car garage and were reserved for the live-in help. They used the back stairs which led into what we called "the little room off the kitchen". There was a large kitchen, a pantry and a formal dining room. A hall ran from the front door to the back door between the dining room and the parlor, as it was called in those days, which held a grand piano. Also, the front stairs led into the hall near the front door. In the back of the parlor was the "green room" where most of the family gathered in the evening after dinner. My father loved beautiful things and our home was filled with antiques and works of art. Both of my parents were avid readers, so our house had large bookcases in virtually every room. I rarely went to the library, because there was no need.

There was about an acre of lawn surrounding our house, interspersed with maple, elm and evergreen trees, as well as flowering bushes. A circular front driveway as well as a longer rear one gave access to the house from the street. In the rear of the house was a large vegetable and flower garden which was enclosed by a white picket fence. My father hired a colored man named Charlie to take care of the lawns and garden. My mother supervised the flowers and their care.

When I was seven years old, my parents hired Katherine to be a live-in maid. There had been others before her, but I have very few memories of them. Katherine came from Ireland and was a few years younger than my mother. She did the cleaning, the laundry and waited on our table. Under the carpet near my mother's chair in the dining room was a little button which, when pressed by a foot, would ring a buzzer in the kitchen. This would signify that mother wanted Katherine to come and find out what was needed at the table. Katherine and my mother became friends as far as their station in life would allow. They shared a love of crossword puzzles and would spend time looking up words in the dictionary or encyclopedia. Katy had a hot temper and we children would steer clear of her when she was mad lest we feel the full force of her anger. She kept track of us as if we were her own, which made my brother and me all the more clever in evading her and my mother.

At about the same time, my parents hired a colored cook named Suzie. She had a house in town, about a mile away, which she shared with her sister, Cora. Suzie spent most of the week at our house, going home only on her days off, which were Thursday and Sunday afternoon and evening. She was a slight woman with grey hair. No one knew how old she was and she kept it a secret. When the census taker came to our door, my mother and Katherine hoped to find out her age only to have her tell the man that she had already been counted at her house. She was an excellent cook using the wood stove in our kitchen. Her pies, without exception, were fine. I can still hear my father exclaim over Suzie's apple pie. My mother baked oatmeal bread and Boston Brown bread and Suzie did the rest of the cooking. She was a quiet, mild mannered person. She was a fan of Joe Louis and joined a club named after him.

My sister, the eldest in our family of five children, went to boarding school when I was four years old. Most of my childhood memories include my three older brothers. We were expected to bathe and dress for dinner each evening. The whole family sat down at the table for three meals every day. My mother felt that hot meals were important so we rode our bicycles home from school for lunch.

All in all, the days passed happily with only minor unhappiness occurring. My only memory of the Great Depression is that my mother told me that my father could not afford to buy me a new winter coat. I was young enough so that this didn't particularly upset me.

We lived in a small New England town where the lines of caste were drawn. My family belonged to the upper crust. It was understood by the young people that children of the tradespeople in town did not belong in our circle. We were to be nice to the others but not include them in our social activities. This division occurred quite markedly when we were in High School. We all went to the public school through the eighth grade and my father served on the Board of education there for a while. My parents believed in higher education. Also, it was fashionable to send your children to boarding school. I went to a private day school in Albany for my first year in High School because there was no room for me at George School, the co-ed Quaker boarding school in Pennsylvania which I attended for the other three years. These were happy years for me. I enjoyed the social life, which was not dependent upon couples to participate, but rather included everyone. We lived in dormitories, two girls to a room. In the dining room we sat at the same table for a semester. There were eight people to a table including a faculty member. Classes were small and there were many extra-curricular activities. I especially appreciated the Quaker influence in regard to their concern for social problems and their attention to the God within each person, which was called the Inner Light. The motto for George School was "Mind the Light". These interests appealed to my youthful idealism. Several times I went on week-end work camps to the slums of Philadelphia with Dave and Mary Ritchie, who had run them for many years. At such a work camp, I worked in a Black hospital doing menial tasks. Another time a group of us painted the inside of a Black family's home.

The contrast when I came home was painful. My parents' interests were more focussed on cocktail parties, bridge, golf, etc. My father was a staunch Republican and against the minority groups. It seemed wrong to me to have so much material wealth and not to be helping others. I objected to his smoking and drinking. One time I came home from school to find cases of Bacardi rum stored in my closet and I made it known in no uncertain terms that I did not want his liquor in my room.

I attended Antioch College in Yellow Springs, Ohio in the fall of 1943. My father would have preferred that I attend Vassar. He offered me a convertible coupe and a fur coat if I would bend to his wishes. One of the reasons I chose Antioch was that I figured if he wasn't enthused about it I would be. As usual, I ended up doing the best thing for me for the wrong reasons.

It was war time and the college was on the quarter system. This meant that the students spent three months on campus completing their courses in twelve weeks. Antioch had the work study program, so ordinarily the next three months were spent working off campus. Since the college had many jobs in various fields, a student could gain experience in a field of their choice. Some of my jobs included selling stockings in Marshall Fields in downtown Chicago, working in an interracial community center on Long Island and a live-in home for dependent and delinquent girls in Toledo, Ohio, and student teaching in two progressive schools.

In retrospect it is interesting to note the events that led to major life changes. Often, in themselves, they are not cataclysmic or dramatic, but rather run of the mill occurrences. Such was the case in breaking the bone in my foot during modern dance class. I had been dating Warren Terry off and on for a quarter. We had taken hikes, bike rides, folk danced and gone to the usual college affairs. He had already graduated from Antioch and was running a local co-op grocery store. Since I had my foot in a cast and had to get around on crutches, I couldn't leave campus for a job when the time came. Warren offered me a job in the store and I took it. For the first four weeks I had to walk a mile on crutches to work. Warren and I worked well together. He was paid $40.00 a week and he paid me $20.00 and the other part time woman $7.00, keeping $13.00 for himself. We later joked that he married me for my money since I was earning $7.00 more a week than he was.

Warren introduced me to the co-op movement, pacifism, and alternate lifestyles. We were a part of a dinner group where we would pool our resources and for a quarter (25 cents) would have a hearty dinner each night. Different members would take turns doing the shopping, cooking and cleanup. Part of the time we met in an old barn and had our dinners there. There was much talk around the table of politics and economics fired with the optimism of youth. One member eventually went to live on a Kibbutz in Israel. Many discussions centered around intentional co-operative communities. We were bound and determined not to be caught up in conventional expectations. Coming from a very conventional, structured home, these topics of conversation broadened my awareness of different approaches to life and were new and exciting. I had entered a world far removed from my family of origin. I was fascinated by it and was drawn to the idealism of it all.

In December of 1945, Warren asked me to marry him. I agreed and we went to Springfield, Ohio to purchase a set of rings. I remember walking in the snowy evenings watching my small diamond sparkle in the street lights. Those were magical days and our friends were happy for us.

I flew to Florida to be with my parents for the Christmas Holidays and Warren hitch-hiked down to ask my father for my hand in marriage. The first evening he was there they sat down to talk. My father was a staunch Republican, capitalist, and prejudiced self-styled realist. Warren was interested in co-operatives, socialism, and intentional communities. On every subject, they were diametrically opposed. It was a very uncomfortable evening for us all. Through my mother, I learned that my father thought Warren was a dreamer. He would have been happier if Warren had been earning $5,000.00 a year so that I could be supported in the manner to which I was accustomed.

Upon the advice of my advisor and confidante, I went home for the Spring quarter in order to prepare for the wedding. The date was set for June 8, 1946 at 4 p.m.-- the proper time of year, day and hour to be married. Warren and I would have preferred to be married in the small campus chapel at Antioch; however, my sister said that since I was getting the man I wanted I should let my parents put on the wedding they wanted. My father had refused to attend my sister's wedding because she married a Jewish man; I was his last opportunity to show the community what he could afford. I was catapulted into selecting pattern for silverware, sending out engraved wedding invitations, deciding on a menu, ad nauseam. I wrote to Warren almost daily and he responded in kind. I needed that touch with my future life in order to go through the myriad of details connected with planning a large wedding.

Unknown to my parents, I sent Warren $10.00 to get from Ohio to New York, and he hitch-hiked all the way. He was quite overpowered by the opulence of our home, but I assured him I was eager to break away from that kind of life.

I had six bridesmaids and six ushers. My sister was matron of honor and my father gave me away. We were married in the Episcopal church where I had attended as a child. I wanted my roommate to sing but the song she chose, "Ich Liebe Dich," was too secular, said the minister. During the ceremony he took off his red stole and used it to bind our hands together as a symbol of our commitment to each other and to God.

The reception was held at our home in the country. There were cases of champagne, as well as many foods. Since neither Warren nor I drank alcoholic beverages, we secretly poured champagne on the plants so it would look like we had sipped our drinks. A small string orchestra played in the front parlor while the guests milled around the back living room and out onto the side porch.

After a short honeymoon camping in the Pocono Mountains in Pennsylvania, we returned to Yellow Springs where we rented the front half of a farm house, a mile out of town. The owner was an old farmer who lived in the back of the house. There was no running water or electricity. There was a hand pump in the yard and an outhouse in the back. We heated with wood, cooked with kerosene and used Aladdin kerosene lamps in the evening.

I returned to school in the fall. I enjoyed my jobs more than my studies, as the book learning became more and more irrelevant. I dropped out the next quarter and took a job as a teacher's aide in the first grade at Frances Parker school in Chicago. Warren got a substitute teaching job in a nearby town. In spring I student-taught at the Antioch School in Yellow Springs which was a private, progressive school. When the semester ended, we gathered some of our wedding presents and other items and had a yard sale. With the proceeds we went west to visit Warren's parents in Washington state. We bought our first car from my cousin in Rochester, New York -- it was a 1934 Chevy coupe with a rumble seat. We paid a hundred dollars for it and drove it across the U.S.

I remember how excited I was to be going out West. Perceptions of distances were different in those days. When I left for college in Ohio it seemed a long way from home. California was over the horizon and almost a foreign country.

We went first to the coastal region of Washington. After meeting Warren's parents for the first time, I loved them because they were so relaxed and warm. Most of their working years were spent in China as Presbyterian missionaries. Mr. Terry was head of the Christian Literature Society in Shanghai until they were forced to leave because of the Japanese-Chinese war. They lost all of their possessions a couple of times and were not tied to material things, as were my parents. There were times when they must have thought I was a bit too worldly because I enjoyed an off-color joke now and then.

Soon after we arrived, Warren's sister was married and the house was full of gaiety. Warren's older brother, was living with his wife up on the hill on the same property, and his younger brother was home for the wedding.

A week after the wedding my in-laws went to Chicago where Dad Terry had a job teaching in the seminary there. Warren was doing carpentry all day and I was left home alone without transportation. I was miserable. We had come from a small college town where we had many friends and here I was stuck out in the country. Blaine is on the Canadian/U.S. border and much of the year it is cold and rainy.

I remember sitting down with a box of fruit to can each morning, listening to the radio while I worked. The house was cold, a penetrating cold combined with dampness. I yearned for community where there was fellowship along with the work.

Warren was having trouble with his allergies and would occasionally inspect the house to see if I had cleaned it properly, thinking that perhaps house dust was adding to his misery. When he'd run his finger over the top of the door frames, I'd feel angry. On weekends I'd be eager to go out and do something different, and since he had been gone all week, he'd like to stay home. Those were lonesome and unhappy days.

As the fall progressed, the weather became worse and the opportunities for work became less. So, just before Thanksgiving, Warren and I set out for California. He had built a wooden slatted platform over our 1934 Chevy coupe and on it we packed our belongings, including all that fruit I canned earlier. We had compiled a list of pacifists, people interested in intentional community, back-to-the-landers, and Quakers. We visited most of these people as we went along. I suppose you might say we were of the counter-culture of our day.

When we entered California we had a picnic near Weed. We were so happy to be in the sun and to be warm and to shed our longjohns. We made our way down the coast and spent Christmas day on the beach near Carpenteria. From there we went to Pacific Oaks School in Pasadena, a Quaker nursery school. They also had a Telluride College program for young men as an alternative to the armed services. I got a job cooking for thirty people each evening. Warren had his business doing handyman carpentry jobs. We lived on the premises and had a warm fellowship with the people there.

In the spring Warren took a trip north to visit several places to see where we'd like to settle for a while. He had a list stating our preferences, such as country living, like-minded people, etc. He returned to say he thought we'd be happy in Gridley, a small town ten miles north of Marysville.

During World War II there had been a group of five men and their families who had formed a co-op farming venture as an alternative to serving in the armed forces. They all belonged to the Church of the

Brethren. One of the families was moving away so we rented their house, a little two bedroom house with a fenced yard, lovely plantings, and a garden space with mature grapes, berries and asparagus. In the back were chicken houses and two acres of large walnut trees. This was to be our first experience of living in the country.

Five months after our first daughter was born, we moved to Forest Knolls in Marin County where Warren had a job with Harold Gregg. Harold and his wife owned a farm camp which they operated in the summer. We lived among the redwoods in a small one-room cabin which was heated by a wood cook-stove. It was the winter of the 1949 and a very cold one. The water pipes froze several times. There was a small bathroom and even though the toilet seat was painted bright red, that did not make it any warmer on a cold morning.

One of the reasons for our move to Marin County was that we were talking with the Brown family about plans for buying a boat with them and sailing to the Marquesas Islands. We felt the U.S. was becoming corrupt and that we might have a better chance to build the kind of life we wanted in another country -- a life where we could incorporate our ideals into our everyday life without the influence of a materialistic society. As the winter wore on we decided not to pursue this plan. The Browns opted for Canada where they bought some acreage and homesteaded there for many years. We returned to Gridley, where we bought an old Army tent which was 16' by 32' and pitched it in back of some friends' house near the dairy barn. We had a wood stove to cook on and heat with. One night there was a big storm with lots of wind and rain. The tent would billow out and then collapse as the gusts of wind played with it. In the middle of the night it billowed out once too many times and the top of the tent split open, letting the rain in. We moved in with our friends for the rest of the night. The next day we had quite a chore fixing the tent and drying out our belongings.

As spring progressed, it became too hot to stay in the tent any longer so we moved into a small house that a friend owned across the street.

By this time we were looking for a place to buy and found eighteen and a half acres on Hopkins Avenue, the next road over from our friends. It had three acres of peaches and the rest was not planted to anything. I laugh now to think how enthusiastic we were about the lovely grass that was waving in the wind, not realizing that it was a field of foxtails. When they dry they stick to socks and any clothing they can. The place had a well and an old fashioned hand pump. There was a grove of eucalyptus trees in the front where we planned to put our house. We paid $8,500 for the property. I had written to my father to ask him to loan us down-payment money. The reply, via my mother, was that he bought one of my brothers a new car that year and didn't have any more funds to spare. My father's idea about his children was that he was responsible for the sons; the girls were their husbands' responsibilities. So, Warren's parents gave us $2,000 for the down-payment. After we had paid some debts there was $1,750 left and the previous owners accepted our offer. We had $100 left with which to start building our home. We slept outside all that first summer under a mosquito net. The mosquitos were numerous because the neighboring rice fields provided excellent breeding grounds for them. Warren built a little crib for the baby and enclosed it with screening as she also slept outside until we had a roof over our heads.

Warren began by laying the floor and framing up the walls. We used the old tent for a temporary roof and the walls were open most of the summer. We hauled our water from the hand pump in two five-gallon milk cans on a wheelbarrow that Warren made. We did have electricity, but it was a year or more before we had running water. In the summer we cooked on a little three burner propane stove that had a small oven with words on the door "Direct Action." It lived up to its name. Everything I baked in it came out sprinkled with rust which flaked off the roof of the oven and I called it cinnamon or nutmeg. In the winter we had a wood stove to cook on and heat with.

Warren was doing carpentry jobs by day and building our house after work and on weekends. We had a large garden and over the years accumulated goats, chickens, and rabbits. We both worked very hard, but we enjoyed the country life, the clean air, and the touch with nature. We were also working toward fulfilling our dreams of being as self-sufficient as possible. We had very little money.

I recall going to the grocery store with five dollars to buy the week's food, schooling myself to ask questions like, "Can I do without this?" or "Can we make something similar that will do the job?" It was a challenge and I soon became aware of how little we really needed to maintain a healthy life.

We would collect orange crates and use them for shelves. If we cut them diagonally at the top and bottom we had a corner cupboard. Cut parallel in half, they turned into medicine cabinets, using the leftover ends for more shelves. Some of them we used for our files and Warren built a frame to hold them. Then he took heavy cardboard and tacked it over the frame. A couple of coats of paint made the file cabinet quite presentable. It still stands by his desk in Lakeport, reminding us of times gone by.

We did have some fun times too. Someone had given us an adult size Dr. Denton suit. It was like a huge sleeper and had a drop seat with rubber buttons to keep it closed. I had washed and hung it on the line while we were living in our tent. Our friend came in from the orchard and saw it hanging there, saying it looked big enough for both of us to get into at once. It really did stretch when it was wet. Well, one night we decided to try it. First we had to cut the feet off the garment because it wouldn't accommodate two pairs of feet. We did manage to get into it and get it all buttoned up, but then we couldn't move or sit down. We laughed so hard it was difficult to get out again, and unfortunately we couldn't even get to tell anyone to come share the merriment, especially our friend.

One time we decided to have a square dance for our neighbors. Most of the people we invited, unbeknownst to us, were fundamentalist Christians who didn't believe in dancing. Some of them stayed in the shadows by the road to see what was going on. The next day a young man from the place in back of ours came over to give us a sermon, replete with many quotes from the Bible about how sinful dancing was. So much for our neighborhood parties!

During the summer our friend, Sue, came to stay with us. Her fiancé was in prison because he refused to register for the draft. We had met both while we were in Pasadena. She introduced us to Gerald Heard's book on meditation. I can remember sitting in back of our house overlooking the garden and trying to experience the life of the spirit. I seem to recall that I wasn't very successful at the time.

As fall approached, it became urgent that we get the roof and walls on our house. Since Warren was needed to work full-time at home, I found a job at Behr's Market. Sue helped with child care and I enjoyed getting out of the house. I couldn't earn as much as Warren, but I was able to keep us in food. One of the clerks at Behr's was threatened by my presence and one day asked me if I was a Christian because I didn't wear any makeup. My answer was that it depended on her definition of a Christian. Also, she didn't like it because I chose to read while eating my lunch in the back room, instead of talking with other employees. When she found out that I had left my husband and baby at home with another woman, it was too much for her. One day she and I disagreed about something and she told me she'd make me suffer. Foolishly, I laughed and said I didn't think so. Not long after that I lost my job. Fortunately, Warren was almost finished with the work at home. Sue left in the spring to join her intended.

That first winter a storm came up with very strong winds and one of the eucalyptus trees fell across the roof of our house. We were all at home when it happened, and once again our belongings were wet. We were frightened but also thankful that nobody was hurt. We moved in with friends for a few days and a group of men from the Church of the Brethren came to help put a new roof on. They did the work in one day and we were very grateful for their help.

During the second summer on our land our second daughter was born. We had running water by then, but no hot water, toilet or shower. In order to wash clothes, Warren would lift a five gallon can of water onto our little gas stove and leave it there until it got hot. Then he would pour it into the washing machine, a wringer type.

The third summer a friend asked if we would take a girl into our home and care for her. Her name was Maryann, a German-Jewish girl who survived the concentration camps in Germany with her mother. The latter lived in Oakland and she thought that perhaps a summer in the country would help Maryann to regain her health and put on some weight. She was eight years old with dark skin and huge brown eyes. She got along well with our family and friends. She ate very little and didn't respond to pressure to eat more, though after seeing her mother almost force us (as guests) to eat what she had prepared, regardless of our own desires, I could well understand Maryann's resistance to food. She moved to Isleton with us, but resisted a new house and a new school. Her resistance was evidenced by vomiting every morning before the bus arrival. After a short while, we decided that she should live with her mother, so we took her back to Oakland. We lost track of her after that. I can't say that we helped her very much except that we gave her the experience of living in the country with a family. Her problems were too deep for a short summer's cure.

We were barely making it financially. Each month we would list the bills and check which ones we could pay and which ones could go for another month. Some of them we would pay only a little so that our creditors would know we meant to pay when we could. The winters were hard because there weren't so many jobs in the wet weather.

Warren got a job teaching shop and fourth grade in Iselton. We just weren't getting ahead financially and felt a steady income would help, even if it wasn't very much. The first year he earned $3,500. Iselton is twenty miles south of Sacramento in the delta region and our small, two bedroom house on the outskirts of town was lower than the levee bordering the Sacramento River.

We had chickens and goats in the backyard. I did not learn to milk. One time when Warren was away on a trip, I took the goats to Tracy about forty miles away where a friend took care of them until Warren returned. That was quite a trip! We had a four-door Model A Ford sedan at the time. I took the back seats out of the car and put the goats in. Our youngest daughter sat on the front seat with me -- no seat belts in those days, so she just sat on the front seat next to me. If we had to stop abruptly, my arm would automatically extend itself in front of whomever was in the front seat to try and keep them from falling. Whenever I took my foot off the gas peddle, the car would backfire and the goats would go baaaaaa. Usually I would take my foot off the pedal when we slowed down to go through towns. What a spectacle we were! One of the goats had horns and when she hung her head out of the window, a man hollered "Watch out -- it's deer season." I'd smile and wave as we tooled along.

In 1952 another daughter was born. Warren liked his job and his superintendent was pleased with his work. He was offered a $500 raise if he would stay for a third year, but we were lonesome for our friends and our own place. So -- back to Gridley we went. We had two cars by this time -- a Model A and a V-8 Ford truck. Warren built a four-wheel flatbed trailer, using an old truck for the frame; we packed all our of belongings, along with goats, ducks, and chickens, on that trailer. We were tired out by the time we left and when we were two miles from home at 2:00 a.m. a policeman stopped us, wanting to see our identification. After some convincing talk on our part, he decided we really were who we said we were and not some tenant running off with the landlord's belongings and animals in the middle of the night.

By working vacations and weekends, Warren had doubled the house by the time we moved back. We had a living room, kitchen, dining room, combined with a back porch where the children sometimes slept. That summer after we were settled, Warren added four bedrooms. Very little of the house was what you'd call finished, but it was more than adequate for keeping us dry and warm.

In the fall Warren got a job teaching forty-two fourth graders in Yuba City. Since we belonged to a pacifist group, teaching jobs were not available for him in Gridley. He did not like his situation -- he had too many children in his classes and the administration was not supportive of his ideas about education. The principal used to open the door of the classroom unannounced. If any child had his or her feet in the aisle, they were reprimanded soundly. His idea of education included sitting up straight with feet under the desks.

Our group of pacifist, community minded people was a way station for people traveling through our area. We had hosted the Rural Life Conference for a couple of years and people would come from all over the state, sharing their experiences of rural living and how they were effecting changes in our society. One man came to our group in Gridley and told us of his community on the east coast which had been flourishing for many years. It had started in Germany and when Hitler came to power, they moved to England. From there they went to Paraguay. The outfit in New York state was a branch of the original community. This man told us of the community's policy of the open door where they would take anyone in who wanted to live with them; not as full members, but as visitors. Warren and I thought that this policy was wonderfully loving and sharing so when a college friend, Karen, wrote that she and her daughter needed a home and wanted to stay with us, we said they could come. Karen had been engaged when we knew her in Antioch, but her fiancé was killed over in China in World War II and she had never married. We put our three girls in one room and Karen and Susie shared a bedroom. It wasn't long before she had a job as a waitress at one of the nicer restaurants in town.

Bill was walking down the railroad tracks when Warren picked him up and brought him home for a hot meal. It was a winter and cold and rainy. He offered to work around the place if he could stay. We always needed more help, so we told him he could sleep in the house trailer which Warren had built. He chopped wood and took care of the animals. He was from New England and knew what hard work was all about.

Another wanderer, Cecil, on the other hand, was full of "I'm gonnas." I'm gonna do this and I'm gonna do that -- lots of talk and very little action. He said he had no other place to stay, so he shared the trailer with Bill.

I was busy cooking for nine people, as well as doing the laundry, cleaning and child care. As often happens, our oldest girl came home from school with the measles. Then the other girls got them. After that our oldest brought home the mumps and the chicken pox. I spent from Easter until almost Mother's Day in the bedroom with one sick child after another.

Nothing lasts forever -- it just seems that way sometimes . . . Bill left, taking the Model A and a neighbor's shotgun with him. Warren finally told Cecil to leave and as he was leaving he said, "You are the first man who has asked me to leave and still shakes my hand." Karen moved out not long after that and married an older man.

Warren decided that he had had enough teaching for a while, so he began his business called "Terry Cabin Builders." He made a model which was beautifully crafted, his idea being to prefabricate the walls at home and then transport them to the location. He parked the model on a trailer near the main highway for advertising purposes and sometimes took it to county fairs. As his business grew he realized he would have to move to a more populous area in order for it to be a success.

In August of 1955 our son was born. That winter Warren got a job teaching an eighth grade class in Modesto. So, we moved again! We rented a three bedroom house and settled into town. One advantage was that I didn't have to transport the children by car whenever they wanted playmates.

It wasn't long until we found a home to buy. The real estate man called it a "dog on the market" and was amazed when we said it was just what we wanted. We paid $7,500 for it and when we first set eyes on it, the weeds were waist high on most of the half-acre lot. At one time it had been a commercial nursery and had many lovely roses and fruit trees. The house was an older one with high ceilings, two bedrooms, a combination kitchen/dining room, and a large living room. By dividing one bedroom and partitioning off one end of the living room, we created four bedrooms.

We stayed 4 1/2 years in Modesto. Warren went to night school and summer school and became fully credentialed to teach elementary, high school and special education classes.

We heard of an opening at Clearlake for a special education teacher. Warren applied and got the job. He enjoyed the freedom to develop his own curriculum as well as the increased salary. Our fifth baby, a girl, was born six weeks before we moved from Modesto to Lake County.

Aside from making a living, most of our energies were spent raising our five children who presented special challenges. Some of these include mental retardation, physical handicaps, mental illness and accidental death. Over the years we also took care of a teenage schizophrenic boy, an abused boy and an emotionally unstable girl as foster children. Because of this heavy involvement with our children we were not acutely aware of many of the current issues, so our emphasis on simplicity was not primarily because of social conscience but of necessity. Raising a large family on a teacher's salary demands creative solutions. We always had a large garden. Sometimes, I would spot fruit trees in someone's yard and we would offer to pick the fruit on half shares. At home, the children would fill the jars with fruit and I would process them in my pressure canner. Many summers we put up over 500 quarts of fruit and tomatoes. Our children were used to wearing hand-me-downs. Two of the girls learned to sew and in this way were able to have more new clothes.

When our children were young and we had little money the challenge seemed to be how we could get the things we needed. Now, as we are older and our children gone, the challenge is how to scale down our possessions so that we don't feel inundated with things. There are times when I yearn for a hermit's life, having a bowl, a spoon, a pot and a change of clothes as my only possessions. In other moods, I crave warmth and quiet and softness as well as beauty.

It is my contention that living simply does not preclude having beauty in my surroundings. I am reminded of the description of Alice Henderson's house in Catherine Marshall's book "Christie." Her home was made of native materials and was furnished with items made by the local people of West Virginia. For myself, I find that I feel more peaceful within when my surroundings are orderly. My home is very important to me and often it serves as a quiet haven for others.

I enjoy the challenge of making something beautiful out of a cast-off. For me, it is more fun to resurrect an old piece of furniture that some one else has thrown away, than to buy a new one. Somehow new things do not carry the excitement a made-over one does. This is not to say that I don't buy anything new, just that there is an extra charge of excitement and creativity to have seen the possibility of a reject and to bring it to life.

One of the lessons I learned from having so little was that I did not have to fear poverty in this country, because so much is thrown away by others. I also came to the conclusion that there is a subtle pressure exerted upon those who choose to be different from the mainstream. In order to withstand this pressure, it seems to me that I need the support of like minded people who share the same values.

At present, Warren and I are involved with using our solar box cooker, as well as teaching others how to make such a cooker out of two cardboard boxes, aluminum foil and a piece of glass. These cookers were developed by Barbara Kerr and Sherry Cole who live in Arizona. The plans for them can be obtained from Solar Box Cookers International, 1724 Eleventh St., Sacramento, CA 95814. This organization is working to get these cookers in use all over the world, especially in the countries where fuel is so hard to get. It can be used to purify water, also, which is another problem in developing countries. I have used my cooker for three years and have cooked, chicken, rice, cookies, bread, granola, etc. This summer I am canning a few jars at a time in it. On a hot day it will heat to 300 degrees. We have helped build six solar box cookers and held a workshop for 14 people. We are excited about the prospects of helping both people and the environment.

There are those who might say that because I was raised with abundance it was easier for me to choose a simpler life, than for someone who had very little. I would agree with them wholeheartedly. However, I do feel that whatever one's background the question is "What are the basic values which determine one's life style?" One can have very little, for example Mother Teresa, and live a full life of service and one can have a great number of possessions and be miserable.

Andrew B. Schmookler writes in *New Dimensions Magazine*, Jan/Feb 1990, ". . . the spiritual damage that we are doing to ourselves with our lust for wealth is far more subtle. Our bodies are not bleeding, they are sleek and well-fed. Our children are not orphaned, for our wealth buys most of us more than the proverbial three score and ten. If there is a deeper way of living than the one offered by our society, it is not so plain that all can see. The mainstream vision of a better future is simply more."

He goes on to say later in the article, "We know from experience that a life donated to compassionate giving is richer than a life of narcissistic taking. We know that a sense of oneness with all living beings and with our mother, the Earth, fills us with joy in a way no amount of possessions could."

THINKING ALOUD

ABOUT

RIGHT LIVING

Jo-ann Jaeckel

Dear Dorothy,

I've spent a great deal of time trying to decide if I deserve a place in your book. After all, I haven't done anything very dramatic or sacrificial. If this book is to touch a wide range of people, though, there needs to be a way for some people to start small and safe like I did. This downward mobility thing is going to have to be a part of everyone's consciousness if we are all to make it through. I hope my story will help the less risk-taking be more open to their own possibilities.

When I began to consider my own story I was confused about the term downwardly mobile. If I was on my way down, where was I from?. What class was I anyway? Until I was ten my parents, grandmother and I lived in a one bedroom apartment. My father only went to 8th grade but he sold used cars (is that white collar or working class?). My mother finished high school and worked as a clerk until she married my father when she was 35. I just found out that my father's father was quite wealthy until the crash of '29, but my father was living on his own at 13! No one of my parents' generation had been to college, and few of my cousins went either. That isn't to say that my parents didn't aspire to be upwardly mobile. When I was nine my parents bought a little two bed-room house. They liked to go to fancy restaurants and most years my parents took a one week vacation with me to some hot springs in southern California.

My mother said my father wouldn't "allow" her to work but made it clear she'd worked in the past and longed to do so in the future. She said a man's ego was very fragile -- that the woman was the boss but she must never let the man discover that. It was our job to keep the man's ego inflated. The message was that openness and honesty were dangerous to women and too painful for men. She never had the experience of tackling an issue openly and working it through successfully. "Why do you always want to dig up old feelings -- they only make things worse." Personal politics, open interpersonal communication, and finding one's moral values were not even concepts in my home.

As I said, my father sold used cars for a living, as did all the men in my family. We lived from one sale to the next. My father felt a lot of pressure to stretch his small commissions, to be the good provider. He often boasted how he could juggle all the different things he needed between customer and boss to make a deal. He was proud to know all the angles. Economics had no moral component, except, of course, not to steal.

I left home at 17 and went to college, lived in the low cost co-op, and worked my way through. Louie and I married when I graduated. His family had more education than mine but seemed more working class. They weren't interested in the trappings (knickknacks, clothes, cars) that seemed so important to my parents. He had just graduated from Harvard Law School and was about to get a PhD in statistics. I was a computer programmer about to get my teaching credential. Were we upwardly mobile?

During those years when we were both students in Berkeley there was always talk of what class you were. I said I was working class but it really wasn't that clear. The thing that was clear to me was that I didn't fit. I didn't fit anywhere! Not at faculty parties, not with the men at BART [Bay Area Rapid Transit] where I programmed, not with the radical feminist therapists with whom I was in counselor training. The people with whom I was comfortable generally seemed to come from similar backgrounds, and I knew I was very uncomfortable with many of my "middle class" friends. Was that learned from my father who had incredibly low self-esteem? or a reaction to my mother whom I judged to be pretending she was classier than she really was? or to my own lack of development? Undoubtedly, it was a combination. What I do know is that even now I feel pain due to the existence of class. I don't trust that I can really be seen by people from other classes -- I fear being categorized, invalidated, trivialized. And I recognize these things in myself and allow myself to be separated from others. Because I don't feel I fit in, I sense this pain almost everywhere. It is a hidden injury not recognized in our great melting pot.

How does all this fit into your book? Well, I can't tell whether I have really been downwardly mobile. Maybe I am just someone who couldn't be comfortable being upwardly mobile. Maybe that's because I don't have a positive enough self-image. As a child, my joys and sorrows were rarely linked to economic wants. As an adult, economics have not been a big motivator in my life decisions. The choices I've made were always in an upward direction of happiness for me. I didn't view them as righteous or self-sacrificing. Now, although our income near poverty level, I live in a lovely rammed earth house, all paid for, in a beautiful spot in the country. The fact that the whole thing cost less than the cheapest house in Ukiah doesn't make me feel any the less rich. I constantly compare myself back and forth between the rich and poor. I vacillate between feeling guilty that I live higher than 95% (a guess) of the world and thinking of material ways to improve my life when I am able. Sage and I are worried how we will manage financially and, at the same time, I'm being very picky about the work I take on. I go back and forth feeling rich and poor, upward and downward. Oh what a jumble of thoughts! Don't worry, if I write for your book, it won't be like this!

A few months later

Dear Dorothy,

It was the phrase, "downward mobility" that was confusing to me. Something about the subject grabbed me in a deeply emotional way. It was nice to think that you valued my opinions but did I really have a right to be in this book? I contacted a friend, who, I felt, would understand my dilemma, to use as a sounding board. As we sat in her kitchen I could feel the tears welling up in my throat.

I think my contribution to your book is not so much modeling a lifestyle as it is acknowledging my process of struggle -- learning how to put my values into action, especially in the context of my primary relationship.

After going through some of my history I began to see the issues more clearly. I have never considered my choices to be acts of conscious economic mobility in any particular direction. Rather I have aimed at my work being right livelihood. By that I mean work that is personally satisfying and at the same time socially responsible and productive. My first two careers (teaching and computer programming) were so personally unrewarding that by the age of 25 I could no longer consider doing work merely for money and/or ego gratification. Being wife and mother during the early 70's with its women's liberation pressures left me feeling an extreme lack of self-esteem. I was groping for a satisfying lifestyle. This is what led me to live in intentional community.

Having grown up in a large extended family, the idea of living and working with a group of people was a fairly natural step. There I found companionship, purpose, and security while material needs took a bottom line on my list of priorities. I spent 15 years in community. After that there was no turning back. The idea of just doing a job for money was totally unappealing.

My mid-thirties was a time of the stirrings of spirit for me. Just what I've come to "believe" in is not nearly so important as the fact that I, indeed, came to "believe" in something. After a lifetime of taking direction from my HEAD came new inner stirrings. Somehow by forty I had developed the sense that I needed to continue to strive to make my life a truer reflection of my best spiritual self.

Now, in my daily life, my head is filled with constant dialogue. I compare myself with others around me. For a professional counselor, I lead a modest life. I work on a sliding scale and some places I volunteer. From a professional perspective I'm low, low, low on the consumer totem pole. Yet compared to the clients I serve, I have it all; the basics are covered and I call the shots. I'm in the upper 95th percentile of the WORLD! One minute I'm feeling like one of the elite and the next minute, tired of scrimping. Every purchase I make I try to consider whether I am worthy, do I really need it, will it somehow be detrimental to the environment, does the manufacturer follow socially responsible policies, should I buy locally, on and on and on. Even the smallest purchase becomes the occasion for an entire personal inventory.

To further complicate matters, I am in a long term relationship. My partner and I make joint decisions about the direction of our lives together as well how we spend the money. While we are not worlds apart in our values, when it comes to working and spending it's hard to keep perspective. I have learned over the years that differences are healthy. I'm learning to celebrate those differences rather than being judgmental. But when it comes to setting priorities on our time and money, things get tough. Up to now I have been telling myself we make so little it really doesn't matter. It must, though, or I wouldn't spend so much attention on the issue. Perhaps focusing on the relationship differences is just a smoke screen. After all, I haven't even come to terms with how I operate by myself yet!

At the time you suggested I write this piece, a new element had added itself to my muddle. Last spring I inherited a house. Within the next few years I am going to have a sizeable amount of money. I will suddenly go from scrimping to not needing to worry. This access to money has been a catalyst for my wanting to become more conscious about my economic dealings by myself and as part of our relationship.

The thought of spending money on this new level has been difficult to come to terms with. At first I would say to myself, when I'm "rich" I'll buy . . . I was so bold as to make a list of things I would do with the money. I carefully kept it hidden so no one would see I was thinking of SPENDING. After a while I found I was allowing myself to think differently than I ever have. I had unleashed WANTING. Living simply, I have not allowed myself to want much. If a thought came in I would quickly tuck it away. Now everything is different. I am learning about a part of me I didn't know existed. How will I accept this about myself much less handle it?

I've lived such a privileged life, I really don't feel that my principles have had a proper testing. I've never worried about being hungry, never worried about a life threatening illness, never had my daughter in a serious crisis, never lacked the funds for adequate shelter or clothes. I vacillate between comparing myself to friends and work associates on the one hand and clients and nameless people in the news stories on the other.

The issue of my mother's house has raised an entirely new set of issues for me. I have unleashed the middle class consumptive demon inside. In the past I've denied myself even the permission to fantasize what it would be like to have this, or that. Unknowingly I've become unaccustomed to feeling the pangs of wanting. I don't know how to deal with those pangs now that I am allowing those fantasies. I find myself lusting after a word processor yet being righteous and judgmental about Sage's wanting a picnic table.

Later

Dear Dorothy,

I think maybe tackling a very specific issue might help me get my thinking clearer. I feel such a strong need to find a harmonious way to approach these value differences so Sage and I don't continue to butt heads over every economic decision.

As you know, we live in the country. We designed our home to be passive solar to be more ecological. Unfortunately to place the home in a sunny spot we had to make a road through the trees. I rationalize that in the long run we'll save more trees by the decision because of the dirt walls and the passive solar. Anyway, the large windows to the west look out on a magnificent view that soothes us in the few hours we're home from stressful work. When the thermometer dips I begin to pile on clothes and Sage wants to make a fire. If she makes a fire, I want to close the thermal shades (blocking the view) so we would minimize the fuel consumption. I value my consciousness and willingness to bundle up but I also know sometimes I just find it hard to believe I deserve the comfort and luxury of a fire (polluting as it is).

Well -- at this point in writing I turn to Sage for her to help put some more depth in this issue, as we have not yet come up with any clever solutions. She says this passage is shallow. I ask her, "What do I do -- say you won't bundle up when it's cold because you don't like to feel bulky?" She says that it's not a good example -- how about the computer and the picnic table? I don't like that one because I can see how silly we've been . . . OK, *I've* been! "Well," she says, "how about our house cleaning issue?" Indulge me a bit here. Sage likes the house much cleaner than I do. I complain she doesn't have enough free time to spend with me. Sage's solution, that we hire someone to clean our house, crashes into my self-image -- I cringe at the thought even though it would make more free time for us.. Click! Sage says I'll trade you bundling up for house cleaning. (Are we playing monopoly?) I suggest that one hour of cleaning equals one fire we don't have. She counters with two hours.

We are still negotiating. This direction has promise. I don't mind paying to keep the environment clean and she can bundle up in order to keep the house spotless.

Later

Dear Dorothy,

Just a final note to wrap this up. We're at the end of the winter now and Sage has accumulated only an hour and a half of housework! She says that the passive solar design kept the house so warm that she didn't have many opportunities to bundle up for ecology. The issue itself wasn't so important, but what it represents is very important to us. We were able to find a solution that met both of our needs. Neither of us feels we've had to compromise. In the future, when, inevitably, more issues arise, we'll have this to look back on for encouragement and a laugh.

You know, I'd like to think mine could be like other courageous stories in the book just by my leaping in. I must admit, I'm not there (yet?!) and I need to respect my own process. I feel good about myself because I'm upwardly mobile on a spiritual plane and I'll keep moving. I think this spiritual mobility is a fundamental task for everyone, upwardly mobile folks included. Perhaps it can be a missing link to economic issues. I hope thinking aloud like this will be of benefit to the readers of your book.

In peace and struggle,
Jo-ann

CANCEL MY ORDER FOR EVERYTHING CONNECTED WITH THE VIOLENT U.S. ECONOMY

Juanita Nelson

Entry . . . My New Year's resolution is to keep the promise I made in good faith to put down our reasons for and experiences of "simple" (simpler?) living. I would do it, I pledged myself, as soon as the garden was put to bed. Well, the last potato was dug long ago, the last jar of beets pickled, the final ear of corn parched; if I don't get to the writing soon the sleeping garden will be jumping out of bed and clamoring once more for undivided attention.

The difficulty is, what is one to say without unwarranted pretension? How is it that Wally and I lay claim to simple living, if I could define it? I'm in no mood today for great philosophic pronouncements. Perhaps a hasty check list of our possible qualifications would be a good start. Wonder if I can come up with ten items? (How am I simple? Let me count the ways . . .)

1. No electricity

2. No plumbing

3. No phone

4. No insurance except for mandatory automobile

5. No bank account

So much for negatives, how about a few positives?

6. Heat and cook exclusively with wood

7. Grow maybe seventy-five percent of our food

8. Earn cash income from the same three-quarters acre on which we produce food for ourselves

9. Make our own soap

10. Built our own house (with lots of help from friends) of mostly salvaged material -- not quite finished yet and probably never will be

11. Live on an income which last year reached a high of over $4,000, more than enough for our day to day needs, probably not for catastrophes

12. Use an outhouse

There must be more, but that's enough for now. A couple years ago I might have added that we cut our wood with a handsaw, felled trees by hand. But since so much is now cut by friends with chainsaws on account of Wally's back and this year his injured shoulder, will have to leave that out. Anyhow I did make the ten points with two to spare.

It adds up to twelve items. But does it add up to simple living?

Entry . . . Took our midweek baths in midafternoon, a day late. It was too cold last night; today the sun shone and it was warm by the window over the tub. Making do with two baths a week, except when visiting family and friends with plumbing, might make a thirteenth item. Sounds ridiculous, but for us it's been a true token of simpler ways. We grew up poor, but clean. I bathed every day of my life and so did Wally, even when he hauled water two blocks to fill a tin tub. Neither of us is that rugged now.

Stripped down living cuts down on soul searching. Don't have to worry about turning off the shower while soaping or about using too much water in the tub. Conservation comes naturally when we pull every bucket of water hand over hand from the well in front of the house. We use about two and a half gallons of water per shower, which consists of soaping up and having your partner douse you with a pail of water. I feel as clean and refreshed as if I'd luxuriated in gallons of steaming suds.

I must admit I'm grateful for the convenience of running-out water by way of ugly, unecological plastic pipes from sink and tub into the fifty gallon drum sunk into the ground. Not as simple as heaving the dishwater out the door. Water was draining slowly today; hope that doesn't mean we should have cleaned the drum this year. I won't worry until there's a tell-tale stink. Ground's frozen so we can't dig to get the top off anyway.

Entry . . . With sun streaming in, snow melted and hills visible on all sides, I am reminded of New Mexico where we began this phase of our lives in 1970. There, of course, we were surrounded by majestic mountains, not puny hills. No matter that the previous day's snows had melted in the next day's sun, there was always snow on the distant slopes. I felt high at 6800 feet, but peaks loomed over us. Maybe a metaphor for how far we'd come but how far from the summit we were, are in this process of getting down to essentials.

I am also reminded that we hadn't thought of what we'd set out for as simple living. I was in pursuit of a life that holds up to the light practically every breath that one breathes in terms of nonviolence, in terms of how the practice matches the preachment. Beyond demonstrations, conferences, tax refusal, on-going though that was and disruptive of "normal" existence. Wholeness.

I mustn't give the impression that all this burst in on us, on me, neatly, dramatic as that would have been. Mother must have passed on to me a bit of that fierce stubbornness which made her act on what she believed, no matter how wrong-headed at times, as I saw it. Even today I rather marvel about how calm she seemed on that trip to Atlanta when I was sixteen. We changed trains in Cincinnati and I was outraged to realize, after settling down, that we were in a segregated car. When I proposed that we change coaches, Mother said she didn't feel like rearranging herself. But she didn't try to stop me when I flounced up and said I was going to sit in every car in that train. She didn't appear frightened, though an aunt had been lynched in Georgia for less. But that was a long time ago and I may have forgotten any anxiety she expressed. I just knew that she felt I had every right to sit where I pleased, so how could she tell me not to?

I got some of Mother's stubbornness, but I didn't get from her my late blooming notion of, as she saw it, "making things so hard on yourself." I was born and grew up in a city slum, among poor people who had left the land, left Alabama and Georgia and Mississippi and were glad to be "shet" of it. Mother sometimes spoke nostalgically of the country, but she preferred to be in Cleveland cleaning other people's houses rather than chopping cotton. I never heard my father praise Georgia or the rural life, hard as his lot was in the north, sweltering in a steel mill.

Once I got into pacifist circles through Peacemakers, I met

homesteaders, dropouts of one sort or another. But even before that, before 1948, there was Wally, who had dropped out of college for a 33 month course in prison as a World War II conscientious objector. I dropped out of professionalism when I quit the newspaper job I held from the time I was 19 until I was 22. (My most important assignment was a story Wally and his friend Joe smuggled out about segregation in the Cleveland County jail; that was where we met.) I knew I had made a significant choice, but I had no conception of where that choice would lead me.

Entry . . . It was Peacemakers which captured my imagination with its talk of "the transformation of society through the transformation of the individuals therein." I've just looked up that sheet, "What is Peacemakers?" and found the initial paragraph continuing, "By changing oneself in accordance with firmly-held beliefs, one person can, in a small, though significant way, begin to change the world." I'm glad I plunged into pacifism through Peacemakers which advocated tax refusal, nonregistration for the military draft, and community. The only other group I had worked with before was the Congress of Racial Equality (CORE); it suited me with its direct action.

What a coincidence that Wally and I began living together in 1948, the year Peacemakers was formed. My education continued. I'd already learned more from Wally than I had getting a B.A. from Western Reserve University. I was fascinated with his jail stories, heard first in person when I visited him in jail, then in letters when his appeal was turned down and he was transferred to federal prisons. (I must have told him about being arrested while a student at Howard University in Washington, D.C. for demanding service at a downtown drug store -- that was in the early forties when D.C. was as segregated as any place in the country. How disappointed I was when the dean of women sprang us after only three hours.) Wally and Joe, who walked out of civilian public service camp with Wally, put me onto Howarth Co-op House on the south side of Chicago where I spent nine illuminating months after leaving the newspaper. I hitch-hiked for the first time, learned about unions from labor organizers who lived in the house, read Thoreau in an audited class at Roosevelt College. A time of growth.

Entry . . . So cold this morning that the red saucepan we cover the well with was frozen onto the pipe; I dislodged it with a blow from a handy board. Rope frozen, too, so I had to make several passes before getting the bailer to go down to water level. Oh, for a hand pump in the house. But our disaster of a 123 foot well just didn't work out for that. Coming from the arid southwest, we had supposed we'd have no trouble finding water gushing from every depression in New England. Just knew we'd have a pitcher pump mounted on the sink. Well, hauling pails of water for twenty years ought to boost one's simple living credentials.

Entry . . . Letter from Ernest saying how they are enjoying making their way through the 120 quarts of grape juice he put up last summer. Made me reflect that I don't always tell it like it is. I have remarked that the only gardening I'd done before New Mexico was a year of tending a half dozen tomato vines, a few bean plants and some lettuce in our tiny Philadelphia yard. Not quite true. I didn't do much gardening in Gano but I was exposed to it.

Through Peacemakers we teamed up with Marion and Ernest to live in community for six years, beginning in 1950, sharing the old farmhouse, income, meals, one car. All tax refusers, we took what employment we could find that wasn't subject to federal withholding. Always Ernest made time for a large garden. Wally, on the road for several years organizing for CORE, didn't have much time for gardening, had he been so inclined. My recollection is that I just didn't have much interest. As I recall, Wally and I would just as soon have lived in town. But Gano was cheaper, and it made all around more sense for sustaining ourselves. Thank goodness the Bromleys were more sensible than the Nelsons.

Wally and I can't be accused of being congenitally practical. We have to work at it. We could have learned so much about gardening and canning by doing more with Marion and Ernest, and thus been better prepared to take a further step. Instead, we left that semi-rural setting, made a detour back to the city, then plunged into a much more rugged life than Gano. A leap frog maneuver. One step forward, two steps back, get your wind, then a great leap forward, landing you maybe beyond where you were previously but not as far as if you'd kept on going. Not much sense to it, but that's the way we did it.

Entry . . . If I make little headway getting these notes down today I can still enjoy a sense of accomplishment. Before Wally's good breakfast of potato pancakes (worth picking all those loathsome beetles every day) I husked the hazel nuts, for once having got to them before the squirrels. What a lot of work for so little, and I have yet to crack open all those tiny nuts. Still, I'm looking forward to eating our own protein, efficient or not.

That question of efficiency comes up often. Like with beans. Until the Mexican bean beetle became unbearable about three years ago, we grew our own supply of dry beans, mostly pinto, soy and kidney. Which is why, casting about for a name for an operation too big for a garden and ludicrously small for a farm, we hit upon The Bean Patch. I must have been thinking back to the days of reading "Mrs. Wiggs and the Cabbage Patch". We were advised to buy our beans, since they're quite cheap and growing them is so labor intensive. But for me that's not the point. I want to produce my own food, not exploit the labor of others or encourage the use of huge machinery and barrels of oil. It gives me great pleasure to serve beans to guests and to pridefully announce that they're our own. I guess that's why James gave us that great sepia print of a bean with the quote from Thoreau, "I determined to know all about beans." Now we need to learn all about bean beetles, so we can grow beans again.

We've had more success with growing our own bird food. Great crop of sunflower seeds, which the birds are devouring from the feeder made from a gallon plastic jug. Maybe I'll finally manage to identify a few of our winged neighbors.

Entry . . . How to explain with a few strokes of the pen just what led us to leave Philadelphia, after a detour of thirteen years? Immediate impetus was the Vietnam War. We were living in Philly during that period in relatively modest but certainly well appointed circumstances. In spite of a bias against owning property, we had bought, after living in three apartments, a three story brick with a $4500 no-interest loan from a friend, the full price. Ernest's reaction was that he hadn't supposed you could get a chicken coop for that amount. (It was less than half what we'd paid for the Gano house and two acres in 1950.) We spent an equal sum for necessary repairs and unnecessary renovations, mostly a 30 x 16 foot living room created by removing walls. A great space for tax refusal clinics, larger than the 16 x 24 foot room in which we now live, cook, bathe, dine, entertain, do everything but sleep. (Still, we have enough room for meetings of Pioneer Valley War Tax Resisters -- must have been about twenty-five last time we hosted.)

We were continuing to refuse taxes, were active with the farm workers, sold pecans to help Koinonia Farm in Georgia exist through boycotts and shootings resulting from not observing a color line. Wally helped form Operation Freedom through Peacemakers, which made emergency loans to southern farmers unable to get run money from banks because of their civil rights involvement.

We were active in the life of Powelton Village, the 30-block neighborhood where we lived. Within walking distance of Center City, it was noted for rehabilitation of its beautiful old residences, reconverting them from rundown apartments to family dwellings. I was secretary of Powelton Neighbors when I was arrested for not giving information to the IRS and was warmly supported even though I noncooperated. But there was a war going on and, much as I enjoyed the ambience, I began feeling uneasy with, among other uneasinesses, having a good bit of my life devoted in a roundabout way to improving property values.

It was difficult to explain why I so passionately felt the need to leave Philadelphia, to simplify. We had made lots of good friends, most of whom I'm sure thought we were a little daft. I remember Hope, a farm worker on an organizing stint in Philly, looking at me in bewilderment. "But you don't live in luxury," she said. "I don't know why you need to be poorer than you are." How easy to be reinforced in holding on to our comforts!

We were for sure doing all the farm workers asked of us: picketing, leafletting, contributing financially. Wally fasted for twenty-one days at the headquarters of a supermarket chain which wouldn't take grapes off the shelves. We didn't buy grapes and lettuce for so long we forgot how they tasted.

We were doing without lettuce and grapes to better the lot of farm workers, but it seeped into my consciousness that with every purchase of anything, I was contributing directly or indirectly to oppression, and especially to the obscenity of the Vietnam War. It came to me with the force of a hurricane that, considering interlocking directorates of corporations and vertical integration, we might well be buying a bit of shrapnel to pierce a child's body with the purchase of a can of tomatoes. I couldn't stop, I knew, at grapes and lettuce. That wouldn't do. I had to look at the whole, at all I produced and consumed. At how Vietnam and the farm workers' struggle were the same struggle, stemming from the same causes. Greed. Profit. Overconsumption. Individual creature comforts above all. Accepting that there shall be classes, that some shall have too little in order that others shall have a surfeit. No, I could not stop with grapes and lettuce.

No, I could not rest with what little I was doing -- then go to the homes of friends or have them to ours and, over dinner, wring our hands and denounce the government and "them", rise next morning to resume life as usual.

I'm getting convoluted and long winded. Time to fill the wood box.

Later: I wanted, in leaving Philadelphia, to cancel my order for everything connected with the violent U.S. economy, and that was everything when it came down to it. It just wasn't possible to continue to denounce so roundly what was going on without making some more extraordinary effort to reduce my own complicity. My grand scheme was to learn to live without money. To produce everything we could and do without the rest, to resist "the system" by making it irrelevant.

Entry . . . We could credit the IRS [Internal Revenue Service] with a pivotal role in booting us out of Philadelphia, giving us the push we needed to leave. Wally was struggling to put behind him the distaste he had developed as a child for anything to do with farming during the three years that his family were sharecroppers. In the midst of that struggle, the IRS was finally closing in, in spite of several moves Wally had made to thwart collection, like getting paid in advance. He had to quit selling for the Antiosh Bookplate Company to forestall collection.   Our indecision came to an end with unemployment. We had to make a move while we had a little money.

Entry . . . Sent in the seed order today.

When I stop to think about it, which I seldom have time to do, I am amazed at myself. City born and bred, never a nature lover, and I find myself doing all these agricultural things, feeling quite at home. Are there many who come to where I am so cerebrally? And then find they enjoy it? Now I work in the noonday sun; in the city I'd have had a heat stroke. I tease Wally now and again about how he thought I was being romantic about farming -- I'd never done it. He now admits he was mistaken, but he was afraid that was the case when we set out for New Mexico in the spring of 1970 at ages 47 (me) and 61, when sensible folk are planning for retirement.   Our Renault 10 was packed as densely as we could manage.   We understood, even I did, that this was a journey of exploration, and so we rented out the house for a year, just in case -- practical for once. We didn't want to be landlords, but decided it was okay if we charged just enough to cover expenses, and if it were temporary, short term temporary.

Really had wanted to apprentice ourselves to some farmer, but didn't find anything suitable. Read rugged enough for me, primitive enough, sufficiently out of the main stream. (Maybe a good reason for pinning the romantic label on me.) We accepted the invitation of a couple who lived most of the time in El Rito, New Mexico, and ran a coffee house in that village of 1100. Peter was convinced that New Mexico, less developed than much of the country, offered the potential for creation of a different ethic and economics.

We wound up in Ojo Caliente, eighteen miles from El Rito, twenty-five miles from Espanola where we shopped. Who told us about Señora Campos and her house? We had searched and searched, and I was exhausting Wally by objecting to everything that turned up: too modern (didn't want to have to tear out the plumbing), too close to the road, bleak landscape, not on a good irrigation ditch. But we agreed on the Ojo place. I'll never forget the interview with Señora Campos. She had been born in "our" house, and had moved a quarter mile down the road when she married.

We had been told the rent for the three-room adobe, with grass growing from its dirt roof, would be twelve dollars a month. I thought that was what Señora corroborated, but because she spoke only Spanish and my Spanish is indifferent, I repeated "doce" after her, just to be sure I had it right; it sounded so little. Apparently fearing we might be objecting to such a high price, she on the spot amended it to "diez", ten dollars.

We had affordable housing in a New Mexico village of 500, a house which more than met my specifications. There was absolutely nothing in it. It was just two wooden floors and one of dirt surrounded by foot and a half thick adobe walls, spanned with vigas of peeled logs. Even the wood cookstove that had been in the kitchen had been ripped out, the parts thrown into the cedar lined well. That was a lot of years ago but I remember how I felt. Challenged. Geographically out of place. Awed by the majesty of the mountains and by the audacity of what we'd done. Bewildered. What do we do now? We did have a few months under our belts in what seemed a different country. In El Rito we had hauled water from the coffee house, been ecstatic about the outhouse from whose throne we viewed the snow covered mountains, washed clothes in the acequia (the irrigation ditch), lived without a phone. But that had been playing at this new way of life. The move to Ojo was a settling in, the real thing. We were committed.

Entry . . . Writing about Ojo yesterday has opened the floodgates of memory. I'd send notes to Señora Rivera and Max and Orlecia Archuleta, except they're all dead now. (Wonder if Señora Campos still lives?) Max rented the ten irrigated acres of the 18 total our house stood on -- all we were entitled to for our ten dollars was the house. Max came one day to invite us, in English more difficult for me to understand than his Spanish, to use all the land we needed for a garden, as his cousin the Señora had indicated he would. He materialized in the spring with a tractor to instruct us that it was time to plow the garden; he had come to do it.

Oh, for at least one more garden like unto that first one, which was all but perfect. It was about a quarter of an acre and it was hard work. Weren't we proud when we learned, under Max's tutelage, how to irrigate from the acequia madre, the mother ditch, occasionally getting water to run in all the rows at once. I raced to the garden before dawn each day, shouting for Wally to come look: the seeds I'd feared had been covered too sparsely, or too deeply, had germinated, I had spied the first pea, lettuce was big enough to thin. Everything came up that year. Neighbors said it was the most beautiful garden ever in Ojo. It produced so much that in order to use the surplus we had a First Fruits dinner, inviting over fifty to a meal that included snow peas -- imagine the luxury of snow peas for fifty! Still seems incredible. Carried on the first fruits tradition for the remaining two years we were there. We've not had such a feast in all our years in Massachusetts in spite of oft stated intentions. Maybe mostly because now we sell all those surplus vegetables. Merchants instead of hosts.

Entry . . . Back to New Mexico. Orlecia lent us her pressure canner and a book of instructions. That's how we learned; canned beans, tomatoes, squash, even chiles with a book in one hand. Didn't buy a canner then because I was hoping to dry or store everything fresh as simpler and not so energy dependent. We did dry a good bit in the New Mexico sun. The year Max's cows chewed the tops off the carrots I grated and dried them on a screen outside. Sweet as sugar.

Orlecia was as helpful as Max; she showed us how to make a floor that mimicked flagstone by applying linseed oil to the dirt surface of our third room. Easiest floor I've ever cared for. There was the late fall day when the señorita next door, sister of Pete who owned the gas station and the general store, warned us there would be a frost that night. She knew because the sky was clear and the stars bright. We ran through the garden stripping every plant, finally having to resort to a flashlight. How unaccountably wise I thought her, acquainted with such mysteries as when there'd be a killing frost.

Señora Rivera, closest neighbor to the south, taught us to make gorgeous ristras of the chiles we learned to grow, though we never became truly adept at stringing the colorful peppers. She gave us the fat for my first batch of soap, and we've bought no bar soap since 1972. No one taught us to use an outhouse, but we didn't feel strange having one since most everyone did -- our Spanish neighbors and the immigrant hippies.

Señora Rivera's brother helped us construct an horno, the "beehive" oven made of adobe. Does Wally remember the time we baked ten loaves of bread in the horno, grinding the wheat berries in our Corona hand mill? That was bread made by the sweat of our brows; I trust the guests weren't able to taste the sweat. I've been hinting that we could try growing wheat again, as we've done two years since we've been in Massachusetts. Not difficult to grow. Wally doesn't seem too interested, but maybe he would be if I could devise some easier way to clean a couple bushels than going over every grain by hand.

One of the regrets I had about leaving New Mexico was the lost opportunity to build an adobe house. There could be no more satisfying way of creating a dwelling than by digging the foundation and using that material for bricks, just the adobe mud, water and straw. I am happy, though, with our salvaged wood frame house, some of the siding milled from hemlock in our own woods.

Entry . . . I am glad we went to New Mexico first. Where else would we have found it a common practice to cook with wood, use outhouses? Standard items in the Española hardware were the pulley for our well rope and the bucket for the well. (Here in Massachusetts no one had ever heard of a bailer, the slender cylinder which goes down into our six inch diameter well pipe and releases the two gallons of water through a spring bottom. Had to send to West Virginia for that three dollar piece of equipment.) We did have electricity in Ojo and I felt deprived when we went to the home of friends that first Thanksgiving and ate by the soft glow of kerosene lamps.

But it was the garden which has had the most lasting effect on our lives, that bountiful first garden. All that surplus food gave us the notion that we might be able to earn our living from the soil as well as provide our own food. I had by that time conceded that maybe we couldn't, or wouldn't, live completely without cash. I still have such fantasies from time to time. I'll make it happen in my next life.

Entry . . . So warm that I hung clothes outside and the bees buzzed me! A relief not to have hangers of clothes all over the room. Afraid we'll pay dearly for this weather. January ending and still no snow. Weather's scheduled to plummet tonight -- a blessing in a way. It's been a chore to cook in this warm weather. Winter is generally a wonderful time for dishes like soup that cook all day, since the fire is going anyway for heat. But there've been some January days when I've almost had to strip when the fire was hot enough for corn pone. Even Wally has occasionally moved away from the fire.

Entry . . . Chuck was over last night, reminiscing about the days when he scavenged food from dumpsters. Found myself wondering afterwards why, if we wanted to simplify, we hadn't just stayed in the city, gleaned food from dumpsters, maybe squatted in a boarded-up house. We could certainly have done without a vehicle, as had been our plan when Wally got off the road as a traveling salesman. A lot easier to do without a car in the city. We know at least one couple who live in the city on as little or less cash than we do. But my concern is that one can live more basically on the land, be more a primary producer. We acquire our clothes as we did in the city, from friends and second hand shops. But here we have the possibility of raising sheep, for instance, and spinning and weaving, clothing ourselves from scratch. Probably won't do it at this point in our lives, but it's possible. I once planted flax with a notion of making linen. Tomorrow I'm having my first lesson with Mary on the book-size spinning wheel for cotton that George and Lillian brought from India. Wool, cotton, or flax, it would be mighty satisfying to have clothes handcrafted by me from start to finish.

Raising food in the city? We could have grown some in our tiny yard and maybe reclaimed a vacant lot. But I doubt that we'd have found space for corn and dry beans and enough squash and onions and potatoes and carrots and beets for winter, or vegetables to sell.

We could have tried. But a city seems to me parasitic. For me, it's important, the difference between living on almost nothing via the throwaways of the society I want to change and attempting to find ways to do things for myself; trying to fashion another way by severing ties with the old rather than by accommodating to it.

Even as I write these brave words I cringe at the wide gap between what I dream of as possible and what we're actually doing. Something I'd rather not scrutinize closely, because the actuality is as pathetic as the concept is heroic. What we've gained most control over is our food. Maybe waste disposal, with our outhouse and our compost pile. A certified outhouse, with a permit. That was a fluke that couldn't be duplicated now that Deerfield has a building inspector. Not that he's ever come to inspect the outhouse, or the house for that matter. We had assumed we'd build an outhouse, but the Board asked that we apply for a permit. What would we have done had the selectmen turned us down?

Entry . . . I wonder where the man is who wrote from New York City to accuse us of being elitist? We had to be rich to be able to flee the city, leaving the poor and their problems in the urban centers. Did I answer him that I don't know how to eliminate poverty in the cities or anywhere else, short of the revolution which I don't see around the bend? I know that most folks who might want to leave the city for a more subsistence type of existence have no access to land because of its price.

We reluctantly left New Mexico because we couldn't afford land. We had sold the Philadelphia house for $10,000, about what we'd invested in it initially, having no doubt but what we could, in essence, trade the city property for a modest acreage in a remote southwest village. Meg and Bob had considered the price ridiculously low and were glad to fork over an additional $4,000. Still it wasn't enough.

We were exceedingly fortunate to work out a Memorandum of Understanding with the Woolman Hill board that gives us lifetime use of three acres and access to natural resources like wood on the entire hundred acres. Our obligation is to use the land responsibly; there is no money involved. The improvements we make (house, well, etc.) belong to Woolman Hill. At our insistence, the board has no obligation to compensate us if we should leave. We have been well compensated. We are able to live as cheaply as we do because of this arrangement. It suits us perfectly since we don't believe in private land ownership with its license for speculation. We'd have fashioned some sort of land trust if we'd bought land in New Mexico.

But even with money not a problem, is there enough land to support everyone living in a fashion similar to ours? That oft-posed question floored me for a while. Then I wrapped my brain around it and wondered how many acres of land are required to support each city dweller. To grow the food, to get it to the cities, to supply gas and oil, to extract raw materials, to manufacture the myriad products needed for even low consumption living. Just to get rid of the waste. I have never been in

New York City without craning my neck to see the top stories of the immensity of high rise buildings, wondering what happens with the flushings from all those toilets. Surely there must be more land used for each city dweller than would be required if each family lived lightly on an acre or so.

Entry . . . Received a strange shaped package today from Jenny. Turned out to be a styrofoam toilet seat, fashioned from material which she assured us was recycled. And she's right -- it is the greatest invention since the wheel. It's designed especially to fit over the hole of outside privies. Really does warm the bottom, or give the sensation of doing so, amounting to the same thing. Much as I dislike plastic, we'll no doubt salvage another piece of foam when this one wears out, or even sooner so we can have one for the twin hole. It has become indispensable for those winter treks, although they're never as uncomfortable as anticipated.

Entry . . . We had a great time at the monthly Hill dinner last night. Great food, and Dave told his story.

What a lot of changes since we came in '74. With the school here, there was a changing population that went as high as thirty. It was a lively place. When the school closed there was an eerie period when no one was on this Hill but us.

The Board solicited proposals for use of the land and buildings. The board itself revived the Yellow House Conference Center, which thrives. Traprock Peace Center was accepted to use the Brown House and last year marked its tenth anniversary. The staff does not live on the Hill, but Hill residents include Dave and Ted, who sublease the top floor of the Brown House from Traprock. Co-directors of the Conference Center, currently Bonnie and Doug, live in the Red House across from the Center. At the southern end of the Hill Rob and Judy and their two children live in the Tan House. They're referred to as the farm family, having come in response to the Board's pledge to make care of the land a high priority. Several years ago Marshall joined Rob and Judy as chief gardener.

So we're the oldest residents, both in terms of age and residency. Sobering thought.

Entry . . . Stan has come and gone. It was wonderful to catch up with their four acres in New Mexico -- made us a little homesick. We talked a good bit about scale of farming. They grossed $35,000 last year. He didn't say, and for once I wasn't crass enough to ask, how much they netted. But I got an idea when he expressed no amazement that Alex and Lance grossed $25,000 and had expenses of $18,000. That sounds about right, Stan said, not batting an eye.

We took in a little over $4,000 and probably netted $3,500 selling at the farmer's market in Greenfield and to the co-op and a few restaurants. On the other hand, I'm sure we worked as hard for our thirty-five hundred as the other couples did for twice as much or more. Wally and I dawdled over breakfast dissecting the question of making a lot of money and having, in the end, such a small percentage left for oneself. Would it be better to farm on a smaller scale? (Not that their operations are large by most standards, just by ours.) We discussed again the question of hired labor and concluded as we always do -- that the hirer inevitably skims off some of the employee's labor. I like the way Jules Rabin put it in an article about the Upland Bakery he and his wife operate in Plainfield, Vermont: "We aren't in the business of paying somebody a wage that is less, as the rule of capitalism goes, than the amount of money the person's labor brings to us." And so they limit their baking to what they can do themselves.

We have certainly had help from time to time, but unsolicited aid from "neighbors" near and far. Unlike Wally, I tend to want to say "no" often, but am learning to be easier with taking what is freely offered. Sometimes, though, it's overwhelming. Wally says I can give but have difficulty taking. And I say I want to know what we can do ourselves.

Entry . . . Last night stopped in at Bill's and Lisa's after the tax refusal meeting. It was cold and Bill finally built a fire. The wood stove is their only source of heat, but they don't use it for cooking as we do. As they rush to leave for work in the morning, it's practical to prepare breakfast on the gas cook stove. Made me realize anew how major shifts are called for to permit what seem even minor lifestyle changes. Sometimes we seem to be on the go an unseemly amount, but we really are home based. Our stove rarely goes out in winter; we bank it at night since we have this marvelously efficient Jotul inherited from the school. So it's easy for us to cook on it, have even slow baked squash overnight.

Our two stoves dominate our living space. The white enamel cookstove, a Home Comfort, sits comfortably in the "kitchen" area. We bought it for $20 from where it lay disassembled and rusting. My hope had been that it would be our only stove, but we shiveringly experienced that first winter that, with all its cracks, it wasn't adequate below twenty Fahrenheit. Now the Jotul is connected to the Comfort stove pipe, but the few inches between them puts the Jotul into the living room. We use it for everything in winter, juggling pots and pans on its limited surface, except when there is baking to be done. And since we've acquired the wonderfully simple top of the stove oven, I often bake in that. Made a great peach upside down cake in it for company on Tuesday.

Since learning to cook on a wood stove I have come to prefer it. I would not trade our range for a gas or electric model. It's satisfying, and often truly more convenient to be able with one fire (in the Comfort) to can, heat dish· and bath water, boil water for tea, while bread and casserole bake in the oven. I've become rather proficient at regulating temperatures by moving pots around. Sometimes I am able to process a batch of vegetables without moving the pressure canner for the required twenty-five to forty-five minutes. When the gauge holds steady at ten pounds, I have a feeling akin to what we had when we got the irrigation water running simultaneously in all rows in Ojo.

Now we have the solar oven to use in summer. Of course it's not so useful during a summer with not much sun. Wonderful to put food in and have it ready with no fuss. There are a few kinks to iron out. I've had squash raw or underdone in an effort to get it just right, and unless one eats before the sun goes down, or soon thereafter, the food is cold.

Entry . . . First real snow of the season! We should have taken the wood off the truck, the wood we collected where the town's been trimming trees. But we didn't get around to removing the barrier from the driveway while it was still driveable. Now we're schlepping a piece at a time whenever we make a trip from Traprock, our winter parking lot.

I was musing last night before falling asleep that everyone has a different view of simple living. Someone who could command (no one could earn so much) $100,000 a year but takes half that amount might qualify as living simply. And a person who's making that much or more, but spends only half of it? Frugal anyway, if not simple, when income exceeds outgo. Billionaires might be considered the most simple livers -- how much more they control than they could ever spend.

A more meaningful musing concerned some of my goals in this "simple living" effort. Not counting the one of completely changing the world with my two bare hands. A more modest desire is to have so little, the bare minimum to sustain myself, that I'd have nothing to give away.

Then I would know that I was taking no more than my share. Not that one can't always share what little one has. Another goal is to be able to ignore any call for a boycott, because I would already not be using any of those banned items, as I inch along toward "living within the bounds of my own productivity." (I had thought we were doing well until we bought a rare box of salt. We took the store brand, knowing Morton's was illicit, only to discover that the store brand was made by Morton's. Next time I'm at the ocean I'll bring back sea water to boil.)   A goal akin to the first: really to act out that there is nothing I will hoard for tomorrow in the face of someone's need today. To trust that tomorrow's needs will be met tomorrow. I might not be here to have a need.

I see this quite directly in the matter of inheritance. I am fond of encouraging that land be put into land trust (with little success), not saving it to pass on to heirs. Somebody needs it now. So often the heirs have no need; I say anyway that we are all equally heirs of the earth.

On that note I'll rise from the typewriter and put potatoes and onions on to steam. Thank goodness for the excellent crops of both in spite of the drought; we have them often. Fortunately it's a dish we relish.

Entry . . . Most snow we've had so far, but hardly the two to four inches predicted. Enough to hide the ice on which I slipped and fell. My great fear was that I'd break the pint jars of corn I was transporting to Nelson's Cove in the Brown House. Traprock has continued the arrangement we had with the school to stash squash, potatoes and canned goods under a stairway in the upper basement. I hate to move the jars from the house, where they add so much to the decor: yellow corn, red beets, dilly green beans, beige sauerkraut, orange/yellow peaches. But they represent hours of hard work and we don't want to take a chance on losing any of it. We don't have to worry about frozen pipes, but last year we came home from our annual trip to find a number of cracked jars.

Even though we were in a great rush to get a roof over our heads that summer of 1974 when we moved to the Hill, we should have taken the time to build a root cellar, I guess. But we've managed without all these years. Amazing how onions can hang in the cold entry way all winter and fare well, as long as there's not constant freezing and thawing.

Entry . . . I had a strange, disembodied feeling yesterday. I left the typewriter where I was trying to get thoughts together about simple living, walked through the woods to Traprock, hoisted myself into our rusting truck, turned the key and drove Wally into Turners Falls for a chiropractic treatment for his ailing shoulder. So what was simple about that? Such divided lives. I leave my outhouse and my gas light and my wood stove and join the throng on Route 5 & 10, and I am indistinguishable. Sometimes I feel triumphant about being "that close" to a utility pole without being plugged into it; still, it might be more appropriate to be buried deep in some backwoods where there is no utility pole. Not so schizophrenic. There was one winter when we didn't use the truck (a different oldie) because we couldn't decide if it was worth fixing, and we could do without it in the off season. We walked into town, often in the snow. The six to eight mile round trip might take most of the day, but we would plan our day around it. I liked it and thought strongly of not resurrecting that vehicle or saddling ourselves with another. But came spring, and we needed manure and lime and wood. . . .

Eveline and Lisa live in town and bicycle mostly, accepting rides with friends sometimes. Susan and Jonathan, older than E and L, got rid of their car some months ago and use bicycles instead of the donkey they had considered. I am sure that if we get to feeling strongly enough about the implications of having a truck, we'll chuck it, then figure how to manage. Until that day comes I'll just fret at the inconsistency. Might be easier to do without than to fret.

Entry . . . Has it been five years since I spoke at Williams College disarmament forum? In response to my remarks on tax refusal, a well dressed gray haired man rose to chide me, "It's all very well for you to take such chances. You don't have anything to lose."

Some years later I attended a talk on South Africa. During the question period I said I was in favor of divestment, as far as it went. But how about divesting ourselves as individuals, by reducing or eliminating our call for those things produced in South Africa, and other places, being less a party to the oppression whose slave labor makes possible our wealth? The speaker dismissed the notion out of hand. We black people, he said, first need to get into the economic mainstream before talking of getting out of it. (Most of the audience was pale skinned, and anyway what did color have to do with the point I was trying to make?)

Two views of who can, should eschew economic privilege. Where does that put me, born into involuntary poverty and an advocate of voluntary poverty?

Entry . . . I ponder the question -- why is it that we seem to go always in the direction of more and almost never in the direction of less? In the direction of development and consumption, never in the direction of de-development? People who earnestly proclaim that riches don't bring happiness, or who coo about how the poor are so often more content than "we" are don't seem anxious to become poor and happy. And yet the law of gravity would indicate that it must be easier to become poor than to acquire wealth; objects fall down, not up.

The difficulty is that whatever one has somehow assumes the status of necessity. That's one reason I so much dislike computers, for instance. Here comes another necessity. (Other reasons I have aplenty: the misuse of resources and of human labor, which could be employed to build houses, grow more food more ecologically, etc.) I've heard so many times, "I really didn't think I'd ever have a computer, but they save so much time!" (Whose time?) So earlier on they had environmental and political and social reasons for disdaining the machine, but then they tried it and it became a "necessity". Sometimes for the laudable purpose of bringing about social change. Doing without the computer could be the greatest social change vehicle available.

I am acerbic this morning.

Entry . . . Would we have considered Woolman Hill if we'd realized from the beginning that we'd have to build? That possibility didn't occur to us until we made an initial ten day visit to inspect and be inspected. We knew it had been a conference center when turned over to the Board that incorporated to receive the hundred and ten acres and buildings, and that it was being used at that time by an alternative school. So of course, we thought, there must be some outbuilding tucked away which we could live in. When it turned out that the school was using every nook and cranny we ran an ad for a small building, one room would be fine, that might be purchased cheaply and moved to the Hill.

The only response was the invitation to take down a four room house. We spent the summer of 1974 doing that. Wally had had minor experience in construction, and both of us learned a lot by way of demolition. Hard work, taking that building down, but not as hard as reassembling it as another dwelling. It's just as well that I can't know how many nails I removed from those old boards, with an initial boost of Katie's help. I think it was Dave who went with us the very first day when we began dismantling by ripping off shingles. We had good support from the very beginning.

Entry . . . Today as I was coming from Traprock I happened to glance up at our partial second story and recalled the time I took a similar glance and realized with sinking stomach the great mistake I had made. I was the "architect" and chose what seemed the easiest type of building: two shed roof boxes joined by an entryway. I was confounded when it came to installing two old storm windows horizontally in the south wall, one above the other, and found we could fit only one in. Walking back that day it came to me in a flash that I had miscalculated and made the roof a foot too low. (We have four roofs and each has a different slope.) Not so bad for us shorties, though I was disappointed not to be able to stand tall at the back of the space, but if any taller tenants take over the house they'll have to bend double until they reach the middle of the room.

The myriad folks who've helped us have put up with a lot. We used no power tools ourselves, but did run a heavy line to the Brown House for helpers addicted to a higher level of technology. One thing I remember most vividly is that with our hand saws we cut on the diagonal boards for sheathing; there's no plywood in our house except for a couple or three old boards behind the tub and sink. And only one half wall of sheet rock, on the east wall of the big room, covered with white wallpaper to relieve the monotony of all-over wood.

Entry . . . One reason I feel at home on this hill is that it's named for John Woolman. What clarity of insight, and how vigorously he tried to live out those insights -- personal visits to the Indians as a peace envoy, laboring with Quaker slave owners, refusing to pay taxes for the French and Indian War. That cogent admonition, "May we look upon our treasures, the furniture of our houses, and our garments, and try whether the seeds of war have nourishment in these our possessions." A concise statement of purpose for living simply. He proceeded to pare his tailoring business because he was, he feared, becoming too prosperous.

Entry . . . Astonishing to note the parallel experiences Wally and I had before we knew of each other's existences. He was recounting at dinner last night how his mother washed clothes for their family of six by hand, and took in laundry besides. During one period Wally and his brother Merrill carried the water from a spigot several blocks distant. We had running water, but mother washed by hand for the five of us. We got a washing machine after I was out of high school, but mother never bothered with a drier. When she visited us in New Mexico she was upset to find me using a rub board.

If I could get through her Alzheimer's now, she'd be happy to know that since the first couple years at Woolman Hill, we've been using a friend's washer. For me it seems a step backwards; I hope to return to hand laundering. We still have the washboard and the bathtub still sits on the platform erected so we wouldn't have to bend so far.

Another parallel experience is that we were both involved in the Congress of Racial Equality. In '41 and '42 Wally was a student at Ohio Wesleyan University, and on vacations in Chicago he'd test restaurants for the just formed CORE. In '43 I was a co-founder of the Cleveland CORE chapter, and was active nationally. We'd no doubt have met at a CORE gathering somewhere if Wally hadn't been sent to prison.

Entry . . . After all these years, there's hardly a full moon when I don't relive the thrill of moving into the first room of our house. It was a palace after the 13-foot trailer that had no insulation. With a bottled gas cook stove, we froze when we were seated, melted when we stood up. So it was none too soon that we were able to get into the 12 x 16 back room in January 1975. We were bathed in the moonlight that came through the south window as we gazed up from our mattress on the floor. Space was so limited that for three and a half years we rolled up our bed each morning. We cooked on the Ashley heater and set up the cookstove outside under a makeshift roof attached to trees. We used it only for canning -- bees abounded when we processed fruit. I declared we didn't have room for the cat who strayed into our household. We fashioned a bed of two cardboard boxes with insulation between and put it under the house. She grew a thick coat of fur each winter and was content and healthy. Evidently we haven't bred out of cats all their ability to care for themselves.

Entry . . . It was a great disappointment, when I went to pick kale a while ago, to find most of it brown and beyond use. It is so sweet this time of year, and I had counted on it as the fresh vegetable for all those folks we planned to have for dinner when we had more leisure. We've plenty of onions, squash, potatoes, canned and parched corn, dry beans (though most of these are not our own), canned tomatoes of all sorts, sauerkraut, pickled beets, applesauce, peaches, even nine pints of our very own blueberries, but no greens. For salad we'll have to rely on that great invention of mine, sauerkraut and pickled beets. I wish I had mulched the carrots sooner instead of procrastinating until the ground began to freeze. But maybe I can hack more of them from the soil -- I managed to wrestle some out a couple weeks ago. Maybe some parsnips, too.

Entry . . . Outside today I was aware of the noise of traffic from Route 5&10, or is it 91? Probably the sounds from both reach us. Our rugged rural life style. We're a mile up the hill from a secondary highway, not much further from the interstate and our hill has a road maintained by the town, even though the road doesn't go anywhere anymore. We're three miles from Greenfield, our county seat and shopping center.

True, we trudge through the woods to Traprock to make phone calls, but what's rugged about that? Not only do we have access to a phone; messages are taken by real people when they're around and by an answering machine when they aren't. Callers may find it trying since only by chance do they get us directly. We use the phone sparingly to save steps (140 from portal to portal) and money. I was happy that this month we spent just around a dollar for extra calls. Greatest use comes when we're doing organizational things.

Not having had a phone in the house for twenty years (in Ojo we used the public phone across the road), I think I'd find it difficult to deal with the intrusion. A bonus is that people tend to drop in on us since they can't conveniently call ahead. So we don't have to make decisions about whether we're ready for company and can feel free to continue what we're doing. If they drop in at meal time we can offer whatever we happen to have without apology. None of the getting-ready-for-company anxiety.

Entry . . . Hurrah for Dvo and Alan. Learned today that they still have a bank account, which many of us tax refusers have given up, but that they don't accept interest on the account. We haven't had money in a bank for years, originally because we didn't want to make it easy for the IRS to collect. We didn't take interest on the last account we had, after convincing the bank that we couldn't be forced to take money we didn't want.

I have come to the firm conclusion that money doesn't earn money - any added value comes from labor. Just as it seems clear to me that the only source of wealth is labor applied to natural resources.

How can money have any meaning if it is not related to labor expended? If I were clever enough to print my own twenty-dollar bills I could exchange them for other people's labor, but it wouldn't be an exchange of my labor for theirs. I find pungently stated truth in John Ruskin's rendering of the case in "Unto This Last": "If all the money in the world were to disappear tomorrow, there would be neither more nor less than there is today. It's just that people's relationships to those things would change." I'd have as much claim to a mansion as the once richest person in the world, since neither of us would have any money.

I agree with Gary that we peaceminded folks, including tax refusers, don't concern ourselves enough with economics. Equal distribution of resources -- that's part of what this simple living attempt is about. I have come to understand that in truth the product of our common labor belongs to all. To me that means that, at the very least, only that which one could, or does, produce by oneself, with help from no other, could conceivably be said to be "mine". So it's all common property -- who in this society produces anything solely on their own?

I had a thought one day in the garden that I couldn't grow as much as I do except that others had fashioned a hoe that I could use, that that hoe couldn't have been made without someone taking the ore from the ground, and the ore couldn't have got to the factory unless someone had transported it, and it couldn't have been transported without . . . and so on and on. Total and absolute interdependence. (As I write this I can hear Wally snort, "Self-made millionaire" -- a phrase that can really get him going.)

Meg says that for a person who hates money so I talk an awful lot about it. True. Once I start, I can keep going; seems so crucial to straighten out our concepts. But I won't keep going now. I'll use that energy to put up that long promised book shelf.

Entry . . . Made my first batch of soap for the year, quite late last night. Diane and Carl generously give us kidney fat from cows they custom slaughter. We've chosen not to have animals (too much trouble, can't imagine killing them and prefer not eating meat), but the decision means importing any animal products we use like fat for soap and manure for the garden. There is something to be said for having a complete cycle of living creatures on a place.

Good to get the soap making underway. I rendered the fat ten days ago, but I'm always uneasy with the first batch. I forget each year just how hot lye gets when poured into water, to over 175 degrees. I set it in the entry way to speed its descent to around 90 degrees, but it took ages.

Had to reheat the fat a couple times to keep it between 120 and 130 degrees. I had the queasy feeling I'd have a greasy mess on my hands, but those floating thermometers are great, and when I poured the contents into the makeshift cardboard box molds, it seemed fine.

Entry . . . What we had thought was just a bad cold sent Wally to emergency last night. Such episodes can evoke our greatest fears -- what do we do in case of chronic illness? (Figure we'll get what we need in acute circumstances.) With no health insurance, with one of us nearing eighty and the other in her mid-60's, it's something to think about, although mostly I don't. We've compromised so far by accepting care under the Hill-Burton bill, which obliges hospitals receiving federal funds to provide a certain amount of free care. That's in lieu of our being on medicare, which would, I think, mean getting on welfare, or just ignoring bills which could equal in less than a month what the two of us earn in a year. Ditto with health insurance, which we've carried only one year of our lives.

Really, our health "insurance" has been the support of our wider community. We were stunned when a potluck supper was staged where enough money was collected to send Wally to Tijuana for treatment of prostate cancer in '86 at a clinic which prescribed laetrile and vitamins and diet instead of the radiation suggested in the States. We actually had enough money of our own for the trip and the treatment, but wouldn't have had a penny when we returned, months before marketing season. Wally's been in remission for a couple of years and thinks it might be due more to the concern which surrounded him than the treatment.

How many people with our income could afford such health care? (A lot cheaper, of course, than regular hospital costs.) Doesn't matter, after all, how much money you have if you can command what you need/want. We've talked some about how much one should accept when it's offered. I generally have more reservations than Wally. I am trying to face the question of what lengths I will go to in case of serious, life-threatening illness. I agree with Greg that everyone should have rudimentary health care, including adequate nutrition and housing, before resources are used for sophisticated life-saving or just life-prolonging procedures. I accept that and need to translate it into what I will do.

Another concern about health is my ability to respond to the needs of others. With mother in a nursing home with Alzheimer's, I reflect a lot on that. It's kind of a moot point right now since Oscar is her primary caretaker and feels she should be in the home, having kept her at her own place as long as possible. But could Wally and I care for her in our circumstances? Would we need to install plumbing, phone, electricity? I don't want those amenities for myself, and anyway how could we afford them? Our scale of living may no longer be voluntary. In a sense, I'm grateful that at this point, at our ages -- as Wally reminds me -- we have few options for changing to another life style, except maybe to win the lottery. Unlikely, as we don't buy tickets.

But for all I protest, I know that if there were no other possibilities, we'd take mother in and do what we could.

Entry . . . Emptying the chamber pot this morning I remembered that lovely ceramic one Chuck found in their attic.   Up until then we had stoutly insisted on going out in the middle of the coldest, darkest, rainiest nights. Wally remained adamant even when he was laid up with his back for two weeks. What tipped the scale was the realization that urine is good for the garden, and we were squandering it.

The ceramic pot is no longer with us. After I'd emptied it one winter day I slipped on ice and the pot flew out of my hands. At least it was empty. Susan wasn't so lucky the time she came down their steps, tripped and splattered the contents of their pot everywhere, including all over the cookstove. I am ever so careful descending our narrow steps with slop jar in hand. Gives me the creeps just to think of a spill.

Entry . . . There are times when all that one does can seem utterly futile. Because it's so miniscule in relation to the immensity of the needs. And because what one is doing pales beside what one is not addressing. What little one refrains from doing that is harmful seems unworthy of mention beside what one continues to do. Sometimes the emotion of futility is brought on by what appears quite trivial.

We went for our $59, thirty-day in advance each way Greyhound bus tickets. For that price you can go across country and stop wherever as long as it's in a fairly straight line, but we wanted to go only to Ohio. The helpful ticket agent happened to remark that, yeah, the tickets are a good deal for the customers and certainly a good deal for Greyhound, which gets to invest your money for an extra thirty days. The observation made me shrivel. No escape. I travel by bus not only to save money but because I'm told that energy-wise it's the most economical mode of transportation. But my pittance goes to garner interest, which I detest, for a big corporation. Besides, I have no idea what the money's invested in.   What do my puny efforts at right livelihood and ecological responsibility amount to? A big joke? Yet I know that not doing what little I attempt would be of no avail. No point in retreating because one can't do much. Try to do more. But surely none of us can feel self-righteous considering how paltry are our efforts.

Entry . . . The calendar is filling up with meetings, a few speaking engagements, potlucks, dinners. I go out too much. Know too many people. In my next incarnation I shall stay in one spot forever.

Entry . . . Went to a movie last night. Chuck insisted that we see "Say Amen Somebody". At least it wasn't a Hollywood flick. I've been to maybe ten movies in our fifteen years at Woolman Hill. Can't bear the notion of supporting the movie industry, with its huge salaries, immense public relations budgets, just plain wastefulness. Not to mention the excise tax. Maybe no worse than other commodities I consume, but this is one I can manage very well without.

What is this insatiable · need for entertainment?   I find myself sometimes listening to our battery powered radio more than I realize. Sometimes I'm not really hearing it; it's just background noise. The mounting pile of toxic batteries shocks me into flicking the on-off switch to off. There again it's the directness that helps me; I'm sure I wouldn't be nearly so aware of the ecological impact of my radio listening if we had electricity and the nasty batteries weren't right there in my line of vision.

Entry . . . Spring approaches. It's still cool, but high time to get thinking seriously about the growing season. The winter hasn't been a good one for our fall planted crops, which could have benefitted from an insulating blanket of snow. The elephant garlic is a complete bust, but some of the regular garlic might make it. The Walla-Walla onions are spotty, though for some reason the bed in the south garden is faring much better than the main planting. Best looking fall planted effort is the spinach, and it's not spectacular. Ah, well, simple isn't always simple, or successful.

Entry . . . I must get the pea fence up so that maybe I can plant some peas by March 27, Wally's birthday, always my target date. Now that the garden is about to awaken, this account must be put to bed. Time for working, not ruminating!

THE WORLD EQUITY BUDGET

or

LIVING ON ABOUT

$142 PER MONTH

Charles Gray

INTRODUCTION

In 1987 Yoshiaki Tsutsumi was the richest person in the World.[1] His public net worth was reported as 20 billion dollars, $20,000,000,000. There was no question that Mr. Tsutsumi was the richest person because he had five billion dollars more than the second richest person in the world. Taikishiro Mori was also easy to place, because he had 6.3 billion more than the third richest, Sam Walton.

In 1987 the poorest person in the world was not identified. We do not know that person's name nor where she or he lived before dying in 1987 and finally attaining a kind of equality with whichever billionaires may have died that year. Please forgive us for not knowing your name, world's poorest person, for you are equal in the sight of God to Mr. Yoshiaki Tsutsumi.

---

1. "Japan Landlord Tops Billionaires," San Francisco Chronicle, Sept. 22, 1987, page C1.

Though we do not know your name, we know some things about you. In dollar terms your net worth was less than zero. You were in debt, perhaps even in debt peonage. Net worth means assets minus liabilities. The calculation was easy, for you had no assets. Your former landlord -- you had been unemployed for some time -- told you what your liabilities were. Your former landlord kept the books and you couldn't question the landlord because you couldn't read. You owned neither land nor shelter nor tools nor animals. What clothing you had had no market value. You had no clean water to drink. You had no medicine, but medicine wouldn't have helped because your sickness was hunger, and you died of it. Your death from starvation was the final qualification to be the world's poorest person. You shared the title with 25 million other children of God in 1987.

There were 200 million persons who tied for the title of the world's second poorest person, those who have nothing and are starving, but have not yet died.

It's too late for the world's poorest person, 25 million of you, but if Mr. Tsutsmumi's assets were cashed in and equally distributed to the world's second poorest person, the 200 million who are starving, each would suddenly have a net worth of $100, less debts, which might keep those 200 million persons alive until Mr. Mori, the world's second richest person, got conscience stricken and also shared his wealth which would keep them alive until Mr. Walton, not to be outdone, followed suit. By then the rest of the top ten billionaires would get in on the act and the 200 million persons would have a lease on precious life for at least five years. By then the revolution in sharing would be upon us. The rest of us who have more than our share would join in and the 200 million and all the other poor of the world would have the basics of a decent life: land, clean water, adequate food, health care, shelter, clothing, education, meaningful work, hope and joy.

THE WORLD EQUITY BUDGET

How was an individual who aspired to living justly and peacefully to respond to this mega-crisis of late Twentieth Century humanity? It seemed to me that if we were to have a decent life, indeed if we were to have life at all, we had to throw ourselves into a struggle to radically change the institutional structure of greed and violence, the high consumption military state industrialism that was propelling us toward oblivion.

How were we to do that? How was I to do that? It seemed to me I had to begin by looking at my own life, to reduce my own participation in the machine that was carrying us to our deaths. If I aspired to a world of justice and peace, it behooved me to start living more justly and peacefully. It seemed to me that to combine peace and justice required a nonviolent economics.

What would a nonviolent economics be? I thought I didn't know. After all, economics is a very complex subject relating to a diverse reality. But I did know. In my heart I knew where a nonviolent economics had to begin. It had to begin on a foundation of equal sharing, an equal sharing of the wealth of the world. I have a feeling we all know that, however deep we may bury that truth with rationalizations and justifications for inequity. Inequality cannot be a foundation for a nonviolent economics. There may be good reasons for deviation from equality, but those deviations must be small and the reasons good. Those deviations must not be based on greed and supported by violence. If we are to be just, if we are to be at peace, we will embrace each other as equal sisters and brothers of a common family. We will share and be responsive to each others' needs. We will share the work of the world and the rewards of that work. I believe we really know that.

Well, I couldn't expect others to live this way if I wasn't willing to do so myself. So how was I to begin? It seemed to me that any deviations from equality must await a democratically arrived at consensus. There was no such consensus as yet. The structure of maldistribution was maintained by force, not consensus. So the only place to start was to live on my equal share, or less. There were many good reasons for living on less than my equal share, considering that I had used much more than that for 52 years. However, I was lenient with myself, as privileged classes usually are. I thought that a good and modest first step would be to neither own nor control nor consume more than my equal share of the world's wealth and to do my share of the world's work to produce that wealth.

This modest and lenient first step did not seem modest and lenient to many of my good friends and loved ones. When I shared with them what I was feeling and intending to do, they were usually shocked. They thought Charles had really flipped. Nonetheless, in October of 1977 I began the effort to live on my equal share, what I now call the World Equity Budget (WEB).

Deciding to live on one's equal share is one thing. It is a rather exciting idea, actually, but figuring out what that equal share is in dollars and cents is quite another thing. My first idea of an equal share was simply to divide the world's total income by the number of people in the world. That seemed pretty straightforward. Soon, however, I realized that future generations should be part of any sharing concept, so I changed to the idea of an equal share of a sustainable world economy. Because world population was growing, and there were more people to share with, I periodically needed to reduce the budget. In 1984 we (there were two of us by then) made a lifestyle adjustment based on the idea that consuming renewable resources was more sustainable than consuming scarce or non-renewable resources. At the end of the first eleven years we finally found information on how we could adjust the WEB to equalize the variations in the cost of living from one country to another. At this time we also added the concept that we should not only live within our share, but that 15 to 20% of that share we would contribute to oppressed peoples and their projects of empowerment and liberation. This would be a form of reparations for the many years in which we were complicit in systems of oppression.

The present WEB is based on the idea of an equal share of a sustainable world economy. Lacking adequate knowledge of what such an economy might be we have adopted a base year of 1960 when Gross World Product (GWP) was about 35% of what it is today. This is crude because it is not only the level of production, but the materials and processes being used that will determine sustainability. Nonetheless, an economy producing at a level 35% of the plundering, polluting and ever-increasing level of today could certainly be sustained farther into the future. Readers interested in the formula used for calculating the WEB can write to me at 888 Almaden St. Eugene, OR 97402.

How does living within the WEB affect the social system and social relations within that system? I don't think the larger social systems have noticed. The dominant social system does its best to ignore the several billion persons, two-thirds of humanity, that involuntarily live on less than their equal share of present world product, and the majority of humanity that probably live under the WEB. So why would we expect it to take any notice of a tiny handful of folks in the First World who voluntarily do so? We do not know the end of the story, but thus far the WEB has not exactly been front page news. The stepping-stones to our shelter have not cracked under the weight of converts flocking to our door.

The most fundamental change in my social experience was the ending of my marriage of 31 years. That happened immediately because it was obvious to Leslie and myself that such a radical change in lifestyle could not happen unless both of us made the change. For two years we had struggled with efforts to find a way. Part of marriage is sharing equal or very similar economic lifestyles. Housing and food are significant parts of one's budget. To cohabit we had to agree on at least the amount to spend on housing and food. Friends might tolerate disparate lifestyles. Spouses cannot. They have to live together to make a marriage. Not all marriages have such premises, but ours did. So our separation was the most immediate change when I started to live on the WEB. I suddenly found myself alone after three decades of companionship. Anyone adopting the WEB might have to face such drastic changes in the relationships that are the closest of all. The importance of other changes in social experience were minor in comparison to the shattering of my marriage.

In the first household I joined after the end of my marriage we didn't share meals. Everyone did her or his own thing. I was not very competent in the kitchen yet, typical of recently separated or widowed American males of my generation, and I couldn't afford many foods, so my meals didn't amount to much. I hadn't eaten meals alone since I was twenty. The evening meal was the worst. Looking across the table at nothing but the wall gave me such an empty feeling I could physically feel it. The emptiness hit me in the chest. I swear I could feel a hollowness there that was so strong sometimes it restricted my breathing. I would shake myself and then I'd weep. I wasn't strong at night and as the winter came on and the nights grew long I was weaker yet. The mornings would revive me. My work with a construction cooperative would absorb my mind, but I did not look forward to the end of the work day except to ease my tired muscles. The end of the day meant returning to my empty room. I could not stop for a beer to ease the pain a little. I couldn't afford beer anymore. It was awfully wet some nights that winter biking home in the rain, pulling my bike trailer laden with carpentry tools. Biking may be morally wonderful, but it sure can be miserable in an Oregon winter. I'd see my working companions get in their warm pickups and drive off. Between the cold drenching rain and my ocean of self-pity I was sure I was going to drown.

One of the first things I noticed after starting with the WEB was that geography became more of a limit on my associations. Travel costs money and/or time. Now I found that I had to allow from four to six hours to get from my home in Eugene to Portland to attend a meeting or to visit friends. I couldn't jump in my car and be there in two hours and return the same day. Hitching meant two days for the round trip. So I traveled less and my contacts outside my home town gradually diminished. Those that were maintained came to depend more on correspondence than face to face meeting. My life became more localized. This didn't happen all at once. During the first four years I remained active regionally, but I no longer could afford to go to national gatherings or to travel across the country to see a friend or across the world to see my children. When I went someplace I tended to stay longer because I couldn't jump back and forth anymore.

This geographic limit cut some folks out of my social circle. It did, however, make space for others at a regional or local level. Even locally, though, my social interactions decreased because I couldn't just jump in the car and whip around town, attend two meetings, see three friends, and do the shopping all in the same day.

Patterns of social interaction also changed because some meeting places became unavailable. Often people meet over lunch, or in a tavern. These are perhaps the most typical places to get together with folks. However, restaurants are pretty much out of bounds on the WEB and there are definite limits of ethics and etiquette covering how often you can let others pick up the tab. It strains some people to come to your home, or to meet in a park or on a bench in the mall. It can happen, but it isn't conventional among middle class associates. It doesn't work well in the winter, either, as far as outside spots are concerned, and if your housing is too cramped or too far from downtown, meeting informally becomes less feasible. Consequently, such interactions, since they can't occur in conventional locations, tend to decrease. Because you exclude yourself from such locations, you tend to interact somewhat more with people on the street.

One day I had hitched to Portland and was walking past a busy downtown corner, Sixth and Morrison, when a middle-aged man asked for some spare change. This day I had so little that I said to the man, "I'm sorry, Brother, I'm just too poor." He smiled and said, "That's okay." I had no feeling of superiority, or condescension, no pity, no guilt, just brotherhood. And it felt good. With that little encounter, I knew a change had taken place. I was a different person.

The content of interactions also changes. Pretty soon, whether I talked much about the WEB or not, the word got around about my class defection. Response to this news took many forms. Some folks avoided me, some castigated me, some admired me, some called me a prophet. The least common reaction of all was to join with me. That was the reaction I would have preferred. The latter finally occurred in the fourth year when Dorothy adopted the WEB.

I think defectors are psychologically threatening to the groups they leave. We are comfortable in the ways we live, or if not, we are at least used to them. When one of our number disavows the pattern, our equanimity is disturbed. I did not seek out those who began avoiding me so I can only speculate on their reasons. Others, at some time or other, made their displeasure quite clear. Some were angry because they thought I was personally selfish in following my own path when that meant separating from my wife. Such action violates deep-seated family values that place personal relationships above the following out of an abstract ideal, no matter how worthwhile or valid the ideal might seem. It is an even greater violation if the ideal seems neither valid nor worthwhile and in fact threatens one's own lifestyle.

Some that seemed angry would not necessarily admit to it, but their arguments against my case had more affect, more emotional charge, than I would have expected from a simple philosophical discussion. I would not contend that all arguments against the WEB are because people are defensive, but some people who opposed me seemed to me to be doing so because they were threatened by the implicit challenge to live up to our shared ideals of equality.

Progressive friends who professed such ideals were perhaps the most vulnerable and the most likely to find a long list of reasons why the WEB was invalid. So part of the social experience of the WEB was to deal with these objections from my friends. Whether or not these challenges were made because my friends felt threatened, the challenges themselves might be valid. So I will comment on the ones that come most readily to mind.

Perhaps the most common response was, "It can't be done in this society. It's simply impossible to live on so little." The argument was often buttressed by a long list of their budget expenses, any one of which exceeded the WEB. Nonetheless, our sixteen years of experience of living within the WEB is a partial refutation of this argument. Many persons are trapped in a variety of familial or other obligations that would at least temporarily preclude living on the WEB. Even with time for preparation it may be that some cannot live on the WEB. For many others, though, it may be more a matter of will than ability. I must admit that with the housing and health care costs in this country, it takes a fair bit of both will and ability, but I think for many it is certainly far from impossible.

Perhaps the second most common was, "Well, maybe you can do it, but I certainly can't." This is followed by a variety of reasons: "My wife wouldn't agree." "I couldn't impose such a regimen on my children." "I am in debt so I have to maintain my high income." "I haven't finished my education." "My job requires full time work." "I would have to change jobs." "I'm too hooked on the good life." "I can't imagine myself crawling into a dumpster." "I could never give up my car, house, (whatever)." When I'm tempted to get impatient I remind myself of the many years I used these same arguments. Such arguments can seem valid. We are not always in a situation that permits us to make fundamental changes in the way we live. We are often locked in our scene, and we don't have all the keys. We may feel that we cannot move without the consensus of our spouses, companions or family. We may not feel emotionally strong enough for the battles such changes are likely to produce.

I also remember how many years it took me to change my own life style, to finally get myself in a position where I had both the will and the ability to change. I was 44 before I dropped out of academia and I was 52 before I took the plunge into the WEB. Dorothy didn't wait as long as I did. Nonetheless, she felt she could not defect from the empire-protected middle class lifestyle until her son was out of high school. After that she felt free to change. Such long delays leave no room for self-righteousness. How many of the world's poor starved while we vacillated? It is easy for the rich to excuse themselves, to say, "not quite yet." After all, they are not the ones who are suffering for lack of food and justice. We, the rich, are too easy on ourselves. The world is being poisoned and we buy another car. Hundreds of millions of adults cannot write their names for lack of teachers and paper and pencil, and we can't write anymore without buying a personal computer. The poor of Latin America are driven off of their lands. A thousand children are dying each day in Brazil alone -- so that we can have our coffee, bananas and hamburgers. Yes, it's hard for us rich to change. It also must be hard to watch your child slowly die of starvation. I think it becomes more possible for us to change when we realize that not doing so makes us complicit in murder. That's not easy to live with, if we really let ourselves think about it.

As for the particular reasons, I cannot answer some of them from personal experience. For example, I did not live this way when I had children to raise. How one might begin to do so would depend partly on the age of the children and what role they play in family decision-making.

It is interesting that we never ask our children when we have the chance to live richer, but we must do so if we see the opportunity or the rightness of joining the poor.   As for imposing a lifestyle on our children, we always do that.

As for the possibility of a family living on the WEB in the U.S., all I can say is that I have personally known families who have, and with three million families in the U.S. with incomes under $5000, many of those, and certainly those with four members, would be living under the WEB. Not having known many of these families personally, I can't say much about how their children fare in this high consumption society, how they handle peer pressure, etc.   The children I have known have been unusually bright, socially conscious, and creative, in spite of, or perhaps because of, their supposed economic handicaps.   It may be that being voluntarily poor has different social-psychological consequences than being involuntarily poor.

As for finishing education, or saving up for your children's college, I would say that living on the WEB might be a better education.   It might keep you from becoming part of an insulated, credentialed elite.   If a school costs so much that it excludes the poor, then it excludes our best teachers.

If your job requires full time work, and you feel that it makes an important contribution to society, you might choose a division of labor so that your WEB companions can do the non-remunerative work necessary for simple living, or you may give your surplus earnings away if you are single, or you may alternate between full time employment and full time unemployment as a way of balancing the WEB budget, or you could take cuts in earnings so your full time work just makes the WEB.   Of course, if you have enough dependents, full time work may be necessary to live at the WEB.   If some of the above cannot be done within your present employment, then perhaps you do need to change jobs or professions. That may cause a crisis, but a crisis is also an opportunity.   Adjusting one's employment can be looked at as a problem to be solved, rather than as an excuse to avoid necessary change.

As for the feelings of shame about crawling into a dumpster, you can live on the WEB without ever crawling into a dumpster if you have access to garden space and/or your other costs can be kept low.   On the other hand, walking right into that shame may be a way to overcome it.

As for your favorite high cost item -- car, house, travel -- you may not need it as much as you think.   Giving it up can be a good exercise in nonattachment. Would you give it up if your children were dying? Well, your children are dying. If you can't give it up, figure out a way to share it with enough people so you can do it within the WEB. That can be done with some houses and vehicles. As for travel, there are many cheap ways to travel. It doesn't have to be given up entirely.

Consensus with one's spouse or companion or family may not be possible. I reported above the choice I made after several years of trying to consense on the WEB. You may not be able to make such a choice if a similar effort at consensus fails. Or you may find some kind of mutually acceptable compromise between your present lifestyle and the WEB. Perhaps better to go part way with your companion than all the way by yourself. As part of a privileged class you still have the power, if not the right, to make such choices.

Do debts hold you to the establishment? Here again, you can look at debts as a problem to be solved rather than as a justification for inaction. Who are your creditors? Are they rich? Some creditors don't do very good things with the money you pay them. Some commit murder, like the U.S. government and multinational banks. Some creditors may have been robbing you for years. Did you have anything to say about how much interest you had to pay? Should you really have to pay for your house three or four times over. As for student loans, why is it the young have to pay to be educated? Is it because social priorities are so screwed up? Did you really get sucked into buying that new car by the psychologically sophisticated fantasy images on the tube? Deeply conditioned establishment morality says, "we must pay our debts", but must we if in so doing we are keeping a murderous establishment going? If beginning on the WEB becomes for you a matter of conscience, you may need to consider bankruptcy as a possibility -- cash in your assets and let your creditors have them so you can start fresh. If you can't in good conscience keep your establishment job in order to pay off your debt, your student loan, your mortgage, your car, etc., then bankruptcy might be your only option. I realize these are pretty radical attitudes. It's a serious challenge to risk giving up one's home, for example, in order to get free of the system. However, the whole concept of the WEB is radical. We are not talking about modest changes.

Another consideration on debt is that we have much greater debts than we realize. Morally we are deeply in debt to the poor of the world for the labor and resources they have been forced to give us by an unjust economic order. When are we going to recognize that debt and start paying it? Why do we only pay debts to establishment creditors -- to those who try to punish us if we don't pay? Is it that we are morally bound or just bound by fear? Perhaps we should look at all our debts and pay first those who have the greatest need, rather than the most muscle, those who have the greatest moral claim rather than the greatest legal claim.

What of debts to family or friends? Some people borrow from parents or children. Are we so hooked on money-making that we make money even off our own family members? Could not some loans of this type be converted to gifts? Might this be done if in discussing such an idea with parents you accepted a responsibility to help the parents when they were needful. If they recognized that you were opting for a simpler lifestyle, they would understand that such help would need to be within the parameters of the WEB. Loans from parents for material acquisitions could be paid off by selling the property. With a house, it might be sold to its present occupant including yourself as a land trust, which if shared by enough people could fit within the WEB. Loans for education might be converted to gifts or at least into interest free loans.

I think the main point is that with debts as with other aspects of our economy, we would do well to clear our minds for some new analysis and we should not just accept debt as one more justification for avoiding fundamental change.

Another cluster of social responses to the WEB have challenged the formula for determining one's fair share of the world's wealth. One of the most frequent of these is the contention that the WEB formula does not figure in the differences in the cost of living from place to place, especially country to country. "But it's a lot cheaper to live in India or Mexico." That is a legitimate criticism and we have now, thanks to the research done by the United Nations International Comparisons Project, incorporated such adjustments into the WEB formula.

Some have felt that some elements of the formula were quite arbitrary, such as the choice of the per capita personal income of the year 1960 as a base for a sustainable economy. They are admittedly arbitrary. I would argue with the statistically sophisticated folks that these choices were necessarily crude, but they were in the right direction and much better than nothing. If the train is taking us to the death camp it is better to act in the right direction, that is, jump off, than to continue talking until a statistically accurate assessment of the risks is perfected. Or, so it seems to me. The rich often argue for more data, more study and more time. That we need data is obvious, but let us err on the side of moving in the right direction now and, if we happen to move a little further than required by the demands of equity, we can make adjustments when the better data is available. It is impossible that we would err so much that we would overpay our debt to the poor.

It has been rather amazing to me that few persons have challenged the most basic idea of the WEB, that we should live within our equal share. That makes me think that, though we don't practice such equality except at times within our families, the concept of equality is deep within our system of ideals. Thus the idea of the WEB has a powerful base, a base of ideals that can be appealed to. In presenting the WEB to people I have argued that equality is the most obvious beginning point for a nonviolent economics. It is the beginning point, and deviations from it should be based on differential needs determined by a democratic or consensus process rather than on conquest, lethal power and institutionalized greed. Few have argued with this position.

A few have said that the present system, or greed in general, is part of human nature. That is pretty obvious. Love seems characteristic of human nature also. Human nature is culturally conditioned and malleable. When and if it becomes clear to us that institutionalized greed is destroying the planet, we are likely to change because the desire to survive is also part of human nature. It could be argued that the desire to survive is motivating liberation movements everywhere. The question for each of us is whether we will be part of liberation movements or part of the resistance to these efforts. Destruction is upon us. If we are to survive we must reckon with the holocaust of world hunger, with the Bomb and with the greed that has produced both. Our capacity for love and our desire to survive may yet move us toward an economically and politically nonviolent society.

Though the goals of equality and a sustainable economy are generally approved, the WEB as a personal lifestyle as part of a strategy for attaining these goals is challenged. Following is a composite that reflects these criticisms: What's the point of it all? I can't see how it's going to help the poor any to have you making such a sacrifice. How's that going to change anything? Not one person in a thousand would join you, so it has no potential as a social movement. We need institutional change, not personal witness.

I have not directly contradicted such criticisms because I think they have some truth in them. I do suggest, though, that none of us really completely understand the dynamics of social change. Even if we think we have a good analysis of some historical social changes, that analysis may not fit our present situation of world wide multi-faceted and rapidly accelerating crisis.

For the very reason that we have had no sure knowledge, social movements usually contain quite a mix of strategies and tactics and much time and energy are consumed in arguing about them, often with much heat and little light. I find myself leaping into such battles with as much enthusiasm as anyone. Occasionally, however, I am a bit more humble. I realize how little I really know. Because we need to learn so much more I think Paolo Freire's concept of praxis -- an alternation between action and reflection so that our action is ever more informed by the periods of reflection and our reflection is grounded in the experience of action -- is appropriate. These writings are partly a reporting on an experience of eleven years and partly a reflection on those eleven years.

I began the WEB and Dorothy joined it, not as a consequence of strategic thinking that led us to believe that this was the way to start a social movement, nor as a kind of personal witness or modeling behavior for a better way to live, but as an effort to reduce the tension between the way we lived and the beliefs we professed. There was a great gap between our lifestyles and our ideals.

Certainly the ideals of equality, equality of many kinds -- of opportunity, before the law, of access to material and cultural resources, of the sexes, the races, the classes, the cultures, the nations, the generations, of political participation -- certainly these ideals are widespread in human society. And equally certainly our social practice falls far short of these ideals. Many must feel the tension between these ideals and the ways we behave. So these small actions that we have taken must come out of a tension that is widely shared, and a tension that is increasing as inequality increases.

We may not deal with that tension in a rational way. We may use denial and all sorts of psychological and ideological mechanisms in an attempt to reduce that tension. But I would contend that such mechanisms won't work because they avoid the real world. The equalities I've mentioned make too much sense to too many people as among the appropriate goals of humanity in this period of history. They are not the only equalities the attainment of which will help us to survive. Others would include reining in our collective material appetite so there is something left of this planet for future generations, a kind of intergenerational equality. In the dominant culture we are not accustomed to looking ahead more than a single generation, if that. With our present power to impact the environment, we need a much longer range view, perhaps the seven generations that indigenous peoples of North America encompassed in their thinking. The reduction of the inequality between social classes and the finding of a sustainable economy (some of the environmental movement is part of this) are two social movements to which the WEB is relevant.

Social movements operate out of a collective tension between ideals and practice. They grow by manifestos and other consciousness raising devices that clarify this tension and that propose programs of action that promise a reduction of this tension by moving the society closer to the shared ideals, or perhaps by moving ideals closer to social practice. Those persuaded of the validity of the analysis and the program then organize themselves to carry it out.

Though we did not consciously see the WEB as a social movement for economic equality, it may have relevance for existing or new movements of this kind in several ways. It speaks to the widely shared collective tension. It accepts the requirement that social movements often put on their adherents, namely that they practice what they preach. This requirement has the advantage of reducing the tension that is likely to be even greater among those who actively organize for the changes favored by the movement. Working in a movement heightens sensitivity to such tension because one is always working with the evidence of inequality and crisis that motivates the movement. Facing it all the time maximizes the tension and presses one to make one's personal life consistent with the professed ideals. Also, if the members of a movement organization practice what they preach, their ability to persuade others and thus gain new adherents is enhanced. Such personal consistency communicates seriousness, commitment, and integrity. The fact that the early Christian communities practiced their ideals of love and equality may have contributed to their rapid growth. Similarly, the personal consistency of the early Gandhians may have contributed greatly to the rapid growth of the Indian Independence Movement and its associated anti-caste, anti-untouchability, and nonviolent direct action components. Many Indians who shared some of Gandhi's goals were long on rhetoric. The Gandhians, at least many of them, were long on practicing what they preached.

The danger of practicing what you preach is that it can become an end in itself, a searching for personal purity or salvation, and forgetting the fact that movement goals are not attained unless the movements grow through organizing and focusing the energy of the collective tension toward program goals.

A movement for a nonviolent economics would have among its

program goals actions that themselves reduce the power of the unjust establishment and reclaim that power for the poor. The WEB is sufficiently stringent that it really becomes a generalized boycott of the economic and political establishment. As such it weakens the establishment in proportion to the numbers practicing it. The WEB also strengthens the poor because their relative bargaining power against a weakened establishment grows greater and because practicing the WEB strengthens the underground economy of barter, subsistence, alternative enterprise, and tax resistance. Such effects are unlikely to be noticeable, of course, until the movement has millions of adherents. However, the intensity of the WEB commitment would magnify the social impact. That intensity is likely to strengthen the adherents as well. Tough training makes tough troops in nonviolent struggle as well as in violent struggle.

To a limited extent, the WEB puts you in the position of the poor so you feel what it is like. Struggle for equality is no longer a head trip alone. You more sharply feel the injustice of the system not as guilt, but as oppression. You begin to feel part of the oppressed. You suffer with them. Your downward mobility may even make your suffering especially intense. Now you are fighting both for yourself and for your brothers and sisters. You not only see, but you feel the difference between the hunger of the poor and the gluttony of the rich. Your resentment of injustice grows. This is a matter of degree and I would not want to overstate the case. The person who has had the privileges and education of the rich cannot ever fully know the experience of the involuntarily poor or racially oppressed. Also the WEB still leaves one at about the midpoint of per capita world income. Nonetheless, in relative terms, you come much closer to an understanding of economic injustice when you renounce many of the material rewards of privilege. That understanding grows as you continue year after year on the WEB especially if you burn your bridges and can no longer return to your previous life. To the extent that that happens you are likely to identify personally with collective struggles as the only means to overcome oppression. You now have a more immediate personal stake in the outcome of such struggles. Focusing your energy on the common struggle is now no different than focusing on your own personal struggle. So your energy is integrated and thus strengthens the collective effort.

Living on the WEB in the U.S., though it still keeps you in the richest third of humanity, definitely places you among the very poor in the U.S. You may, because of access to the Great American Garbage Can, have a fairly comfortable material life, but you experience some of the psychological oppression and social discrimination of being at the bottom of the class system.

I have, perhaps more than Dorothy who has kept her nursing credential up to date, experienced a growing identity with the poor. Many of the bridges to my past life have been permanently cut. I have been too long away from my academic profession and I am now too old and too radical to return to it. My age now limits my earning capacity and employment opportunities.

The basic concept of a nonviolent economics includes the idea that one not only does not own or consume more than one's share of the world's wealth, but that one does not control more than one's share. Consequently, to avoid the unequal power that such control would give, we need a World Equity Wage (WEW) that does not produce a surplus over the WEB.

The WEW is based on a guess that an adult without dependents with an intermediate level of technology, about the level of the ball bearing and the bicycle, could produce his/her share of what is needed for a simple, but decent, life by working about one-third time. At first that may seem too low, but when we subtract the work that goes into the weapons and luxuries and junk and waste in our culture, that estimate of necessary work seems about right to me. That would mean twelve or thirteen hours a week. Wow! The WEW starts looking better. We or our community would adjust this time to cover the needs of dependents.

How much do we charge for this one-third time, or perhaps one-half time if we are more conservative in our estimate of the waste of the present system? We charge enough to pay the WEB. Our hourly pay, or WEW = WEB / hours per month at one-third time. If the WEB is $100 and our estimate of one-third time is 50 hours a month, then WEW would be $2 an hour. As the WEB changes the WEW needs to be adjusted. During the first sixteen years of the WEB my WEW ranged from $1.21 an hour to $2.90 an hour.

In order for a growing identity with the poor to be meaningful in movement terms, the time to do movement work is essential. The WEB liberates time. As we have seen, even at the World Equity Wage, (WEB/one-third time) sub-minimum by U.S. standards, it only takes a third of full time work to meet one's budget needs. Labor intensive gardening or reclaiming dumpstered food can add some to that, but one still has at least half of one's time free for other pursuits and for movement work. Also, because one's material needs are modest, one is freer to do movement work for pay without straining the movement budget. In both these ways the WEB can free one to help in the struggle for justice.

As movement people come to adopt the WEB their lifestyles will more closely approximate those of activists in the Third World and this greater equality is likely to give more reality to the "our brothers and sisters" rhetoric. Some of the present barriers in solidarity work will diminish. We will become part of the solution instead of part of the problem.

In the early 1980's Dorothy Granada and I became involved in the Fast for Life. I was doing a workshop on the Fast For Life proposal at the summer conference of the Fellowship of Reconciliation at Seabeck, Washington. I also participated in a workshop on simple living where I talked about the WEB. Dan Berrigan was on that panel too. Dan said the WEB was not for him. That was a big disappointment to me.

At the conference I got better acquainted with Dorothy Granada whom I had originally met during the occupations and subsequent trials at the Trojan Nuclear Power Plant. Dorothy liked me, the WEB, and the Fast proposal. She didn't know quite what she was getting in for, but she went for the whole package. That was the end of my loneliness. What a joy it was to have a personal companion again. What an unexpected treasure to have Dorothy to share this lifestyle and this demanding and exciting fast organizing. I had thought that being alone was one of the costs I would have to pay for the WEB. That was true for awhile, but now perhaps that was over. I luckily came along at the right time. Dorothy had previously decided she was going to adopt a simple life style and she had already decided to become active in the efforts against the Bomb. In December of 1980 Dorothy moved to Eugene.

Dorothy's adoption of the WEB was a very sudden plunge from a car and a three bedroom house in the suburbs of Portland and a $25,000 a year salary. It quite amazed me. I had taken several years of psychological preparation and practical sorting out of financial affairs before I had managed the change. Dorothy, on the other hand, did it all in one big jump.

1982 and 1983 were years when we felt completely taken over by the preparations for the Fast For Life. In Washington we came in contact with the Community for Creative Nonviolence. We were deeply impressed with their work with the homeless. We met some of those homeless who were living on the sidewalks in front of the White House. The contrast between their hungry faces and the impassive faces in the chauffeured limousines pulling into the White House driveway became another of the foundation images supporting the importance of the WEB. The concentrated greed and the concentrated poverty, the latter because of the former. A year later an ordinance was passed prohibiting the homeless from sleeping on that sidewalk. The powers that be must have been threatened by that juxtaposition. That very visible truth was too stark for them. That experience deepened our resolve to have the Fast become a *s*ymbol of the connection between world hunger and the arm's race .

The Fast For Life was a profound experience for us. We knew we might starve to death. We spent a lot of time preparing our spirits for that possibility. As the Fast progressed we felt a deeper and deeper identification with the hungry of this world. In one sense at least we now felt at one with the poorest of the poor. We were starving. During the time when we felt we might die, the difference between ourselves and the world's starving, namely that our action was voluntary and theirs was involuntary, lost its meaning for me. Given the condition of the world, our fast did not seem entirely voluntary. We were compelled by the world's crisis to take such an action.

We felt spiritually strong in the Fast. This was in part because of the outpouring of support the Fast generated. It reached very deeply into many people and sparked new energy. In part I would attribute our strength to the preparation we had made. I felt that the several years of the WEB was a clarifying kind of preparation, a way of life consistent with the Fast. We entered the Fast feeling in tune, that in a sense it was a logical extension of our path.

While fasting our personal expenditures approached zero though the organization was spending a fortune to get the word out to the media and to a mailing list of many thousands. It struck me funny, like the story of Gandhi's rich friend who was reputed to have said, "It costs me 10,000 rupees a year to keep Gandhi in poverty."

The Fast officially ended after forty days. All fasters survived, though several were pretty sick by then. Our high goals were not attained nor were those of the many other efforts that year to stop the missiles, or to get a freeze.

After recovering from the fast and reporting on it, Dorothy and I went to Guatemala and then Nicaragua to work. Twice we returned to the U.S. to educate people here about the realities of life in Central America. At present I am doing Central America solidarity work in the U.S. and

Dorothy is again in Nicaragua establishing a health clinic in Mulukukú.

To summarize, living on the WEB can help the poor both directly, by reducing our own demand on available resources, and indirectly, by strengthening movements for justice. Because the WEB boycotts much of the establishment, we make our living more consistent with our goals, and thus we persuade others by our lives as well as by our words, thus gaining more adherents. The WEB enhances solidarity work because our lifestyles more closely approach those of persons struggling for change in the Third and Fourth Worlds. The WEB gives us a greater personal stake in the collective struggles for justice. Justice is no longer a head trip. Finally, the WEB frees up time to do more movement organizing. Increased energy plus the time to use it means more movement work gets done. My evaluation is that we have done more movement work and higher quality movement work in the years on the WEB than in most of the previous thirty years.

I see the WEB as a way to clean up, strip down, and move. Purity is not the goal. The goal is to prepare ourselves to collectively move the world. We can't do that if we insist on dragging The American Dream Machine along with us. Shed it! It's not only unjust. It's killing us.

As I said previously, we wanted to experience the WEB before suggesting it to others. Consequently, we have not organized an effort to persuade others to adopt it. It may be true that not one person in a thousand would opt for stripping down in this fashion. Actually, it would be pretty impressive if one in a thousand did so. That would be a quarter of a million persons in the U.S. Perhaps one in ten thousand, or 245,000 persons, would be more in the realm of possibility. We don't have the first dozen yet. Shall we form an Order, the Order of The WEB? How's that? Join us. Get poor now. Avoid the rush later.

Joking aside, it may be true that people will not flock to the WEB. Historically, the evidence suggests they won't, at least not in large numbers. However, as I see it, however many do, whether it's 24 or 24,000, they and the movement for justice will be that much further ahead. Historical evidence may not tell us much in this case since our present multifaceted crisis is unique. The sheer size of this crisis may, as has sometimes happened in the past, stimulate new religious movements relevant to survival. Sustaining the planet and living within one's share could be among the core beliefs and practices of such movements.

Some of our friends have expressed the fear that living on the WEB will result in our becoming marginalized. We have experienced this to some degree. Sometimes we feel that we can't talk to friends and acquaintances about our lifestyle or about the WEB in a language they will understand or be able to identify with. Thus, useful dialogue diminishes. However, moving to the margin of one group may move you closer to another group, a group that may be more significant for social change organizing than the privileged class you have left. Though we have experienced some marginalization, we accept that as a problem to be worked with. Who knows? We may be marginal to 1993 and central to 2093. However that may be, we seek to live some approximation to truth as we see it whether it puts us at the margin or at the center. Cutting edges are marginal, though I would not argue that all margins are cutting edges.

These have been some of the largely verbal reactions we have gotten from our friends and others who have come in contact with our lifestyle. In our discussions we have sometimes found that we have answered one objection after another only to find that there is always one more. At such times we suspect that our friends are not moving toward change of this sort, and that they are defending their status quo by simply adding to the infinite list of possible objections. Fair enough, we all do that at one time or another when we have no intention of changing our position on a particular subject.

For the most part, we have not felt ostracized from community groups. An exception to this is the exclusion we experience when we can't afford conference fees. We don't, in our view at least, aggressively push the WEB idea even though we feel very strongly. That is either because we are shy or we have learned it doesn't get anywhere, anyway. On one occasion, a conference on the international debt crisis, I did propose the WEB as well as participation in reparations payments to the peoples of the Third World for all we had stolen from them. My approach was personal and definitely at the margin of the generally academic calls for institutional reform. I later learned that some of the audience were furious, accusing me of putting a huge guilt trip on them. As I saw it I just laid out the facts and asked people to assume some personal responsibility. If they felt guilty, perhaps it was because they were guilty. Living on one's share is just a practical nonviolent economics and debts are debts. Guilt is not the point, nor is penance. We aren't trying to punish ourselves.

Because our movement activity has generally not focused on the WEB, but rather on resisting the Bomb and the Empire's wars, we have not developed a network of people focusing on the concept of equal sharing. Nonetheless, part of our social experience of the WEB is that we have become more aware of persons doing this sort of thing. There are quite a few voluntary simple livers out there. I imagine, if some of these writings see the light of day, we will become more a part of a network of folks moving in this direction and the social experience of the WEB will become more of a community experience. Even thus far we have learned most of our ideas and practical applications from others.

Another aspect of our interface with the middle class has been the question of gifts and subsidies. Some of our friends look on our life as too austere. They see that we pass by the restaurants, movie theaters, concert halls and conferences that are part of their own lifestyles. In their generosity they sometimes invite us to such places. Also, at times it may slip their minds that we cannot afford such luxuries, and they suggest that we do such things together. These situations cause some awkwardness occasionally and at times, if people treat us too often, we have to, as courteously as possible, tell them that, though we appreciate their generous spirits, their picking up the tab is inconsistent with our effort to not consume more than our share. We sometimes encourage other ways of being together such as a walk on the beach, or a meal shared in our homes. Friends can rediscover the fact that you don't really have to spend money to be together and have a good time. Newly purchased material gifts are also beyond our budget, generally. We have tried to get our family and friends to reduce the gift exchanges to simple greetings, a bit of hand work, something recycled, a poem, some food from the kitchen or garden. This has worked pretty well, though some of the goodies from the kitchen can get pretty fancy.

I'm sure at times our friends love to corrupt us a little. And we, for our part, love to be corrupted. We don't want to come off as fanatical purists. We aren't interested in sack cloth and ashes. We want to enjoy the material things of life as much as possible within our equal share. So we try to keep the corruptions small and not too frequent.

At times we accept gifts for our work, either equipment used directly in the work itself or gifts that add to our personal comfort in places where working conditions are hard. Enjoying comfort as much as the next person, we have often happily accepted these generous offerings. In some situations, though, as in Nicaragua, certain gifts have set us apart from those we are working with and tend to perpetuate the image of the rich North American. It's something of a dilemma because certain very useful items are not easily come by second hand. In a place like Nicaragua where all equipment is in short supply, it is nice to have new equipment that won't break down and that can be given to Nicaraguans when we leave. The dilemma is one we have not resolved. We deal with each situation as it occurs. Perhaps we should accept useful equipment for the work itself, but try to keep to the simpler old hand-me-downs for our personal life.

One of the problems in our social experience with the WEB is that it has been easier to change our personal lifestyle than to change our work style. Much of our experience has been and still is with the predominantly white middle class peace movement organizations. Our associations, skills, and opportunities have been largely within this milieu. We find ourselves living in two environments, a middle class one while working and a much simpler one in our personal lives.

We feel clashes here. The most important perhaps is that we mobilize financial and other resources to carry on the work. These resources then give us power over more than our equal share of wealth and thus violate one of the principles of the WEB. We have not yet devised methods for sharing the decisions over these resources so that the principle of equal power is put into practice.

Though perhaps less important rationally, the sometimes posh hospitality we receive when we are on speaking tours seems particularly inconsistent with the WEB. We feel this so sharply because when we are on tour we are often surrounded by affluence night and day. We are guests and we gratefully accept and enjoy the queen sized bed and private bath. We also appreciate the generous spirit in which these luxuries are shared with us. I think many of our hosts would share with the whole world if they could somehow see the way. Yet the affluence makes us uncomfortable. We are often gone from home for months at a time. We have no balancing simplicity, no getting on our bikes after work and returning to our simple food and shelter. We often yearn for the old bicycles.

Yet, in spite of these dilemmas, we are reluctant to give up this access to the middle class. We can learn from our dialogues with them and our generally more radical analysis and experience with the WEB may have something to contribute to their lives, including such ideas as the WEB itself.

We have accepted some free health and dental care which the donors have seen as a kind of barter for the peace and justice work we do. Recently I have pulled away from this as an unjustified subsidy. Barter for our work should go directly to the work and not to us. However I could see trading health care for movement educational consultation with the health care provider on an hour for hour basis.

Most of the social experience I have written about so far has dealt with our relations with family, friends and associates in the peace movement. Another major interface is with non-familial social institutions like education, government, health-care and business.

Though we have had friends in the health care field, we have also had the more usual impersonal contacts with doctors, dentists and hospitals. Because of high and, in our view, exorbitant costs we have avoided such health care professionals and bureaucracies whenever possible. At other times, hospital staff have looked at our income level and our lack of establishment employment and legally classified us as indigent. Funny word. We might be working ten or twelve hours a day to stop the arms race, but in the warfare state that's either subversive or indigent. We haven't had life threatening health problems where we had to choose between paying for high cost treatment as the society expects, but which most certainly violates the WEB, or dying, as the society abhors, in order to maintain our commitment. That will be a challenging day.

Our more frequent contacts have been with dentistry. The teeth continue to decay even on a fairly low sugar diet. Our teeth just don't realize what a bite they take out of our budget. On beginning with a dentist I explain my lifestyle and point out that I can't necessarily go along with his/her advice if I cannot afford it. As explained elsewhere, I avoid cosmetic dentistry and saving a tooth no matter what the cost. This is shocking to some dentists. It's bad enough that I usually refuse X-ray, but to be willing to have a hole in my mouth rather than put out from $400 to $600 to save the tooth seems beyond their comprehension. Once when a crown was recommended to save a tooth and I was told that a root canal might be involved also, I asked the dentist to figure out something cheaper. An interesting conversation followed. He said that he had gotten so used to the usual American idea, a recent one actually, that no effort or expense should be spared to save a tooth, that it hadn't occurred to him to consider any other options. Keeping a tooth for a dentist is like keeping a person alive for a doctor -- don't spare the cost! He thought about it for awhile. Some dentists don't have time to think. They are too busy getting rich. This one, though, was known as the "hippy" dentist, I suppose because he was rather laid back and didn't schedule so tightly that he had no time to reflect on what he was doing. He decided not to build up a crown so I would have a biting surface, but to clean out the decay and put in a cheap filling which he would look at again in the future. A couple of years later he suggested, contrary to the going root canal/crown craze, that I have the tooth pulled out. So now there is a gap where I can store an extra peanut now and then. If I smile broadly, as I often do, my World Equity mouth shows. It's the only really obvious evidence that I have parted company with the medical/dental save-it-at-all-costs ethic, an ethic I see as part of the maldistribution of health care. I now feel an identification with the often gap-toothed smiles of my Nicaraguan campesino friends. Our solidarity is just slightly greater.

We are pretty much a generalized two person boycott of the business establishment as far as level of consumption is concerned, though I don't think they have noticed. We feel a little odd when we sometimes join a specific boycott protest vigil since our whole lifestyle is a boycott of the American Dream Machine and the specific boycotts don't change our own patterns at all. We've been boycotting them right along. Consequently, they don't experience any new dip in their daily take on our account.

As for government, we no longer produce much wealth for the establishment so the only income tax liability we have is for social security. This tax falls very heavily on the poor since anyone earning over $400 a year is liable for a considerable chunk. It's the biggest tax paid by the poor, taking between 7.3 and 13% of the gross income with no exemptions. Because social security reserves are invested in U.S. government securities which help fund the warfare state, we refuse this tax, so we are still hassled by the IRS even though we are below taxable levels for the income tax. To avoid seizures we keep just enough in a credit union to keep an account open so we can cash checks. Dorothy once had to quit a job to avoid having wages garnished. When we can, we opt for self-employment to avoid this problem. Our present practice is to not only refuse any IRS claims, but to have nothing the IRS can seize. When the IRS collection agent comes around and finds no car, no VCR, no TV, no hi-fi, but just a few books, clothes, fifteen year old bicycles, a 30 year old manual typewriter, I think he'll scratch his head and cross us off his list.

A major local government institution is the building inspector who would think ill of our various forms of substandard or illegal housing; that is, if he knew about them. We do not recognize his right to deny us the right to shelter ourselves. We feel that what he doesn't know won't hurt him, and that we have no moral obligation to educate him.

Since to live as poor as we do, by American standards, means we must, at times, live outside the law, and because we engage in occasional civil disobedience in our resistance work, we also come up against the criminal "justice" system. There our real poverty and political solidarity with the poor means we will stay in jail rather than pay bail or fines. We have not actually spent much time in jail. Often the actions we have participated in have been large enough that the courts have dismissed charges or given probation to avoid the expense of jailing a large group. The now frequent court restrictions on adding new inmates to overcrowded jails have put the sheriffs in a bind. Presently lots of new prisons are being built to satisfy those on the right who want to lock more people up and the liberals who want locked-up people to have less crowded conditions. Our budget has somewhat limited our participation in civil disobedience actions that are far from home because of the costs of travel to far places for court appearances.

For the most part we have remained independent of government welfare programs. The exceptions have been rather minor: a hospital bill written off because I was classified as indigent and some Ronnie Reagan butter and cheese. I suppose some government program picked up the tab on the hospital bill. We do not want to become dependent on welfare. We do fully utilize parks and libraries and streets and city water so in this respect we benefit from the public wealth of the society. We don't feel we benefit from police forces, however. We do not call on them for assistance. We consider them generally to be agents protecting the interests of the rich. They pull people into a criminal injustice system that is more likely to professionalize the "criminal" than to rehabilitate him/her. How do you rehabilitate anyone with jail cells and guns? How could agents of the American Death Machine be expected to improve the behavior of anyone? We prefer to use what nonviolence skills we have and to cooperate with the nonviolence skills of others to deal with anti-social behavior rather than depend on a police force. Such a force uses violence as its ultimate tactic and sometimes as its first tactic if it is stressed or racist or if you challenge its authority in any way. Our own ability to deal with violent anti-social behavior has been tested several times in high crime neighborhoods in U.S. cities and also in accompaniment work in Guatemala and Nicaragua. Partly by good luck and by being observant we have so far managed. People fantasize violent chaos without police forces. I doubt it could be worse than the concentrated institutionalized violence of the National Security State.

The social experience of the WEB has included not only the interface between the WEB adherent and the rest of the world, but the relations between the WEB adherents. I spent three years on the WEB before Dorothy and I began living together. During that time I developed the basic principles of not controlling or consuming more than an equal share of a sustainable world economy, the concept of the World Equity Wage and a person's labor obligation, and the ECO Dollar indexing system. So Dorothy essentially adopted a plan that I had previously developed; I was the originator and Dorothy was the joiner. That background was one influence on how we interacted on the WEB. Another factor was our quite different personalities. I tend to be a planner, meticulous on details and somewhat of a purist. Dorothy is a doer and more concerned with general ideas than details. Dorothy is spontaneously generous and flexible. We have had lots of good fights over the WEB. I assume this would be characteristic of any couple or community of WEB adherents.

We have somewhat different bottom line ideas. For me, living on a rational WEB is itself the bottom line and lifestyle must be modified to fit within whatever the WEB is. Consequently, the WEB is the first priority for me. I have not been tested as to whether this bottom line would hold if it meant risking my life or seriously risking my health. The first sixteen years have not put me to such a test. I may have needs that would take priority over staying within the WEB, but thus far whatever needs I have had I could meet without breaking the WEB.

Dorothy states her position somewhat differently. She says, for example, "I'm not willing to live on the street and I refuse to do without a few little luxuries like wine and coffee. That's my bottom line." In practice we have managed to accommodate Dorothy's bottom lines within the WEB.

At times it has been very difficult to keep the roof over our heads and it has taken most of our budget. I actually place high priority on having a fairly secure shelter also, though I would try to live on the street if that were necessary to stay within the WEB. Living within the WEB is a kind of moral Absolute for me and of course a person with a moral absolute can put up with a lot of discomfort. At any time we could face a housing crisis that might pose a choice between breaking the WEB in order to shelter ourselves or living on the street. At that point we would have to deal with the conflict between our bottom lines.

An area that neither of us has resolved completely has to do with those times when we generate more income than the budget requires. Sometimes this occurs because, though we are working at the World Equity Wage, we are working longer hours than the budget requires. Sometimes we have done this on purpose, as when we worked full time to put together and tour with an exhibit of Nicaraguan photographs and poetry. The project paid us a stipend equal to double the WEB because we planned to not work for an equivalent period of time after this project was turned over to others. Thus, on average, we would be conforming reasonably well with the WEB concept of devoting one third to one half one's time to provide for material sustenance. We figured that after the project was done we wanted time for reflection, for learning more about growing our own food and sheltering ourselves and for educating and training ourselves for future work, things we couldn't do while working full time. We consensed rather easily that such an averaging was a reasonable application of the WEB principle. During such periods of higher income we still stay within the WEB as far as consumption is concerned.

At other times we generate surplus income because we cannot always control our wage rate. As a nurse, Dorothy sometimes has to accept the going wage. Also she is not as keen as I am on the sub-minimum World Equity Wage.

The generation of surplus income violates the WEB principle of not controlling more than one's equal share of a sustainable world economy. One may redistribute it and not consume it, but the redistribution itself is a type of control. This bothers me more than it does Dorothy. She feels that such surplus can be given away without exercising more than a very modest amount of power or that it can even be used to subsidize our own projects. I have not been comfortable with this, but I'm the purist.

I imagine that any community adopting the WEB would have such problems. It's hard to be so relatively austere, to have to consider the cost of every little thing we do, in the high spending environment of the U.S.A. I can see the formation of High Consumers Anonymous (HCA), with folks getting together and testifying as to our past high consumption life and how long we had been off the "bottle" of wasteful and unjust living, and how when we backslide or are tempted to do so, we call on our HCA support groups to help us back onto the proper path. If it worked as well for HCA as it has for AA, we'd soon have millions of members and the revolution would be getting underway.

So these have been some of the aspects of our social experience with the WEB. That experience continues to unfold, to pose new questions for us. Our lifestyle has primarily been a challenge to ourselves. It has perhaps been a small challenge to a few of our sisters and brothers. The WEB has put us in a special kind of dialog with our still rich friends. We ask them to personally reckon with the institutionalized violence of the worldwide maldistribution of wealth, to consider living on their equal share as a step toward a nonviolent economics and a more peaceful world. Some have responded by finding flaws in our reasoning, some by saying 'someday, but not yet', and others by saying they are starting to move toward the WEB or some modification of it. So, give it some thought, dear reader.

LIVING OUR FAITH

Judi Buchman and Richa

Simple living? We are two people, at times living by ourselves in an urban 5-bedroom house -- complete with full basement, attic, and garage/warehouse -- that is practically overflowing with AWFULs (Articles Waiting For Use Later; sometimes known as Junk). We are fairly self-sufficient if that means living mostly off our society's discards -- including our house, most of our food, our clothes, our transportation, our furniture . . . our welcome mat, our electric organ, our yacht paint, even our incense. And, of course, because life is so simple for us, our lives are completely peaceful!

Well . . . we do have our share of struggles and problems . . . though we also certainly have our share of satisfactions and joys. As we learn and grow, we have more of the latter and fewer of the former. And basic-ally we feel grounded, alive, and purpose-full.

In what follows we will first separately relate influences upon our lives, up to the time we began living together. We will then write of our lives together, starting with our home, extending outward in community until it encompasses our world and something of our dreams and faith.

We can hardly go into much detail in such a short piece of writing and some things are simplified or left out due to our differing ways of seeing -- they become too complicated to easily explain. So we invite people who are interested in knowing more to contact us.

Note our use of the word "co" herein, a non-gendered personal pronoun which substitutes for "she", "he", "him", "her", or sometimes "it". "Cos" is the possessive form, substituting for "his", "hers", "her" or "its". This term was coined over 20 years ago as a non-sexist, easy-to-use alternative to generic male pronouns in cases where gender was unknown.

Judi uses it in that way. Richa, believing that gender (like race, which has no special personal pronouns) is secondary to basic humanity, and that language should reflect that belief, uses the term generally. We have used it generally in our writing herein.

For lack of a better alternative we use Gregorian dates herein. We are aware that there are calendar systems other than the dominant Gregorian system favored by Western "culture", and that the Gregorian system is not necessarily any better than other calendar systems.

Richa

By and large my upbringing did not prepare me, either practically or spiritually, for 'simple living'. Our White middle-class family lived in an almost exclusively White middle-class suburban wasteland near Washington, D.C., where my mother cared for us children and my father worked at a government job. I had little exposure to other lifestyles until after leaving home. Yet while still at home i realized that there was something important missing for me in that environment -- a sense of purpose.

I felt that school was stifling. I happen to be directly descended from Horace Mann, "the father of modern education", and from an early age used to tell my classmates, in a disgusted tone: "My great-great-grandfather invented school." I had enough common sense, even then, to realize that i was not responsible for the acts of my ancestors. Some of what i learned in school was, and remains, useful, but as i became more aware and critically reflective, school seemed increasingly irrelevant and oppressive.

Neither school nor home taught me much about physical labor -- working with my hands and body. Nor did either one help me very effectively with social relationships.

Of great influence was the fact that my parents practiced corporal punishment. The injustice of that penetrated early and deep, causing, or at least significantly contributing to, a strong sense of discomfort around, fear of, and distrust of 'authority figures'. They weren't intentionally cruel, simply doing as they had been taught and acting in conformity with predominant standards that accepted (and still accept) hitting children under certain circumstances. But i felt it as a terrible injustice.

In my blind anger, i in turn hit and otherwise abused my younger siblings and the family dog, though i would often feel terrible afterwards, for i also had a keen empathic sense. It wasn't until around the time i entered my teens that my sense of justice extended far enough that i stopped such abuse.

Sometimes i would see friends or others fighting. Despite my own bullying behavior at times, fighting scared and repelled me. I didn't understand it, and avoided it.

My parents and some teachers helped me to learn and appreciate certain positive values. Being honest. Checking things out for myself, rather than automatically accepting whatever i was told or read. Persistence. To some degree, fairness, i.e. a sense of justice.

Even those values were not always seen as positive, as some people would say that i was blunt, critical, stubborn, impracticably idealistic. I later learned to modify some strong tendencies in accord with the dictum 'moderation in all things'. ('All things', i should point out, includes 'moderation'.) But those values certainly contributed to my rebellion against and rejection of much else i was 'taught', allowing and helping me to see some things as irrelevant or unsound or harmful.

Many in my generation (i was born in 1947), myself included, huddled in school hallways in practice drill, to protect ourselves (!) from a nuclear bombing. We were very young; we could not understand very well what it was about. Nevertheless, it was largely the fear engendered by threat of nuclear war that prompted me as a teen-ager to seriously consider some aspects of living simply -- very simply! Having been brought up to intellectually value "individualism", i decided to study and practice wilderness survival skills. I checked out books (including a U.S. Army field survival manual!), went on small forays, and did lots of experimentation, especially on edibility of wild plants. I did it in order to be prepared to go off into "the wilderness" and survive in the event of a nuclear war. Having survived my self-experimentation, i later came to see the whole idea for the craziness it is. However, i am aware that it still does not seem crazy to quite a number of people.

In my late teens, while still dependent on my parents, i looked for ways to gain more independence, and to experience more of the world. One way i was able to do that was by traveling on my own, mainly by hitchhiking. This not only enabled (and sometimes forced) me, in small measure, to practice survival skills, but it brought me in touch with deeper poverty. In rural Georgia I saw families living in shacks so run-down i was appalled. But i also remember warm, open hospitality being extended to me -- a complete stranger -- by very poor folks in West Virginia, and later elsewhere. Those experiences, at a time when i was searching for meaning, had a profound effect upon me.

The military draft played a part in causing me to think about and change my lifestyle. People consistently warned me that if I refused to be drafted i would not be able to get a good job, and would have a hard time later in life. That scared me at first, but bringing it to my attention helped me to decide that if such were the case i would simply have to accept such consequences.

The draft also resulted in my imprisonment for two years, which threw me in with two sorts of people i had had practically no contact with previously: people from backgrounds of poverty and violence, and other people who resisted militarism. It was also by far my most intense first-hand experience with institutional brutality and gross injustice. I went to prison opposing war and the draft, and emerged soured on and opposed to American institutions generally and practically everything associated with those institutions. While still in prison, i wrote to the "Injustice Department" and renounced my citizenship. It wasn't until nearly ten years later i decided that voting was justified and valuable in certain instances and claimed it back.

I had already firmly decided, by my mid-teens, that i would never join any military. My increasing awareness of and profound dislike for violence, as well as for "authority", were crucial to that decision. But it was not until somewhat later that i thought seriously about taxes. Being supported by my parents while going to school, it was not something that even came up until much later. But my eventual questioning of taxation, and my decision to resist it to at least some degree, turned out to be one of the most important factors leading to a life of "simple living", even though it led there in a backhanded sort of way.

Part of my opposition to taxation stemmed from opposition to violence, knowing that much of tax money went to support militarism. But that opposition also stemmed partly from the feeling that nobody should have the right to take somebody's earnings, or to tell someone how co must spend cos money. This admittedly simplistic and individualist stance was reinforced the more i found out how tax money was actually spent. Having profound distrust of government by then, i determined not only to resist payment of taxes to military, but to refuse to fill out tax forms, to not get a social security number, and to avoid payment of taxes generally.

I learned how limiting that was when i looked for paying jobs in my early twenties. Many jobs that otherwise would have been open to me, were not. I had to stick with small jobs that i found through personal contacts, and had to live frugally in order to get by on the relatively small amounts i earned. But that turned out not to be so hard. I had little desire to obtain expensive things, and seemed to have natural talent for spending wisely and stretching limited resources. Though i lived frugally by American standards, i knew i was well off compared to the harshness of prison, of nature, and of much of the third world. Nevertheless, it is quite possible i could have settled into a more money-centered lifestyle if it were not for these limitations.

In my mid-twenties i did a lot of traveling, not staying in any one place for very long. But after a few years of that, i wanted to be more settled. Having lived in both urban and rural settings, my preference was for a rural place where i would be surrounded by natural beauty and could, i thought, be more self-sufficient. Feeling by then that land should not be a commodity to be bought and sold, i started looking either for an unused place to settle, or for a donation of land. While asking for the latter in a real estate office, a customer overheard me and ended up offering me a sizeable farm in rural West Virginia. Around that same time i visited Judi, and we renewed in a major way a relationship that up to then had been off-and-on. Judi was quite settled in a residential section near the downtown of a moderately large city: Grand Rapids, Michigan.

Judi

Unlike Richa's suburban background, i come from a rural farming community. I feel that my family rooted me in the ideas of conservation, living closely to the land, and family and neighborhood recreation. I remember with pride the wool shorts i made from a skirt that came from a dress that was remade from the dress of an older cousin who worked in Toledo and could afford nice clothes. I loved the stories about all the things mom made from printed feedbags -- pajamas, shirts, dresses, aprons. She'd have dad pick out all the bags with the same prints so she'd have enough to make things. There were times when money came our way more easily because my dad now worked at a factory in Toledo during the nights and farmed during the day, a common practice among farmers at that time. During those times we'd go shopping. I would almost be disgusted by the prices, knowing full well that my mom and i could make this same item for practically nothing. Those were the days when you could buy material for a dress for one or two dollars if you watched for specials. I'd draw the dress and mom would cut it out. Sometimes she'd end up with a handful of material left over. We'd both feel so good that we hadn't wasted. It was like a game -- a game that i enjoy to this day.

So when we talk about our lives changing to simple living that's not quite accurate. However, my siblings and father enjoy the standard middle class style today, while my life is very different. I guess the real question is: Why didn't i grow in the same direction as my family when the economics of mid-America changed? . . . Several thoughts come to mind. One, money was always pretty meaningless to me. Although we were never rich, we had plenty to eat, we had a home and enjoyment of family. I never felt poor or "beneath" anyone. I was greatly loved and cared for. And although, like everyone, i see family behaviors that i can be critical of, the love and security i had while growing up were the pillars of my constitution.

When I went off to college, my parents paid my way. I was the only one in my family to graduate from college, so it's rather a joke that i'm so poor and have the college education.

I left college to teach at a Lutheran summer camp. It was one of those experiences that mark your growth. I came in contact with all types of people -- people with conviction, people from inner city Detroit, migrants working in the local fields, many men dealing with the draft, several draft resisters. This opened up a whole new arena for me. Through my church groups, we discussed issues, we journeyed to Detroit, we met a new world that expanded our limited small town experience.

The next year i started my first year of teaching in an all Black school in inner city Toledo. I entered not having any idea of where to begin. I learned a lot -- about teaching, about life, about disparities. I loved the kids, who taught me a lot. But mostly i didn't like myself in that situation. I needed the community of camp, the support of others. Money was no reward for emptiness, zombie Sunday nights, despairing, eating binges.

So after spending the next summer at the same camp, i made a decision not to go back to teaching full time. I could sub. I could do other things. So when several other people at the camp were in transition also, it was natural to migrate to Grand Rapids and live together in community. Although i had first been startled by the suggestion, it didn't take me long to warm to the idea. I had always lived with lots of people -- a big family, cousins, neighbors, and friends. So why not live with the people i had grown to love from camp?

Those years were the start of my politicalization. We journeyed to Canada to meet with Cambodian, Laotian, and Vietnamese women whose visit there had been organized by Women Strike for Peace and the Canadian Voice of Women. We marched with the many in Washington, D.C. We started a community paper, bringing out the issues of poverty and the Vietnam War. It seemed like a natural step from the security of home into a world that cared for others. I had been nurtured and i felt it to be horrible to see the products of war, including the toll on my brother, who was in the Marines, and other young men like him.

Somewhere along the way i decided that not only could i live off a small amount of money, but also that i liked doing so. It started with a decision that i could not pay for war. But i didn't feel like i had many choices. I didn't feel comfortable declaring extra dependents or other techniques that some tax resisters used to avoid having tax money withheld. I had little needs, so the natural thing for me was to live below taxable income. Perhaps this was also my decision because i've never been heroic. I can be outspoken when i see injustices, but i'd just as soon stay out of the newspapers, hate cameras, and am embarrassed to talk about myself. So this method also seemed low risk.

However, at this same time, i was becoming more aware of the injustices due to the privilege of birth. I was inheritance rich because i had good nutrition, love, education. I was brought up trusting and believing in myself and that i could make a difference. Others didn't have that beginning. I decided that i wanted to live below or at the poverty level for more that just tax reasons. I wanted to try to equalize in some fashion. I wanted to take less jobs. I wanted to be free to do some of the many tasks that needed to be done to help turn this world around. And twenty years later i still want to do that. In fact i feel the many rewards and i advocate this choice for others.

House Tour

The sidewalk in front of the house has been cracked, chipped, and uneven for quite a few years. The City legally requires homeowners to maintain property, including sidewalks, out to the street, and some years ago demanded that we replace, at the cost of several hundred dollars, most of our sidewalk. Their justification was that poor sidewalks are dangerous. While there is some truth in that claim, there was also an unstated motivation: sidewalks that "look better" help to raise property values, which in turn brings more money into City coffers. Patching the chips and cracks was not allowed: if a section of sidewalk was damaged, the whole thing had to be replaced. We went ahead and patched ours anyway, which made it reasonably safe, even though not as smooth and even as some in our area. We informed the City that we could not justify using up resources or spending money for something that was not a clear need as long as there remain people throughout the world with their most basic needs unmet. The City threatened us, but as sometimes happens with bureaucracies, never followed through, and our sidewalk remains cracked and patched. This may seem trivial, but such 'trivialities' are part of what gives life meaning, and many of them added together can make a real difference to our world.

When we began living together in 1975 most of our yard space was covered with grass. We have replaced most of that over the years with trees and flowers, using leaves as a mulch.

On the east side of the house is our cement cartway (formerly a driveway), which leads to our "warehouse" (formerly a garage) in back. Along both sides of the property are strips of earth a meter or so wide where we have planted raspberries, comfrey, tansy, roses, jerusalem artichokes, and various herbs, most of which have multiple uses. For instance, we use some of the rose hips for eating and for tea, and we harvest "jay-chokes" all winter to eat fresh, alone or in salads.

The main part of our garden is in back (to the south) of our house. Vegetables, usually peas at first and winter squash later, grow up along a home-built solar wall during the growing season. This wall is built over ten inches of recycled insulation, and is connected to the second-floor greenhouse. As our home is located in a "historic preservation district" we had to fight with a historic preservation board over that wall. Probably because the wall was not visible from the street, they eventually let the matter drop.

In the rest of the garden we usually grow tomatoes, kale, and broccoli, as well as a little of whatever else strikes our fancy. The broccoli and kale are highly nutritious and are said to be anti-carcinogenic. They also last well into the cold season -- we typically harvest kale well into January, sometimes February.

We eat a fair amount of the "weeds" that grow in our yard, mostly in salads. They are organic, and some of them are highly nutritious. These include sorrels, purslane, peppergrass, mint, lamb's-quarters, dandelions, daisies, and chickweed.

Behind the garden is a peach tree and at the back of the yard are two compost piles and a wood ash pile. We have plenty of material for the compost piles, partly because we deal with a lot of salvaged food.

The garage-cum-warehouse serves well for storing lumber, glass, insulation, and other large items, most of which we have retrieved from the trash somewhere or other. Some other things it houses are a push-cart that Richa built for a peace walk in 1987, and that we now use sometimes for nearby hauling; a substantial amount of new molding that a neighbor was going to throw away; and a canoe, complete with a home-built folding cart that enables us to carry it by bicycle.

We store bags of leaves along one side of the garage, and use the leaves for our garden and compost piles. In front of the garage and along the edge of the cartway is our woodpile, which we have easily kept well-stocked from what others near us throw away.   In fact, people keep offering us wood to the point where we can afford to be quite selective about what we take.

Coming back to the front, there is a large front porch, where we often sit when the weather is warm.   In fact, the porch is our summer dining room, essentially.   It is filled with trash-picked furniture and various plants.   Ivy pokes in at some of the window edges.   Located on the north side of the house, it is often the place to be on hot days.   We keep it open to the breezes during summer, and close it in during winter.   Others on our block have similar porches, which facilitates interaction with our neighbors.

Entering the house you may be struck (nonviolently!) by the woodwork, which is mostly stained oak.   The two entryway doors are oak with panes of cut glass.   The house was built in 1910, and at that time, apparently, ours was a fairly ritzy neighborhood.

Just inside hangs a two-person saw, which had belonged to Judi's grandfather.   That and a bowsaw help provide much of our heat.   We deliberately do not use a chainsaw, mainly due to the chemical pollution, noise, extra material consumption, danger and cost.   The time we spend sawing by hand does not usually feel like a burden, but rather a chance for exercise and meditation.

The living room is typical of other rooms in that it contains reclaimed furniture, shelves, and lots of other items, including games and a treadle sewing machine.   Often there are boxes of food, clothes, or other items to be given away.

One of our traditions is to invite friends over for a gathering and potluck around the time of the winter solstice.   We fill the house with candles and gather in the living room following the meal.   Usually we will have a short group silence followed by a sharing time -- each person who wants to shares things important to co about the past year, or plans/hopes for the future, or whatever else co is moved to share.   It is always a very good connecting experience for most, at least, of our friends and acquaintances who make it.

A wood stove, which we put in the dining room several years ago, provides our main source of winter heat.   When weather is cold we not only eat in the dining room, but congregate there when we want to read, write, talk, or just relax.   The rest of the house is generally cold during the winter.

Off the back of the dining room is a large bedroom which we have generally used for hospitality, i.e. for people who need shelter on an emergency basis. More on that later. It has a single bed and a set of bunk beds, which we built years ago for some former hospitality guests. There is the usual stuffed chair (half the rooms in the house have a least one trash-picked stuffed chair), a dresser filled with clothes that folks may use while here or take with them, and a box filled with toys. Off to the back is a small lavatory with a toilet and sink.

The kitchen, off the dining room, is filled with salvaged, donated, and home-grown food, including lots of spices and herbs and teas. There are several containers for recycling food scraps, metal, glass, paper and plastic. We keep two bins by the refrigerator filled (usually overflowing) with recycled bags. And a bucket by the sink is used for extra water, which we use for plants, or sometimes to flush the upstairs toilet.

Throughout the house Richa has built shelves, in some cases having torn out walls to make use of previously unused spaces. We have accumulated a lot of things, and it can be a challenge sometimes to figure out where to store them all. This may seem very materialistic. But most of the things we accumulate are things we make good use of, or believe we or others will make good use of in the future. They are also mostly things that others have discarded, or would have discarded. And having all these things means we hardly ever have to go to a store to buy something, and that we are often able to supply friends and people in need with the things they are seeking. It saves us and others time and energy that can be well used elsewhere. What it amounts to is that our house is something of a de facto second-hand free store.

On the door to the basement a small salvaged chalkboard usually displays a quote that one of us has thought up or otherwise considers special. A sample of past quotes· "Beauty is diminished by injustice; en-hanced by love," "Our every action helps make history," "Love conquers all without conquering anyone," and "True spirituality is rooted in our everyday relationships."

A full basement provides a workshop space, storage for food, bicycles, recycling, and odds and ends that we use for various projects, often with children.

On the stairway to the second floor are two large mirrors, on the walls opposite each other. Retrieved from a dumpster (one had to be cut to match the other), they provide some fun entertainment, especially for children.

There are three bedrooms on the second floor, all large, one of which we use. Our second floor bathroom has a tub and shower, and a small washing machine (presently not in operation), as well as a sink and toilet. We typically save bath water, or let shower water run into a plastic tub, then use it to flush the toilet. We also keep a plastic bucket under the sink, with the drain pipe disconnected, and use that water to flush the toilet or to water plants.

A small study leads to our second-floor greenhouse, built from locally discarded materials, which covers what used to be a flat roof. The greenhouse not only extends our growing season, but helps to insulate the rest of the house, and often provides significant additional warmth, especially in late winter and early spring. Even though it is not a particularly efficient greenhouse, it gives the lie to those who claim that solar energy is impractical in our area due to the cloudy winters.

Household Community

Our sense of community is very important to us, and very related to our lifestyle. That community starts with the two of us. In some ways, we are two very different people. Some of the differences we readily appreciate; others we have simply had to learn to live with. That is not always easy, but we work at it. We are both upset that our childhood educations did little to prepare us for dealing with interpersonal conflicts. Many things we have had to learn the hard way.

The things that draw us together have, so far, been stronger than those that tend to pull us apart. We are drawn together by desire for intimate companionship, sexual attraction, sense of security, caring, sensitivity, and commitment to peacemaking and justice through simple living and direct action. By joining forces we have been able to help each other, not just by giving each other our love and energy directly, but by helping each other to grow, by sharing and to some degree teaching each other our strengths, by dividing work according to our preferences, and more.

Our house, being big, is appropriate for several people to live in. Our more immediate extended community has consisted of people who have lived in the house with us. This has included 'housemates': people who live and work with us and do not have special needs that are overwhelming; and 'hospitality': people who need shelter on an emergency basis, and often need other support as well. The distinction is sometimes vague, but we will focus here on housemates.

As we have become older, clearer about what we want and don't want, and, especially, more focused on peacemaking from a global perspective, it has become more difficult to find people we wish to live with. In fact, we have been the only two people in the house during several periods in the past few years. That has presented a dilemma for us, as both of us have wanted to share our lives, not to mention our house and other resources, more with others, yet we have not wanted to put a lot of energy into living with folks who basically want a cheap place to live and who share little of our values. There has been no simple resolution of this dilemma; we keep on re-evaluating, questioning ourselves and each other. One thing we have learned is not to expect people to stay with us "forever", or even for a long time, and that that can be just fine.

When we originally decided to live together, we had a choice: to go to the rural land Richa had been offered, or to stay in the big urban house Judi and quite a few other people lived in at the time. We decided to stay.

The other people at the house were long-time friends, or friends of friends, of Judi's. Some of them, including Judi, were in the process of trying to buy the house cooperatively. Richa plunged in, helping to pay for the house, asking for and getting formal acceptance as part of the community, and generally trying to fit into household routines and to enhance the community.

Most of the people there were even younger than us, and did not have any clear long-term commitment to the group. People frequently came and went, until we had been there longer than anyone else. Other people continued to come and go, and still do, though less frequently nowadays.

We've had a number of college students stay with us, usually for no more than two years. A number of other folks have come as well, from various situations. One early housemate who desired to live more self-sufficiently and in harmony with the natural environment moved down the street, and with our support, fixed up an urban homestead. Co still does hospitality on a regular basis, and we still consider ourselves part of a wider community of people who value and co-relate simple living and peacemaking.

One of our original household members, who had claimed a long-term commitment to us and with whom there had been tension after Richa came, suddenly left one day, literally refusing to talk. Reconciliation proved impossible, and the rift was not only traumatic for us, but reverberated through our circle of "peacemaker" friends. We have had to realize that those of us who want to be peacemakers sometimes cannot overcome human limitations or other obstacles. And that there are some deep differences that divide some of us who try to work for peace, which are not easily, if ever, surmounted.

Our household relationships have generally become more positive over the years, probably in part because we have become more cautious and less quickly trusting. Many of our difficulties have come about from what seem like small things, but which, over time, become large in people's feelings; things like differing standards of cleanliness. We have learned some things from these and other experiences: Make our expectations as clear as possible. Decide what things are really important to us in living with others, and let other things go. Don't expect long-term intimate, committed relationships with people, regardless of what they say, on the basis of a short-term relationship.

One former housemate, one of the more gentle, loving, and solid people we have known, had also been a victim of a serious rift, before living with us. This person took legal custody of a teenager whose family had had problems, so we also had a teen ager living with us for nearly a year.

This got us involved with the public school system. In checking out the public high school system, Judi, who was somewhat familiar with it, was not particularly surprised, but Richa was appalled. Fortunately we discovered an alternative high school that was just starting, and managed to slip the teenager in. Three of us were on the school's first governing board, composed equally of students, staff, and 'parents'. That was a good experience for all of us. Probably our most significant accomplishment was curbing the military recruiters who had flocked in like vultures; we established an equal time policy for peace-oriented folks.

That teenager is now in cos twenties, doing well the last we heard. The gentle, loving housemate married someone co met at one of our potluck gatherings, moved away, and is now raising two children.

We have had several people live with us who have been involved in solar energy and other ecologically viable energy systems. There is a college nearby that specializes in that field. Besides being fine people to live with and get to know, they have helped inspire us and teach us to be more energy conscious. Many of our present friends are people who have lived with us at one time or another. That history of sharing helps to create a special bond.

Generally we have not had children living with us as housemates. Judi, before we began living together, made a decision not to have cos own biological children. This was basically because co felt that there were already plenty of children on an already strained planet, many of them with unmet needs. Also, because co felt committed to working with children, being the extra hands that are useful in the best of situations. And not having cos own children would allow more opportunity for other pursuits. Neither of us has regretted that decision.

Hospitality

Shortly after we started living together we started taking on hospitality, and have been doing so ever since. It started through friends of friends, and word spread. Soon we were getting calls from all over, often from people or organizations we had never even heard of, on behalf of folks needing emergency shelter. For several years we remained open to whoever expressed need, though through experience we increasingly learned to set limitations and to be clear about what those limitations were. The limitations developed partly because we decided that hospitality could only be a part-time activity for us; there were and are too many other things we want to do with our lives.

Our basic rule is: Respect the peace and dignity of everyone else in the house. This means, among other things, no weapons and no violence, whether verbal or physical (we have learned that we must specifically say that that includes spanking). When guests start resorting to verbal or physical violence, which is often out of habit or because they do not know other ways of handling various situation, we explain and model nonviolent ways of relating. It is most frequently a problem between parents and their children.

Other policies and expectations, which we are looser about, include asking people to clean up after themselves, to eat whatever food they take, and to avoid most drug usage. We do not allow smoking inside the house.

Our first hospitality person was someone, married with two young children, who was questioning co's marriage and wanted to explore other relationships. Co stayed several months, then went back to cos family. They are still together, and seem to be happy.

Several prostitutes stayed with us for fairly long periods. This opened up a new world to us. One woman would go out in the middle of winter wearing a short skirt and a thin blouse and start "hitchhiking". It took us awhile to catch on. At 18 co had been prostituting since the age of 10, had been raped a dozen or so times, had suffered some traumatic health problems, and generally had lived through more pain and seen more of the hard side of life than some of us do in a lifetime.

Another young woman, who occasionally did prostitution, stayed with us on several different occasions, sometimes for fairly long periods. Co kept getting into relationships with different men that proved abusive and destructive. This was an introduction for us to a pattern we have found to be very common among victims of domestic abuse.

A Black male prostitute who stayed with us most of one year would sometimes invite cos friends over to "dress up". They had lots of fun, and it gave us new perspective on behavior we had looked at askance previously. This person was highly sensitive and talented in obvious ways, and wanted to get away from prostitution, but had a hard time -- it was hard to find other meaningful activity that could provide anywhere near the comparable excitement co seemed to want. But co left with new plans and more hope, and while here co brought us in contact with a "mini-culture" we would otherwise have hardly been aware of.

We took in a number of people just out of jail or prison. Both of us, having done at least a little jail time, could relate to some of the special hardships they faced.

A number of young people and families without places to stay would stay with us until they were able, one way or another, to come up with something. Often their coping skills were not very good. They would often spend money, when they had it, foolishly. It seemed helpful to some of them to get to know people who did not think highly of acquiring expensive or unnecessary things, and whose values and practices reflected other ideals. For many that was clearly a new experience.

Richa knows a little Spanish and a little Sign, just enough to carry on very rudimentary conversations. That has been helpful on the several brief occasions we have had Spanish-speaking people stay with us, and with one deaf person, who stayed with us off and on for about four years before finally getting a place in low-income subsidized housing in a nearby city. That experience gave us some knowledge of the deaf culture, and of special problems associated with deafness.

Judi has long had a particular interest in and fondness for children. Over the years co has learned effective ways of relating to and dealing with children. Co has developed a store of both knowledge and materials that help children to relax and enjoy themselves in a strange place, to learn, and to develop skills. This has been quite important, as we have had a lot of children stay with us at difficult transition times.

For a period of time it seemed as if the same people kept coming back to us. We would see people leave with a promising start, but then something would go wrong and they would be back. This has probably helped us learn to have more patience.

It may be that our own marginality in this society helps us to better identify and empathize with others who do not cope well. Clearly, in our minds, there are some good reasons why folks do not -- and in a sense should not -- cope well with our society.

For a number of years we limited our hospitality mainly to victims of domestic abuse, being a 'safe home' that was an extension of a local shelter. We felt good about it, as we were clearly able to make a difference for quite a few people. That ended when we lost our phone in 1990 after one hospitality person racked up about $200 in charges through AT&T, which is, among other evils, a major military contractor. There was no way we would pay them, and our local phone company, which collected for AT&T, disconnected us. As of this writing our house remains full, and people have generally been staying with us longer.

Problems have seemed relatively few over the years, and we have learned from them. Things have occasionally been taken -- once a person we found to have been on drugs ripped us off rather badly before we discovered what was going on. There have been occasional threats of violence. Differences in lifestyle, culture, expectations have caused tensions at times. Such experiences have made us more cautious, but have never made us decide to give up doing hospitality work. We figure that, in a long period of taking in people who are down, often because they have suffered severely over long periods of time, it is to be expected that we will suffer a certain amount of abuse and loss. But overall that is relatively rare, especially considering the degree of physical and/or emotional abuse so many of our hospitality folks have suffered.

One of the important assets we have for hospitality work is that we are both good listeners. We have found that people in crisis are often almost desperate for a listening ear. We may or may not give much feedback; that often seems to be of secondary importance. We have learned to keep projects around that we can work on while talking or listening: knitting, sorting the wheat from the chaff, putting our dried herbs and teas in jars, etc.

Because our lifestyle is so different from that of most other Americans, some people feel uncomfortable here, and not infrequently people who hear a little about how we live decide not to come at all. Many bear with us because they do not have other options. But often the differences, though strange at first, are appreciated. Children often discover they prefer active involvement in things over sitting in front of a TV, and they tend to respond quickly to respect and caring without violence, even when we are firm in ways they aren't used to. Parents sometimes remark on how well the children respond. What is sad is that quite a few women who have stayed with us have told us that Richa is the only gentle man they have ever known. It reminds us how much in our society needs to change.

The expansion of horizons is definitely a two-way street. We have been blessed to witness and learn a little of the beauty of movement in sign language; to meet people who have suffered terrible abuse yet continue to care about and seek to aid their assailants; to see the strength and resiliency of children who have been exposed to violent and/or neglectful situations all their lives; to keep in touch with many of those who suffer due to the militaristic, materialistic, and violent nature of our society; to know we are of concrete help to at least a few people; and simply to meet and share parts of our lives with a variety of other people.

Neighborhood and Region

We live in a racially mixed and economically and otherwise diverse urban neighborhood. We generally like it here. We are just inside the border of an "historic preservation district" that extends to the north. This area has suffered a good deal of "gentrification". To the south of us there is more poverty, more trash, more run-down houses, and the population is predominantly Black.

Street crime has been a reality for us. We are cautious about going out at night. We have suffered several break-ins over the years, as well as uninvited entries and rip-offs by people we have let in. On occasion we have been personally threatened at home or in the neighborhood, and have had rocks or other items thrown at us, but we have so far managed to avoid actual harm. Listing the problems makes it sound worse than it is. All told, we generally feel safe here, though we recognize that in order to be truly safe and secure we need to continue our work for global justice as well as our neighborhood involvement.

Politically the Grand Rapids metropolitan area is perhaps even more reactionary than most American metropolitan areas, though it is not as bad as some. Amway is headquartered in a nearby town and exerts a considerable influence in the area. That will explain a lot to those who know about this company. If you don't, read Steve Butterfield's book, *Amway: The Cult of Free Enterprise*. There is a strong and pervasive presence in the area of people who call themselves Christians. Judi emphasizes that many 'Christian' people in our area care for other people and otherwise have positive values that are not immediately obvious. Richa, who agrees with that as far as it goes, also believes that hardly any 'Christians' in our area make a serious attempt to practice the teachings of Christ.

There seems very little consciousness or concern over ripping off of third and fourth world peoples in order to increase the consumption that increasingly endangers us all. Of course, in this regard our region is not much different from other regions in the USA.

Despite the problems, we feel rooted here. We have made many friends and become involved in many activities. Over the years we have seen in many ways how we have helped to make a difference. We believe we will continue to do so, in part because we have built a base of trust and respect and friendship in our neighborhood and region, despite being far from the mainstream in some important ways.

Recycling as a Way of Life

As you will have gathered during the "home tour", we recycle/reuse practically everything. We put out a bag of trash to go to the landfill perhaps once every two or three weeks on the average. Along with that may be one or two large items -- a worn-out bicycle tire, a broken plastic bucket, etc. We are actively working at reducing that amount.

Most of what we do throw out, or recycle for that matter, has already been discarded by someone else. Our retired neighbor across the street brings us cos old newspapers every week or so. Richa usually skims through them, and sets aside articles that co thinks may interest Judi, before putting them in the recycle pile. We habitually check certain trash bins in the area, and frequently pick up items from curbside trash. In fact, sometimes on trash days Richa will go out "shopping" and is often able to find things we want.

For the most part, recycling and reusing whatever we reasonably can, as well as generally limiting our consumption, is the extent of our personal power to limit the waste generated by excessive production.

Take mail, for example. We make good use of the mail for networking and sharing information. Much of our mail we pass on where we see that it may be of use to others. When we don't have particular places in mind to pass on mail that has good information or networking possibilities, we put it in a box in our living room and periodically invite people to sort through it and take whatever they want. We reuse many envelopes, though that is harder now that computer codes are stamped on many of them. Those envelopes can be torn open and the insides used for writing, however. We also reuse paper when only one side has been used. Such paper serves as our writing paper, for notes, for children to draw upon, etc. We deal with junk mail in several ways. Some of it we burn. We have contacted places locally and otherwise that send us a lot of junk mail and asked them to cease doing so. Sometimes that works. When it doesn't we drop it and other junk mail in a post office box after writing on it something like "Return to sender -- ecologically damaging, unsolicited mail", or "obscene mail". The post office claims that it must deliver all mail, but we figure that attitude might change if enough of us send the junk back and force them to deal with it.

An important factor in our lifestyle is our appreciation of what is already available, and our decision to use materials from that pool of resources. For instance, rather than go out and buy expensive 'mountain bikes' we waited until an abandoned mountain bike frame appeared nearby.

Rather than first decide how we wanted to build our greenhouse, we saved up lumber, glass, and other materials adequate for the job, and then figured out how it could be done using those materials.

Rather than decide we want black bean soup, asparagus, and garlic toast with margarine for supper, and go out and buy those things, we will take from what we have -- perhaps fish from the food bank that was stored in our freezer, broccoli from our garden, and toasted several-day-old bread from the co-op's throw-away pile, with oil (far purer than most margarine, which melts on the toast anyway) given us by a friend who moved and did not want to take it with co. Also, when we use recipes we use them as guides, substituting for items we don't have or simply leaving them out. This provides no end to use of our creative talents, and we have become a lot better at it with practice.

Up to the point of real need, material goods are crucial. A little beyond that, they may enhance our relationships more than hurt them. Beyond that they do little at best, and at worst are clearly destructive of relationships with others in our human family. Sometimes it is hard to give up certain privileges or material things, but it becomes easier for us when we remember or are reminded that our relationships are of the essence.

A native American friend of ours was asked for cos solution to the ecological catastrophe our species and planet now face. Cos answer was succinct: "No dumps." We can envision the way to a world of no dumps, partly with improved recycling, but largely through improved production: more durable and carefully made products; less packaging and what there is designed to be reused; easily repairable goods, with standard fittings and parts; and many fewer items produced overall. All this will, of course, require significant changes in consciousness with accompanying political/economic changes.

Regarding such changes, we are aware of the danger of becoming too dependent upon the social structure we wish to change. For instance, one of our original housemates rejected the suggestion that we even talk to grocery store managers about setting aside usable food they were throwing out, feeling (certainly with some good reason) that doing so would jeopardize what was at that time our main source of food, the store's dumpsters. The managers might have taken steps to prevent us from continuing to retrieve that food, had we alerted them to the fact that we were doing so regularly. That decision was more or less taken out of our hands, as will be explained shortly.

Knowing we are totally interdependent with others, we try to keep ourselves rooted spiritually, and to act in ways that benefit us all. So if today we can obtain food by 'harvesting' what others throw away, great, as long as we don't let ourselves become dependent on it, and we retain our vision of where we want our world to be and our willingness to risk our comfort of the moment if necessary in order to work toward that vision.

Food and Water

Our household's regular runs to supermarket trash bins came to an end one evening after the manager of one store and two police confronted the two of us, demanding that we put back the food we had just loaded. We refused, and were arrested and jailed. Next day a number of people demonstrated at the store in protest, and three of them were also arrested and jailed. On the day following all but Richa were released. Richa fasted and was released nearly two weeks later. Meanwhile other protests were mounted, in other cities as well as in our area, and there was some dialog with upper-level management as well as local management. All this generated quite a bit of publicity, which was surprisingly favorable to us. Some concessions were made as a result.

This episode brought out some serious differences in our household. Richa had brought an increased sense of outrage and militancy to the salvage operation, which continued. But others were drained, and backed off from further such confrontation.

It did two good things for the Grand Rapids area generally, however. One was to raise awareness about food wastage -- quite a number of people were surprised, if not appalled. And apparently because of the publicity, the director of a then newly-forming group that coordinated and worked to expand 'food banks' wrote and sent literature about what they were doing. Richa passed this on to a local hunger task force, some of whose members initiated a process which eventually led to the establishment of a food bank here in Grand Rapids.

Our household maintained membership in a local food co-op. For years we got our food from a wide variety of places including the co-op, a local farmers' market, our garden (some years we had two or three gardens), wild food (mostly greens and mushrooms), other food stores, and still occasionally from garbage bins.

At some point we became more active in the co-op, and Richa quickly became concerned about some of the items the co-op sold, particularly some of the third world cash crops. Co started a committee and worked hard to raise consciousness on issues related to such sales. Despite some success the majority of the co-op membership continued to support those sales. Eventually we left the co-op and tried on our own to avoid purchasing items from anywhere or anyone who sold items tainted by severe oppression of other people. This meant we could hardly buy anything, relatively speaking. We were able to find more than enough to survive on, but in the midst of superabundance, and having gotten used to that, it was particularly hard on Judi to be so limited. So we relaxed that after a year. Later we discovered that the food bank in Grand Rapids was throwing away usable food. Richa, with long experience salvaging food, was able to volunteer sorting salvage and, in exchange, was allowed to keep much of what had previously been thrown away. After several years that was no longer allowed (and even larger quantities of good food were thrown out by the food bank). We've now gone back to a combination of gardening, a bulk buying club, and salvaging on a small scale.

Most of our water comes straight from the tap, supplied by the City. It is highly chlorinated, and our understanding is that ingestion of much chlorine can be hazardous. But we also understand that the chlorine dissipates if the water is boiled for a few minutes, or allowed to stand overnight. So we let it stand for straight drinking, and boil it for tea. We have considered getting a water filter, but believe that working to remove environmental pollution by promoting a more sustainable society is the more responsible way to protect and improve our water.

Shelter

We have lived in the same house since we began living together in fall of 1975. We paid the cost of buying and fixing up the house in 1979, and the major expense on it since then has been taxes, which are high for us, but affordable, and relatively low as urban housing goes. We have done quite a bit of work on the house, using mostly recycled materials.

Some years back a group of us from five or six households talked about establishing an urban community land trust that would include our homes. That never got off the ground, but it "in deed" had an effect, inducing us to add several provisions to our deed. Those include the following: the land may never be sold; the structures may never be sold for more than $10,000; the property may not be rented for profit, nor used to support any part of the military or militarism; the owner shall use and maintain the property in ways that do not damage or contaminate the environment

The city has charged us taxes based on an assessment well over $10,000, which Richa appealed, but the appeal was unsuccessful. People who speculate on real estate seem to have a pretty good grip on our governmental system.

The house has provided not just simple shelter, but a base to work from, and space to keep all the things that aid our lives and our work. It is a place we and others have been able to depend on, and has served, directly and indirectly, to help many people besides ourselves.

Now, due to our decision not to pay property taxes to local government, we expect to be evicted sometime in the next few years. Actually, we didn't expect to be here *this* long. It seems that the bureaucracy has been the biggest thing in our favor! More on this later.

Heat/Utilities

Utilities tend to be expensive for us, nor do we feel good about paying for them because of the style of life (high salaries and other costs) we are helping to pay for, and for other reasons. We have avoided the biggest utility expense by heating with wood, which we get free, but that is not very satisfactory either, because we are contributing to pollution by doing so, even though we mostly avoid burning items that contain particularly dangerous known toxic chemicals. We have put quite a bit of energy into insulating and solarizing our house, but we have a lot of blockage from trees, our designs and materials have not been the best, and the area we live in is very cloudy during most of the time when we need sun for heating purposes. In sum, though our work on the house has helped quite a bit, we still burn a lot of wood, and we consider that to be a problem.

Transportation

When we first lived together one house member had a car, which co shared for household purposes. We used it for many of our trash food runs. As our housemates changed, sometimes there were one or more cars, sometimes none. Different people were more or less free about letting others use their vehicles. At one point we bought an old van to be used as a house vehicle. But several house members around that time insisted on having their own vehicles as well, which made the van seem superfluous, if not ridiculous, so we got rid of it. After that we became more discouraging of having motor vehicles generally, and have been clear that we do not want one ourselves. We have, in fact, turned down three or four offers of free cars since then.

Generally bicycling has been our main means of transport. When we first lived together we walked a lot. Walking is wonderful: It allows easily for immediate stopping, is good for conversation and physical closeness, provides good exercise, is non-polluting, and is slow, which helps us keep in touch with the environment of our neighborhood. But when a departing housemember left behind a bicycle, we both began bicycling more. Bicycling allows us to range farther and carry more, yet retains most of the advantages of walking while avoiding most of the disadvantages of motor vehicle use. Not least of all, bicycling is fun.

As we lived here longer, we began finding bicycle frames and other bicycle parts thrown away in people's curbside trash. Richa retrieved many of these, and learned how to put the good parts together to make usable bicycles. So co not only replaced and improved our old bicycles, but built many more to pass on to others.

We tried various ways of carrying loads. A children's red wagon was our main load carrier for awhile. The van lasted for a year or so. Then Richa experimented with carts. The first one was a flop, but a valuable flop, because the second one, which could be pulled by hand or by bicycle, is still hauling loads up to 275 kilograms after several years of heavy use.

Richa bicycles virtually all year. Judi frequently takes a bus in the winter. On rare occasions we will borrow a car or truck. When we travel long distances together we will sometimes bicycle, sometimes find people going our way, and sometimes hitchhike.

One thing about not having a motor vehicle is that we do not so often travel long distances, or even moderate distances (by the standards of most of those around us) for that matter. We miss that sometimes, but consider the loss almost trivial compared to all the problems involved with owning and using a motor vehicle.

In the saner society we envision, motor vehicles would have a definite place. But now we consider them a cancer that contributes to the misery of many of the world's poorer people, and to the choking of the planet.

Luxuries

Because we are Americans of middle-class backgrounds, and especially because of our lifestyle, we have lots of time to work for peace in various ways, to goof off, and to do whatever we feel like. We certainly spend some amount of time, money, and energy on things and pursuits that are not necessary to our survival, or to the survival of others. How do we justify this, considering that some people do not have their basic survival needs?

In a way, we can't But we are products of our society and culture, and do not easily reject all our habits, feeling, and connections that arise from that. We travel in order to take breaks from the city and our urban routines, we play music, we buy little things we don't truly need, we read to escape, etc. Such things seem to help sustain us.

That is not to excuse and let us rest complacent with all our privileges. The fact of tremendous injustice and suffering is a constant and deeply felt presence in our lives, and over the years has served to make us devote more of our energy and resources to doing something about them. We want and expect that to continue. And we learn to integrate, to some degree, our luxuries with our work. A few examples: in going to rummage sales, suggesting that people donate leftover items to Nicaragua or to local domestic abuse victims, which also means talking about the issues involved; writing and singing songs that reinforce and help bring to others our commitment to peace; and going on a peace march for "vacation".

Fitting In

To live as we do, we cannot be too concerned about maintaining an image that allows us to easily 'fit in'. Most of our neighbors still have yards of grass, for example, while ours is a hodgepodge of various plants. Nor are we very good about keeping things neat and trimmed. Fortunately our neighbors have never seemed to mind. Also we try to minimize painting on or in the house, most paints being moderately to highly toxic. So if paint is peeling we are in no hurry to paint over inside the house, or outside if no bare wood is exposed.

Judi tends to be more concerned about fitting in than Richa. Our room is usually somewhat of a mess, which is sometimes an embarrassment for Judi. Judi is more particular about haircuts, though co has become brave enough to let Richa cut cos hair. Judi is not about to shave cos legs, but in certain situations will wear pants to cover them. And co maintains a larger, fancier, and more carefully tended wardrobe than Richa (which is not saying much).

With some people Judi especially is more hesitant to talk about certain aspects of our lifestyle, such as federal tax resistance, or property tax resistance, or the fact that we are unmarried partners and mates. But over the years these and other things have become more integrated into our total lives, and both of us have more freely and easily shared with others the less generally accepted aspects of our lives.

Work and Recreation and Exercise

Our lives center largely on our work, which in turn centers on direct service, various other forms of peacemaking, and recycling. All of these connect and overlap. The same can be said about our work, recreation, and exercise. We have already touched on the work and recreation connections. In addition, if we travel somewhere to relax and enjoy, we frequently meet people we otherwise wouldn't meet, and it is natural for us to talk about our work -- and talking about our work is part of our work!

With frequent bicycling, gathering and sawing wood, salvaging and distributing food, clothes, and other items, maintaining our home, working and playing with children, etc., we get at least a moderate amount of exercise. We sometimes go out for more recreationally center-ed exercise as well: going to parks, swimming, canoeing, or throwing a frisbee around.

Sometimes when friends or acquaintances have talked about joining a 'health club' or some such nonsense, we have invited them, free of charge, to get some exercise on our woodpile or some other project we have at the time. Occasionally folks have even taken us up on such offers.

Income

We have structured ourselves and divided responsibilities to suit our differing skills and temperaments. Judi likes cos time structured, is highly social, and tends to like a lot of outside activities. Co has generally earned most of the money for the two of us, and in recent years practically all of it. Richa is more a homebody who likes to have a lot of unstructured time. Co brings in most of the "recycled" items, takes primary responsibility for being with hospitality folks and everything connected with that, and does most of the house maintenance and cooking. We divide cleaning more or less equally between us.

We earn a total of between $3000 and $4000 per year, generally, which comes out about equal to the world average. We give away some, and we have saved somewhere between $500 and $1000 per year on the average, which we pass on as no-interest long-term loans to peace and justice oriented organizations that need capital. That is our only monetary insurance, and our hope is that we will never ask for it back. But we are well aware that we are still far better off than most of the world's poorer people, who don't have access to all the 'trash' and other benefits we take advantage of.

For instance, a Guatemalan laborer who works 12 hour days six days a week, 52 weeks a year (work is not that reliable for most Guatemalan peasants) picking cotton or bananas under conditions of extreme heat and humidity and under brutal bosses, making the minimum wage of $1.80 per day (many make less), would earn less than $600 in a year. Judi, who works three days a week with summers and holidays off, working eight hour days at a creative and fulfilling job that is not overly hard, and who takes a very substantial pay cut to remain below the federally taxable level, makes six to seven times as much money as the Guatemalan.

We are motivated to spend as little as we do on ourselves largely because of our knowledge of such inequities. Several factors help us to do so without feeling significant sacrifice: our lack of desire for a great abundance of goods or services, our willingness to recycle and reuse, and planning to anticipate our future needs and desires.

We have decided neither to pay nor accept interest, which favors people who are already rich, allowing them to profit without working, which means that they profit at the expense of others. It is an option most people do not have, at least to any significant degree.

Between us we have received about $30,000 inheritance money from various relatives. The IRS, so far, has not even attempted to collect taxes on this. To have kept any of it for ourselves, we feel, would have been unjust and racist. We have passed it on to people much more in need, or to groups working to help those in need, especially in the third world. The amount would have been more, but Richa's parents stopped passing on money after learning we were not using it 'for ourselves'. At present Summer, 1993 we are working on establishing a community group to make the decisions about where such money will go, with a focus on making the money work for long-term justice and systemic change. We hope, thereby, to encourage others to similarly pass on some of their 'excess' wealth.

Property Taxes and Global Justice:
A Challenge for Ourselves and Others

We have generally not paid federal income taxes or telephone taxes (when we had a phone), and in some measure (Richa particularly) have not paid other taxes. We should owe money to several different governments by their criteria, and, in fact, have been summoned or otherwise approached by federal and state treasury officers on three or four occasions, but we have yet to be prosecuted or have assets seized.

In 1986, however, we decided to stop paying the money taxes on our home, a decision we were reasonably sure would not be ignored. Instead we have done work that promotes global justice, as well as local service work. For instance, we took in a disabled person for over a year, thereby likely saving thousands of dollars in local government expenditures. We have also re-directed the money itself in ways that we believe help to balance the scales a little toward both local and global justice. For instance, we have given money to a local recycling effort as well as to oppressed people who are working nonviolently for social change in Mexico, Palestine, Honduras, and elsewhere. So we are actually paying at least double our share, though we feel good about that.

The decision to re-direct the property taxes was initiated by Richa, with Judi initially agreeing to it largely because it was important to Richa. Richa had been learning more about USA government policy in the third world, particularly in Central America, and had felt a desire to take stronger action. Though strongly drawn to indefinite fasting, co eventually rejected that option, feeling that risking cos life was not the best approach, all considered. Later co did research for and printed 5000 copies of a 30-page booklet on sexual abuse in Central America. Doing that brought the issues out even more starkly, and co decided that non-payment of money property taxes would be a good way of drawing connections between the American lifestyle and the extreme injustice and suffering in much of the third and fourth (native peoples) worlds.

An explanation of the connection between our property taxes and third/fourth world suffering is warranted here. We have found that even many of our friends and acquaintances who have been active with peace issues do not readily understand that connection. The following information is according to our understanding. Much of it applies equally well to why we attempt to "live simply that others may simply live."

Annual income for most people in many third world countries is a few hundred dollars or less. Those people face hunger, malnutrition, and other conditions of extreme poverty. Many die as a result, especially children. Children as well as adults are frequently the victims of military and police violence, including murder, torture, and rape. Land and homes are systematically taken, by deception and by force, by wealthy people in order to grow crops or otherwise produce for export. The USA government, backed principally by the military, large corporations, and extremely wealthy people, is primarily responsible for this state of affairs in many countries, and partly responsible in virtually all countries. That government (supposedly our government) has militarily intervened directly all over the world on numerous occasions, and has continuously intervened even more widely in recent decades with covert forces, military aid, and otherwise. It continues to help fund military and police forces within many countries that keep atrocious, in some cases genocidal, policies in operation. And it continues to train those forces in techniques of killing, torture, deceit, and other means of repression and intimidation.

People do not normally voluntarily leave secure communities where they are free and able to make a living for themselves, in order to have a tenuous chance at survival by competing for jobs under huge landowners who pay one to three dollars a day for extremely hard work under conditions of virtual slave labor, or to scrabble to survive off the garbage piles of the wealthy, or to turn to drugs and prostitution and stealing. Large USA business concerns profit obscenely from this state of affairs, and all of us in this country benefit to some degree from it -- we are able to obtain cheap cotton for our clothes, cheap fruits and vegetables, cheap minerals and manufactured goods, etc. However, we only obtain third world products cheaply in terms of money -- the human cost, and often the ecological cost, is steep indeed.

It is widely thought that the American people, steeped in the tradition and practice of freedom and democracy (at least to some substantial degree), would not tolerate, if they generally knew about it, the USA government's systematic subversion and suppression of those same values elsewhere in the world. We hope and believe that is the case. However, a powerful mass propaganda effort by that government directed largely toward USA citizens keeps the reality hidden. People in third world countries who work and fight for the same freedoms we have, and in the same ways that we have worked and fought, are labeled 'communist', 'violent', and other loaded terms, and are falsely said to be a threat to us and to those same freedoms. In the early 1950's the CIA started systematically infiltrating major USA media. Over two decades later a Congressional committee found that the CIA owned outright "more than 200 wire services, newspaper, magazines, and book publishing complexes", and subsidized many more, according to Michael Parenti's book, *Inventing Reality.* Co also writes: "The CIA runs the biggest news service in the world with a budget larger than those of all the major wire services put together." So is it any wonder that the American people are not accurately informed? And that most Americans implicitly believe that local taxes, if not federal taxes, are for the good of everyone?

Recognizing that our American lifestyle is in part dependent upon the severe exploitation of the majority poor in much of the third world is the basis for our challenge to property taxes. Those taxes are coercive, and help to reinforce our exploitative lifestyles. They support yearly salaries in the tens of thousands of dollars, or more, while many people who help create and support that level of wealth are receiving hundreds of dollars yearly or less. Americans get upset about the threat of having 30 rather than 28 children in a classroom while children elsewhere have no schooling whatever and remain illiterate. Many of us eat too much protein and waste considerable amounts of food while children elsewhere die of starvation. Why should one child have plenty while another faces poverty, violence, and frequently an early death, due to the accident of birth?

For us, deciding not to pay money property taxes, and simple living generally, are ways we can help promote justice. Simple living is a means of helping to preserve our planet as well, though that is also, in part, an act of justice. The majority of the world's people have been denied much, if any, real voice in the actions that are leading toward destruction of our planet.

We have found that many of our friends and acquaintances who have been active in "peace" work do not easily understand why we risk our home by re-directing property taxes. On the other hand many faith-centered people we have talked with who have little or no 'peace' work background have readily understood and even been supportive.

A friend of ours has helped some to better understand by likening our action to an action of Thoreau's. Our friend wrote: "Thoreau wound up in prison for not paying a state poll tax. Though his state had no slavery laws and the federal government, not the state, was at war with Mexico, he could not support his state which tacitly supported an unjust system. 'I quarrel not with far-off foes, but with those who, near at hand, co-operate with, and do the bidding of, those far away; and without whom the latter would be harmless.'"

In 1989 a real estate agent bought the tax lien for the 1986 taxes. In talking with co later we learned that cos intention had been to support us. Co, in fact, did *not* buy the lien for the 1987 taxes, offered at the 1990 County tax sale, nor did anyone else. We were happy about that, as it was an indication of support, and left the responsibility where it should be -- on the shoulders of state and local government.

From the beginning we made clear that we would resume paying property taxes when local government took its fair share of responsibility for ending third world oppression. One attempt toward that end was trying to convince our County government to establish a 'Department of Global Concerns' that would do things such as discourage military activity in the County, establish sibling community relationships with areas of the second, third, and fourth World, promote ecological sustainability, help develop peace and justice curricula in the schools, inform County citizens about the various direct and indirect effects of military spending, lobby the federal government and other bodies that make decisions affecting us, and help provide support to oppressed people throughout the world.

Some ideas behind this project were: To take steps toward rectifying injustices between our part of the world and most of the rest of the world; to create a vehicle for effective action that truly represents the interests of people in our community; to provide a model for other communities; to increase awareness of global interdependence. We have received minimal support from County government for this idea, and are not actively pursuing it at this point.

Assuming we are eventually evicted for our action, some likely possibilities for us are that Judi would stay with friends, while Richa may attempt to return, take over an abandoned house, and/or make some other public challenge to the process. This will likely involve some jail time, which has always figured as a possibility in our lives. We do not expect the changes we are seeking to come easily.

This action, while scary, is in some ways positive for us personally. It presents new challenges to us and to our faith. Clearly we face some difficulties, which may even threaten our relationship, but we also hope and expect to see some real change.

A home provides a place to relax and escape for awhile the tensions that sometimes threaten to overwhelm us. It also provides a sense of security, and a space where much that is of value to us both can be shared. Losing our home would force us to learn more about our sense of rootedness -- to what extent that exists in our home, in ourselves, in our faith, in each other, etc. But "to choose to risk is to choose to live".

Peacemaking Outreach

Our property tax challenge is one specific example of our peacemaking outreach. Generally, the way we live we consider to be in itself a major part of our peace outreach, besides being a basis for our other peace-related work. Our direct service is also a major part of our peacemaking work. Beyond that, our peace outreach is predominantly educational, though it involves strong direct action and organizing/networking aspects.

Our focuses and styles differ, and we usually work on different projects. Sometimes that has been a source of tension between us, but we generally support each other, knowing that we complement each other and are basically working for the same things.

We usually have a number of peace involvements and projects going at any particular time. Right now, for instance, Judi's projects include: getting set up for the next school year (Judi teaches in a private school with a strongly peace-oriented curriculum); helping to publish a calendar and global resources newsletter of peace education primarily for local schools; planning for the "Children's Creative Response to Conflict" workshops; and helping staff the IGE (Institute for Global Education, a locally based peace education/outreach group) office. Richa's major outreach at present focuses on publishing, with friend and fellow activist Jeff Smith, a small 'alternative' newspaper that focuses on issues of basic justice.

We help each other on these projects, whether directly or indirectly. There are also lots of other ongoing and smaller projects and activities, and we both have lots of creative ideas for more. So our regrets center around things like having to sleep, there are only 24 hours in a day, there aren't more of us, etc.

Our lives and our peacemaking are built on a strong sense of global awareness. But we are also concerned about and work on neighborhood issues. Judi has done volunteer work in the public elementary school nearest us, and has helped conduct a "reading club" for neighborhood children during summers. Richa has helped start a block club, supplies many recycled items to people in the neighborhood, and helps neighborhood children with bicycles, various projects, etc.

We have built good relations with most of our immediate neighbors, especially those who have lived here a long time. There is at least some sense of neighborhood community, which includes trust and friendship, looking out for and helping each other, and to some degree shared values and goals.

Reaching Our Vision

We envision a human society based on caring and justice. Nobody is hit or otherwise treated abusively. Decisions are made by mutual agreement of all those involved and able to express themselves. The environment is cared for so that it will be left at least as clean and whole for the following generations. Technological advance is encouraged, but slowly and with care, and only to the extent that it contributes to human and environmental well-being. Each person born is guaranteed loving care, basic physical requirements, opportunity to fulfill cos creative potential, and a reasonable stake in humanity's total existing wealth.

Living simply is a crucial means for attaining this vision, eventually. But doing so also allows us to attain part of that vision now, at least for ourselves. This is no small thing, for living in a way that is compatible with justice and a decent life for every human being feels good in a way that lasts.

Many people regard simple living and self-sufficiency as being similar if not identical. We don't, nor do we hold self-sufficiency as an ideal. We see it as valuable in that it allows people to more easily withdraw support from institutionalized violence. But we do not know any person or small group who is completely self-sufficient, nor do we think that substantial self-sufficiency is practical or even desirable for the great majority of folks. But we do believe it is desirable and practical for 'ordinary' people to challenge and change institutitionalized violence by withdrawing support from that violence, at least to some significant degree, in our personal lives. We all can do that individually and collectively, and many of us can help others to do so more than they would be able or willing to acting alone.

We prefer to work for change primarily on the personal and spiritual levels, though we are certainly not unaware of structural problems. We believe that living our lives lovingly, and with concern for fairness to all others, has a positive effect upon those with whom we interact, and that that effect spreads and grows. We are first concerned with changes of the heart, which we believe will lead to changes in structure.

Faith

Our faith, in large part, gives our lives value and meaning. It can best be described by listing its major elements: basic respect for all people; caring for the environment that sustains us; recognition of our profound interdependence on many levels; 'nonviolence' as a way of life; constant seeking of truth; belief in each person's power and responsibility to work for good and to effect change.

We are very grateful for all we have, which is a lot. We also feel very deeply the need for certain changes in our society. We know we do not have much control over how others live, and essentially we do not want such control. But we can control, to a significant degree, how we ourselves live, and, because we live very interdependently with others, we know that our lives affect the lives of others. In fact, the way we live is essentially determined by the relationships we have with each other and with our total environment.

In the context of that environment, our lifestyle is a natural and necessary extension of our faith. It feels like a wholistic way of constructively confronting a world situation that desperately needs to be changed, rather than getting hopelessly confused trying to decide to support one boycott and not another, giving money or energy to this cause and not that cause, and ending up feeling like we are trying to plug a crumbling dike with our fingers rather than working to rebuild it. Our spiritual, political, and personal lives are one whole, inseparable.

SIMPLE LIVING

AS SIDE-EFFECT

Dorothy Norvell Andersen

The story of changing from a "good" income to a low one is all interwoven with so many other stories. To follow the thread of downward mobility through the fabric of life for two years I find that I must describe a few other threads as well.

Steve Norvell and I were a young married couple living in Oklahoma in the fall of 1950. Steve was a medical doctor on the staff of a cooperative hospital and I was the teacher/director of a parents' cooperative nursery school, when suddenly we emigrated to Canada.

The Korean war had begun, and doctors were being drafted along with others. Steve had served in World War II, and had emerged from that experience with strong pacifist objections to entering the military again, even though he, as a doctor, would not have been called upon to kill others.

Called before the local draft board, he cited the recent Nuremberg trials in which the defendants, Nazi officials, had been found guilty of breaking international laws against genocide despite the fact that the orders they had obeyed were legal at the national level. Especially since the use of the atomic bomb, Steve argued, warfare itself had become potentially genocidal and he felt a responsibility to not participate in it. He stated that he was willing to do alternative, non-military service, but no provision had been made for that in the doctor-draft law. So, what he was asking for was official conscientious objector status.

However, to the men on the draft board in this small town it seemed clear that a doctor who had received his medical training while in the army during World War II should serve in the next war. The board members were accustomed to respecting the religious beliefs of Mennonites, who believed they would go to hell if they sinned. The southern Baptists on the board didn't see military service as a sin but they could understand those who did. However, this young doctor, who wouldn't even claim that he believed in a Supreme Being, seemed beyond their ken.

They simply didn't understand this man, nor did they act as if it was their job to try to do so. I was present at the meeting of the board when Steve was questioned. The hostility of the board members toward him remains vivid in my memory even now. I, who had been thinking about conscientious objection to war all through World Ward II and back to the time I was about ten, was so choked up in response to their scorn that I would have been unable to speak if I had had the opportunity. We had already thought of emigrating and had made some tentative plans. This interview tipped the scales.

Thus, in one week we changed from being a young couple with an income of about $10,000 a year, which was good in those days, and a position of considerable status in a fairly prosperous town in the country where we had always lived, to being strangers with no income, no job, and, for Steve, no license to practice the profession for which he had so arduously trained. We found ourselves living in a log house in a remote valley in British Columbia without electricity, and dependent on a nearby spring for a water supply.

Perhaps I am being overly dramatic. The decision to leave and the transition were, indeed, sudden. However we had been making preparations; we had known for two years that the doctor-draft law made no provision for alternative service and that Steve was not likely to be deferred. We had bought a farm with some friends who had emigrated to Canada about a year earlier. Our friends were living in Toronto when we arrived in British Columbia. We lived on the farm for several months with Mr. Skribe, the elderly man from whom we had bought the property and who had built the log house.

For both Steve and me it was an adventure to learn new ways of living. Mr. Skribe was an old hand at homesteading, and he proved to be a delightful person to get to know. He was liked and respected in the sparsely populated, impoverished valley and, since he liked us, the people there accepted us quickly. Everyone there had an "old country"; Austria was Mr. Skribe's; the U. S. was ours; most countries of Europe were represented; these people were used to welcoming strangers.

However, for Steve there were intense worries which I didn't have. Whereas my parents had understood and approved of our move, his parents had not. As a Friend (Quaker) I had grown up expecting that at some time in my life I would be in prison for civil disobedience as so many Friends had been in the past for refusing to accept the laws of earlier times. Emigrating seemed mild compared to that. Steve had had no such expectations. And the problem of getting a license to practice medicine in a new country loomed large for him.

In addition to these current new problems Steve and I had had a lot of tension in our relationship throughout the two years of our marriage over matters which do not belong in this story. Despite the tension, somehow the thought that we might separate had not occurred to me during our marriage. I remember now that about four years earlier, when we were first engaged, I had been the one who suggested that we have some plan for how we would separate if either of us should want to do so. Having once voiced the idea, I seem to have completely forgotten it. Thus, when Steve announced one night, about two and a half months after we had arrived at the farm, that he thought we would have to separate, I was stunned, shocked, silent, and physically cold for hours. In retrospect, I understand his feelings. I didn't then. What to do?

For the next several days we hardly spoke. I tried more than ever to please. Neither of us knew how to communicate well, nor did I realize that we didn't know. It was January and very cold. The kitchen range and a Franklin type stove in the living room were the sources of heat for the whole house. Our friends from Toronto were expected to arrive in a few days, so Steve and Mr. Skribe were working upstairs to make some rooms out of a good-sized attic. They had cut a hole in the ceiling above the living room stove as a way of heating the upstairs. As part of my non-verbal effort to please, I tried to keep them warm while they worked by putting lots of wood in the living room stove. Mr. Skribe had told us that you use cedar to get a fire started and beech to keep it going. He probably had told us why and I'm sure he had shown us the difference between the two. I had not paid attention. I heaped both on the fire. The sparks from the cedar flew up the chimney and landed on the old cedar shake roof. By the time we realized that the roof was ablaze it was too late to save the house. The spring was no higher than the roof of the house so there was no water pressure at the level of the fire. We carried buckets of water until we realized it was useless. I rescued Steve's medical bags from upstairs but there was no time to get clothing, blankets, and other possessions. We saved some of Mr. Skribe's furniture and clothes from the ground floor.

We stayed with neighbors that night. The next day we looked at the ruins. The metal stoves must have been there but all I recall seeing was a hot water tank and a pipe somehow related to it. The log walls, the roof, the floors -- everything Mr. Skribe had built -- were charred ruins partly covered by new snow. Yet all Mr. Skribe said was, "Now if dot ain't good for bedbugs, I don't know what is." What an amazing person he was!

Neighbors came to our rescue with jars of home-canned fruit and vegetables, clothing, and blankets. I remember especially a coat with a lining in shreds which I wore for the rest of that winter. None of them said, "Careless greenhorns!" They said, "It could have been us." We lived for a few months in the vacant house of the farm next to Mr. Skribe's, which was for sale. Our three friends from Toronto arrived, as did a couple from North Dakota, and we all shared this house until spring. Steve doctored and I nursed Mr. Skribe through pneumonia. Mr. Skribe told us later that he contemplated suicide at this time but refrained because he realized the guilt we would feel.

Steve received a temporary permit to practice medicine from the B.C. Medical Society. We moved a few miles away from our friends to a slightly larger settlement where there was a Red Cross Outpost Hospital. Fixing up a rented cabin to live in and remodeling a room in the basement of the hospital for an office took all our energy. I became his office nurse, receptionist, and bookkeeper. Although a couple of years later I was happy to return to work for which I was better prepared, at that time I was glad to be useful in those ways. It was a time when I privately gave myself a new middle name -- "Adjustable". My reasoning was that I wouldn't mind adapting my own plans, wishes and hopes so much if to do so was a goal I had accepted. This attitude was widely recommended as a feminine virtue in those days. Now I see that there was something false in it. Now, being adjustable is just one option to be considered. In any case, years passed before we talked again about separating.

During the year that followed we had many expenses and very low income. When I figured the income tax for that year we didn't owe any; our income was under $3,000.

The next winter a new crisis was upon us. The B.C. Medical Society wrote to Steve that he would not be permitted to take the examination for a permanent medical license because there were already enough doctors in

B. C. and because he was a conscientious objector to war. After some deliberation we posted a copy of the letter in the local post offices of the three rural settlements where his patients lived. People rallied quickly. They had really appreciated having a doctor in their midst, and many were very fond of Steve in particular; the nearest other doctor was forty miles away on winding mountain roads. The local groups, including the Canadian Legion, wrote letters to their Member of the Legislative Assembly in Victoria. The Member raised the question in the Assembly whether the B.C. Medical Society should continue to have the right to decide who was eligible to take the Canadian Council exam. The medical society reversed its decision and the people in our communities rejoiced. I felt deeply grateful to them all. Steve -- able and conscientious doctor that he was -- passed the exam and was certified to practice medicine anywhere in Canada.

I had grown up as a child with the idea that there were people (like Friends) who acted on the basis of good principles and then there were ordinary people who didn't. With a child's limited vision I assumed there was no other explanation for the fact that most people approved of killing others in wars. In my teen years the good people who acted on principle had expanded considerably to include those in the consumer co-operative movement, and college experiences had further broadened my outlook. However, here was a community of "ordinary" people who had banded together to right an injustice and had succeeded. It would be hard to overstate the blessing they bestowed upon our lives or the lesson they taught me about the wrongness of labelling and prejudging people.

The uprooting from our homeland, the fire, the ordeal for Steve of obtaining a license to practice medicine -- all that was part of my first experience of being "downwardly mobile".

Twenty five years later I again made a sudden shift from a high material standard of living to a much lower one. The circumstances were very different.

"Last night she slept in a goose feather bed with the sheet turned down so bravely, O. Tonight she sleeps on the cold, cold ground, For she's gone with the Raggle Taggle Gypsies, O." I pointed out to myself that the foam mattress in the tiny $200 camper-trailer we had bought was not the "cold, cold ground", nor had I left a castle with servants all around, nor was the child I had left behind a baby -- he was a capable, nearly grown-up 15 year old. Still, fragments of the old ballad persisted in my mind as my new loving companion and I travelled through one state after another, left the trailer and some belongings behind, took a bus and finally boarded an ocean liner bound for Europe. "Gypsy" was almost the right word.

What had happened to bring about this second radical change in my life? During the eight years following our time in the Arrow Lakes Valley of British Columbia I had worked in various interesting social work and teaching jobs while Steve did a residency in surgery in Alberta and then a registrarship, also in surgery, in England. Back in Canada we began to raise our two long-awaited children. How can I briefly say what that meant to us? Steve's mother once said, "You both treat the children as if they had come straight from Heaven," and Steve, who labeled himself an agnostic and whose mind was steeped in scientific explanations, replied, "Of course, where else?"

Once the interneship and residency were over, Steve's income was such that money was never a problem. We bought nothing on credit except a house, and that we paid for in three years, as I recall. I felt rich, partly because I had never before had so much money and partly because through my work in a head-start type pre-school I was in touch with very poor people. But there were lots of strains between Steve and me, as there had been for most of our many years together. Now that we were "established" we could no longer attribute them to stresses imposed upon us by the long training period.

In the early summer of 1978 I met a man for whom I felt an immediate attraction and a great sense of shared values and interests. I began to wonder why I should stay with a man who said I was making him unhappy when someone else whom I admired really wanted me. My daughter had already decided to leave home for the last year of high school and I learned soon after the separation that she had wondered for several years why Steve and I had stayed together. In deciding to leave my husband it seemed to me that I was setting him free, clearing the wife-space for someone with whom he would be happier. My son was the one for whom this sudden move of mine would be a great shock. It was not fair for me to break his trust in me by leaving when he pled for me to stay -- yet I left. How I wish I could have done so without hurting him.

Al, my new partner, the "gypsy" of my song, was a philosopher, a Friend, a man who had recently been released by his wife from their marriage vows. He was a profoundly serious person and yet, with him, I felt as if I was living in a light opera for he whistled and sang and solved a myriad of problems with such delightful good spirits. He was the "Merlin of my everyday", my "gentle Viking".

He was also a tax refuser. I had for years felt guilty about paying taxes which were used for war preparation. Kier Hardie had said, at the turn of the century, that wars will cease when men refuse to fight. Now, it seemed to me, that wars would cease when people refused to pay for them. Al and his first wife, after many years of dialogue with the Internal Revenue Service, had had their house sold at auction. He had for years had a varied and unpredictable income, so he was familiar with many ways of saving money. I quickly came to enjoy sharing ice cream cones, buying clothes from second hand stores, and, later, furnishing an apartment from yard sales. I remember how cheered I was by a sign in the first second-hand store where I bought clothing for myself -- "Neighbors helping neighbors with dignity".

At the same time, Al was, and is, a person who sees all kinds of possibilities. Why not go to Denmark to be with his father on his father's ninetieth birthday next month? We would go by sea, of course, because Al had a scruple against jet travel. We tried to book passage on a freighter, but we found that freighters no longer took passengers. The luxurious Queen Elizabeth II seemed the only option. This temporary luxury didn't change Al's simple living ways, so, that's how it came about that he bought a suit for $5 in a grim Salvation Army store near the docks in New York City just minutes before we boarded that deluxe ocean liner!

This second change of economic status was, for me, a rather incidental part of an emotional sea-change of momentous proportions.

Now, about fifteen years later, we live in a mobile home in Tucson, Arizona, for more than half of each year and in a motor home in Eugene, Oregon, for the rest of the year.

We chose the dry and sunny winter climate of Tucson for health reasons, but after living there for eight winters we have many ties. Now we are among the long-term residents of a trailer park, which is a friendly neighborhood for those who reach out to make it so. We bought our mobile home, furnished, for $6,250 about six years ago and paid another $1000 to have it moved onto the site we rent in the park. We marvelled that we could own a home "free and clear" for less than $8,000 in this day and age.

There are other attractions in Tucson. Al makes great use of the University of Arizona library. We both find that belonging to Pima Friends Meeting gives opportunities for meaningful work, fellowship, and spiritual quest. And in Tucson we are very near to the Third World. Refugees from oppression in Central America and poverty-stricken Mexicans continue to arrive despite all U.S. Government efforts to prevent them. Most winters I do some volunteer work; several times this has been with people who help refugees.

Our motorhome, in which we live during the summers, is a medium-sized one, 24' long, and is second hand, of course. A carpenter-neighbor in our trailer park remodelled it so that we have a large desk for our computers, the typewriter, the laser printer, a television set, two video cassette recorders, and a fax machine. Solar panels on the roof supply us with electricity. It has happened more than once that we are turning out minutes, reports, and position papers for a conference we are attending while parked in some parking lot. Other conferees besides ourselves find the equipment useful.

That is the pattern of our lives right now. I am grateful that income from selected investments combined with our variation of simple living leaves me free to work on projects which seem to me worth-while and fascinating -- such as the editing of this book.

HOW DO WE ENSURE

HUMANE & EQUITABLE

USE OF POWER ?

Alfred F. Andersen

As I sit down to write my contribution to this volume it was twenty eight years ago that I received the following letter (dated March 24, 1965) from the chairman of my PhD committee at the University of Pennsylvania. I quote the entire turn-down letter because I will be referring to it in the course of this chapter. Its content will help to illustrate how our modern universities are at the heart of the mounting moral dilemmas, today bordering on crisis, which we increasingly face in this super-technological civilization.

Dear Al:

I am delighted to have your letter and to know of the important and exciting things you are doing in Berkeley.

I talked your letter over with Dr. McMullin. We are both of the opinion that "The Humane Use of Power" is a book that needs to be written and that you have the skill and the training and the background to do it.

On the other hand, we feel that it is not a suitable topic for a doctor's dissertation, which, as you know, is a student effort circumscribed by many rules and restrictions which I shall have to impose to get you through the final oral examination. What I am trying to say in effect amounts to this -- that you are really beyond the PhD dissertation in your intellectual and philosophic maturity.

If you should want a PhD for its prestige value, <u>or</u> as a union card for entrance into a university faculty, you will need to set your book aside and select some corrigible topic which can be fitted into the pattern of the PhD dissertation and can be completed in a reasonable length of time.

I hope you will let me know when you are coming to Philadelphia so that we can renew our friendship and talk about this and other topics.

In the meantime, please keep me informed of the things you are doing, and don't hesitate to ask any questions about the PhD requirements.

As can be seen from the title of this chapter, my concern for "the humane use of power" continues to this day. As this same title suggests, that concern has expanded to include equity as well as humaneness. I consider equity to be the most essential ingredient in humaneness, where the term 'equity' -- not to be confused with equality -- is almost synonymous with 'fairness' and 'justice.' It might be said that equity is justice "with mercy." An action which is both humane and equitable softens the implied hardness of raw justice still more. Humaneness implies a further expansion of "justice with mercy" to the fullness of social responsibility. In what follows I shall be using the term 'justice' in this expanded sense.

On the other hand, to be humane and equitable is not necessarily to be compassionate or loving. These latter qualities go "beyond the call of duty," and thus of justice as this term will be used here. No matter how strongly I feel compassion for someone, I cannot justify coercing others into acting on my compassion. I can only justify using my coercive powers against those who caused, or are causing, injustice. And it is in the employment of *coercive* powers that I am most concerned that justice with equity and humaneness be "ensured." I grant that some *forms* of coercion are *sometimes* morally justified in order to prevent or remedy injustice, but some of the greatest injustices have been perpetrated by coercive measures ostensibly designed and employed for this worthy purpose. They have been perpetrated in the course of carrying out previously made commitments. In short, they have been perpetrated in the course of administering economic and political *structures.*

I do not, therefore, join anarchists in rejecting all coercive structures. I am not willing to let anything but trivial injustice go uncoerced. The challenge is to design -- and implement -- economic and political structures whose implicit commitments ensure that when justice requires coercive means, these will not themselves violate the very sustainable justice they ostensibly are designed to ensure.

I will not undertake in this chapter to address that challenge in anything but a very limited way.[1] Here I will focus on (1) the role of research universities in meeting that challenge, and (2) on a major change needed in political structure if the present trend of rich getting ever richer and the poor ever poorer is to be reversed. The biographical accounts given will be those I consider most relevant to addressing these aspects of my total challenge.

* * * * * * * *

The above-quoted letter makes it clear that my PhD Committee was eager to accommodate me. The informality of the letter is indicative of the friendliness of our relationship. Despite this, and despite their acknowledging the social importance of the topic, they felt so constrained by the rigidities which had become built into the academic structure under which they were operating that all they could offer was a perfunctory way to get a "union card." No wonder their letter didn't inspire me to set aside what had become my basic commitment in life.

It was a commitment which emerged out of many hours of meditation in a prison cell, and it had grown during the two decades between being released and receiving the above-quoted letter. I had been incarcerated during World War II for refusing to cooperate with conscription. I never doubted the rightness of my refusal to bow to the power to conscript, but I was thereby forced to consider what kind of power could be justified, and how such a power could be established in the world. My main purpose in pursuing a PhD was to expedite that commitment. So, it would have been unthinkable to set that commitment aside for the sake of admittance into an intellectual club whose credentials in moral responsibility were increasingly suspect. In fact, at that time I was deeply involved in confronting one of the most prestigious PhD-granting institutions, the University of California, for its role in administering **all** research and development of nuclear weapons for the US military.

Thus, my decision not to continue my pursuit of a PhD degree was not a choice in favor of downward mobility as such; rather it was a choice not to pay the price of upward mobility in the academic world.

I continued to be so involved in social issues of one kind or another, in Berkeley and elsewhere, that it was not until twenty more years had passed that I was able to eke out the time and energy for writing what I

---

1. I do address this challenge in considerable fullness in a forthcoming book, called *Toward Sustainable Justice, Local to Global.*

had hoped would be my dissertation.[2] But the delay did serve a purpose, because in the meantime I was storing up concrete experiences which greatly clarified and enhanced my basic thesis.

Over the intervening years I have become ever more firmly convinced that the seeds for the moral dilemmas and gross injustices we see today can be found in two identifiable sources:

(1) the moral flaws in the US Constitution (largely the result of the subtle and manipulative "coup d'état" which established it over two centuries ago[3]) and

(2) the complicit role played by US universities in promoting the very "military industrial complex" which retiring President Eisenhower warned us about, and which the implementers of that constitution have "legalized" over the intervening two centuries.[4]

As for the moral flaws in the U.S. Constitution, the only one I will deal with here to any great extent is its failure to ensure a just distribution of the benefits of what I call "our common heritage of productive capital": namely, all land and natural resources, and all technology -- including urban infrastructure -- contributed by previous generations. Income from this common heritage is now all but monopolized by an elite few -- primarily the most aggressive and acquisitive -- and permitted to be so, even encouraged, by the U.S. Constitution. I have calculated that income in the United States from what should be considered our *common* heritage yields this legalized elite about two trillion dollars a year. If we had a political structure which "ensured" that this income from our common heritage was collected by a Common Heritage Trust, and then distributed equitably among the population, the average annual income from it to each resident of the United States would be about $8000.

No wonder the rich are getting richer. They not only get income from whatever capital they generate themselves, but also from their near-monopoly ownership and control of our common heritage. It seems only fair that a person get income from capital s/he has generated -- made a

---

2. It was published by Transaction Books, Rutgers University, 1985, under the title, *Liberating the EARLY American Dream*, presently available from Tom Paine Institute, 3120 N. Romero Rd. #39, Tucson, AZ 85705.

3. *Ibid.* Chapter XIII, for those interested in the justification for this statement. No such justification will be given in this paper. Rather, I will focus attention on a major economic inequity which is implicit in the resulting *structure* of the US Constitution and which threatens to engulf all life on earth in the near future.

4. *Ibid.* Part I, especially Chapter IV, for those interested in the justification for this statement; except for the "clue" given in the following paragraph, no such justification will be given in this paper.

better mousetrap, worked harder and saved more -- but from our common heritage s/he should get only her or his fair share.

One of the assumptions upon which the PhD program is based is the same one upon which all economic and political philosophy has been based for the past two centuries: namely, that anything which contributes to the total economic output of a society is good for everyone in that society. It emerged out of the Utilitarian philosophy and a simplistic formula which reads, "the greatest good to the greatest number." As applied to political structure it was assumed that such a "greatest good" was best determined by majority vote. During the twenties, then President Coolidge expressed it as follows: "What is good for General Motors is good for the country." Today that whole set of assumptions is implicit in "trickle down economics." And despite its denials, it seems that the present administration has largely embraced the same set of assumptions.

As a way of beginning to see how all of the above related to the relationship of the knowledge industry to the corporate world and its beneficiaries, we remind ourselves that the entire industrial revolution so central in modern, technological living, is based on two phenomena: (a) the scientific discovery of Nature's laws, and (b) division of labor in applying those laws to increasingly more efficient high-tech production. Since such scientific discoveries called for careful intellectual research and reasoning, universities naturally emerged to undertake that particular specialization. And the various PhD programs became a still further step in the division of labor.

The above-quoted letter contains a clue as to how complicity with "trickle-down economics" on the part of what former University of California President Clark Kerr called "the knowledge industry."[5] manifests itself. The granting of PhD degrees seems harmless enough until one realizes how splitting up the total field of knowledge into narrow specialties serves the military industrial complexes of the world in several crucial ways.

1. The knowledge industry supplies these complexes with a constant supply of knowledge about how to employ Nature's laws in the service of their purposes, which include retaining the advantages of their near-monopolistic ownership and control of our common heritage.

2. The knowledge they supply is largely "tailor made" to meet the purposes of those complexes. This includes breaking it down into narrow bands in order to accommodate the various divisions of labor

---

5. See *The Uses of the University*, by Clark Kerr, Harvard U. Press, 1963

in the industrial world.

3. Such divisions into bands of knowledge -- corresponding to PhD specialties -- tends to assure that the concepts in terms of which each band is presented have no moral dimensions implicit in them.

4. Narrow concentration of focus within each PhD specialty tends to make the academic specialist in each such "discipline" oblivious to the complicit role it plays in facilitating the ultimate purposes served.

5. The overall consequence of the above-stated causal factors tends to make the knowledge industry and its practitioners oblivious to the extent of their complicity with military-industrial complexes, because no band of specialists is able to rise sufficiently above its narrow focus to make an overall evaluation in terms of social responsibility.

There was some initial resistance to such PhD narrowness, especially around the turn of the century. But evidently it couldn't prevail against the combination of "greatest good for the greatest number," the industrial revolution, the subsequent scientific revolution, "what's good for General Motors, etc.," the greater efficiency of specialization, and "trickle down economics." So, as this is being written, the PhD programs in the various intellectual "disciplines" centered in the our universities divide up not only university activities from undergraduate to graduate levels, but intellectual life at the preparatory colleges and even back into secondary and elementary schools. About the only level of education free of its influence is the kindergarten level. Even the field of Philosophy, the one last bastion of intellectual monitoring and holistic thinking, has succumbed to PhD specialization. The various specializations in Philosophy have still not formed separate departments, but it may be just a matter of time before we see them in the already specialized areas of Metaphysics, Ethics, Epistemology, Logic, and History of Philosophy. Whether that happens or not, the hope that Philosophy will save us from the ominous blinders of specialization seems slim indeed.

As stated in #4 and #5 above, precisely because the various PhD programs have populated our universities with experts in narrow specialties, most practitioners fail to realize how the concentrated narrowness of their respective disciplines tends to deny them the overall perspective which might otherwise alert them to the way they and their colleagues are so often being "used"[6] by those who primarily benefit from the resulting knowledge-power.

Even those who come to realize the causal connection between "the

---

6. See *The Uses of the University*, by Clark Kerr, Harvard University Press, 1963

knowledge industry" and the gap between rich and poor are dissuaded from writing about it because they cannot claim such analysis as their professional specialty. *Therefore, they cannot do so at the level of professional standards to which they feel committed.*

Thus, an economist is constrained from commenting on any output from the political science department, and vice versa. Similarly, professionals in all departments are reluctant to give anything approaching a professional opinion regarding our civilization as a whole.

Additionally, their research tends to be justified on the grounds that it adds to "the sum total of human knowledge," a phrase which every PhD candidate will recognize as a major requirement of that program. It is a requirement whose establishment was based on an assumption characterized by what has been called "The Age of Enlightenment," of which the entire scientific and industrial revolutions were logical outcomes. It is an assumption which even has its roots in the Platonic dictum that a certain kind of knowledge assures virtue, and in the gnosticism which followed. It not only implies that more knowledge is necessarily a good thing, but that more knowledge will necessarily *ensure* good things.

It seems to me an assumption resulting from incomplete moral thinking. It certainly is true that the greater the knowledge the greater the *potential* for goodness of many kinds, including justice. But potentiality is not actuality. The potential goodness implicit in knowledge derives from knowledge as a kind of *power.* And "power tends to corrupt." So, the potential for good implicit in knowledge-power is only realized to the extent that safeguards against the *misuse* of such power are developed along with and comparable to the power itself.

An important prerequisite for the necessary safeguards against misuse of power is a special kind of knowledge: namely, knowledge about what constitutes injustice, how to prevent it from occurring, and how to remedy that which isn't prevented. Until this special kind of knowledge is not only developed but effectively applied, I urge the knowledge industry to place a moratorium on generating and distributing any other kind.

Insufficient restraints on the indiscriminate production of knowledge-power is the basic contributor to the kind of run-away *pace* of life we are witnessing today all over the world. Careful analysis will show that such out-of-control pace in misuse of power is largely determined by university-produced knowledge-power constantly catapulted into an already morally confused world civilization of ever-mounting moral dilemmas. The result is that those who are sincerely striving to develop safeguards against the *mis*use of such power simply cannot humanely and equitably cope with such a pace. It takes time and careful process to develop safe-guards of any kind. So, when the pace at which power is developed outpaces the pace at which it can be equitably controlled the result is that power gets used in *in*humane and *in*equitable ways.

There is yet another ominous result of constantly feeding university-generated knowledge-power into the minds and hands of those corporations which have near-monopoly ownership of means of production. The resulting "labor-saving" which technology delivers generates ever more profits for the corporate owners and less jobs for those who are thereby replaced. Increasingly, therefore, those who must get all their income from their own labor find themselves competing with each other for fewer and fewer jobs at ever decreasing pay.

Nor does the solution reduce to the simplistic one of generating more "jobs." We must beware of being seduced into that mind-set, so vigorously promoted by the US Government and its elite benefactors. In an increasingly capital intensive economy income from capital -- in the form of ever more labor-saving facilities -- will inevitably become an ever larger percentage of total national income, and income from labor an ever smaller percentage. Indeed, the way the present US administration pro-poses to generate such job-increase will accelerate this trend. Even the jobs which will be created will be temporary, and will result in less jobs than ever when completed. A closer look will reveal why this must be so.

The Clinton administration (like all administrations before it) proposes to "create more jobs" by encouraging the near-monopolists of productive capacity to "invest" in even more labor-saving facilities. To be sure, such investment will require the employment of certain skills, and thus generate some jobs in those particular skills. They will also make corporate owners better able to compete with their counterparts in the global marketplace, and this will generate more jobs in the industries which expand to meet the growth in market demands. But let us consider what kind of jobs will be created, and how permanent they will be.

First as to the kind of jobs. They will be jobs in the high tech industries and their supporting subcontractors. To be sure, there will be some unskilled jobs. But cheap labor in "less developed countries" and competition among unskilled workers in this country will provide them with mere subsistent wages -- and even these will be only for those fortunate enough to find one of the decreasing number of unskilled jobs.

Consider next the permanence of those jobs which will be created by such investment in high tech and by expansion into the global market-place. The jobs *constructing* the more efficient facilities will necessarily be temporary because once the more efficient, labor-saving technology is in place the builders of it will no longer be needed.

It might be argued that constant expansion through constant investment in ever more high tech will generate ever new jobs, and that the Clinton Administration's plans for "Lifelong Learning" will assure a continuing flow of skills to fill such jobs. But there are several realistic factors which would prevent such unlimited expansion. One is limited natural resources. Another is the need to end ecological destruction. Still another is the need to reverse pollution levels. Then there are the limits to energy sources, now that the dreams of unlimited supplies from nuclear energy sources have been all but smashed. Finally, and perhaps most important, are the human limits, such as our inability to maintain safeguards against misuse of the power being developed at even its present pace. *No, the continuous expansion we so desperately need, as noted above, is in knowledge about how to cope in humane and equitable ways with even the present pace of life.*

Some of the elite owners and controllers of means of production will share with "labor" in suffering from the above-outlined agenda. But most will not, because they still be participating in near-monopoly ownership of the facilities essential for producing human needs. The major beneficiaries among the global corporate elite may not have the market they would like among "ordinary working people," because survival-level persons are poor customers. But the elite can trade with each other, and provide markets to each other. That's what they are trying to do by way of breaking down the "trade barriers" around the world. This explains the push for "free trade agreements."

In any case, until there is a change in the near-monopoly ownership of means of production by the most aggressive and acquisitive no amount of job increase will meet our need for "the humane and equitable use of power." As long as the most aggressive and acquisitive retain the support they now have from the US and similar constitutions, and from the various knowledge industries around the world, they will control the entire economy, including whatever jobs are generated in that economy.

Just how they exercise such control is complex, and sometimes extremely subtle; one well known way, of course, is by way of their financial contributions to the manipulative political campaigns of politicians who are willing, in return, to continue to legalize their near-monopolistic economic status.

From all that has gone before, then, it must now be clear why Dorothy and I don't so much seek income from "jobs" as from means of production and other forms of capital which we have accumulated, which **we** control, and which we continue to add to as a way of generating power for a way of life which is socially and ecologically responsible. Thus, though we live simply in a certain sense, buying almost all our clothes and most of our furnishings from secondhand outlets and yard sales, we do not make a virtue of downward mobility as such. We don't attempt to limit our income, whether to stay below taxable level or some national or global average income. We salvage as much capital as we can by way of simple living, and get as large a part of our income as we can from capital while attempting to do so in ways which are "socially and ecologically responsible." Since our major activity is educational in nature we invest in the best facilities we can get for that purpose, thereby reducing somewhat the near monopoly ownership and control of them by the most aggressive.

This is why the close quarters of our mobile home (winter quarters in Tucson, AZ) and our motor home (summer quarters in Eugene OR) are filled with desk top publishing, a FAX machine, other technological wonders, and solar panels on the roof. Incidentally, these solar panels are generating energy for this computer as I write, and will generate energy for printing out all the camera-ready pages of this book by the laser printer resting under the desk upon which I am writing. All this technology is God-given by way of Nature and natural laws. It is the basic source of power in this world, power which we are meant to use for humane and equitable purposes, and which should not be nearly monopolized by the most aggressive and acquisitive. The challenge addressed in this chapter, therefore, is to indicate how to bring about economic and political structures which will ensure such humane and equitable use of power. I begin to address this challenge by picking up again the autobiographical threads with which this chapter began. And the remainder of this chapter constitutes my answer to it in my personal life.

My Political Education Begins

The first stage of my political education came in 1944 when the Federal Reserve Bank of New York foreclosed on a loan to my small manufacturing business in Bridgeport, Connecticut, and declared me bankrupt; I had no choice about it. Even my personal car was confiscated.

I had graduated with a B.S. in Mechanical Engineering in 1941 and had immediately joined my father in a two-man manufacturing operation. Gradually, over the course of a year or so, we expanded it to about twenty employees; and soon thereafter my father retired and I took over completely. I had worked a year after high school, and had worked summers as a tool maker while attending college. So at graduation I was well prepared in the mechanical field, both practically and theoretically.

Mechanical and mathematical things had always been easy for me, but that wasn't where my heart was. I had grown up during the Great Depression, and had seen my father, one of the best tool makers in Bridgeport, work for $12 a week, and be glad to get it. I had seen the bank foreclose on the house my father built, and had myself sold magazines, cookies my mother had baked, and berries I had picked in order to supplement the family income. So I knew from personal experience at a very young age that something was basically wrong with our modern technological society.

But the event which finally threw me headlong into dealing with these concerns philosophically was, strange as it may seem, my switching to a major in quantum physics my last year in college. It was 1940. Some of the philosophical implications of the revolution that was taking place in physics sent my mind spinning! They challenged the very foundations of materialism as a theory of what constitutes basic reality. From then on I was incurably a philosopher, and my views of how society could be better structured were approached philosophically as well as concretely.

My studies in philosophy continued in a token way even while I was deeply involved in the details of running a small business; I commuted to two courses at Yale and one at Columbia, and I inquired into entering Harvard Graduate School. William Ernest Hocking, who was chairman of the Harvard Department of Philosophy at the time (1942), advised me not to enter graduate school, but to continue studying, thinking, and applying my philosophy as it developed, saying that graduate school programs were for people who didn't know what they wanted. Later, when Hocking became my mentor in philosophy and a personal friend, I came to understand better his advice; for his philosophy emphasized alternation between theory and practice, meditation and social outreach. Also, his wife, Agnes Hocking, later told me that Ernest, as she called him, had said to her once that whereas he at one time could think his own thoughts, now he could only think other people's thoughts. Apparently he attributed this regrettable situation to his studying the philosophies of others before his own thinking had matured.

In any case, after those token courses at Yale and Columbia I stayed away from further graduate work for several years, and returned, in the meantime, to seeking ways to apply my emerging personal philosophy in my business venture, including involving the employees more democratically in its operation.[7] I worked long hours, and the business prospered until a large contract my father took on just before he retired, and which had to be financed by a huge loan from the Federal Reserve Bank of New York, soaked up all my remaining assets before we achieved an efficient level of production in fulfilling the contract.

In retrospect, it would have been wiser to have rejected this opportunity for "upward mobility," but I especially welcomed the contract because it was for making a product (piston pins for airplanes) which many other firms were making, and I saw it as an opportunity to demonstrate that a democratically run business could function more efficiently than the other more conventional firms which had contracted for the same product. What I didn't know at the time was that these other firms had enough other profitable contracts to absorb their losses in making this product. It was a case of making too big a leap into the unknown. Up to that time I had had success after success in my life. I learned from that experience that I too could fail. And I have tried to keep that lesson in mind ever since.

I learned another important lesson also, a lesson about the myth of patriotism in the financial halls of the US Government itself, because it was a US Government bank which shut us down. Despite the fact that we did finally reach a profitable level of production, the Federal Reserve Bank of New York concluded that we had not sufficiently met the requirements of one of their impersonal financial formulas, and decided to throw me into bankruptcy. The callousness with which this financial arm of the U. S. Government made their move in such complete disregard for not only myself personally, not only for our young family, not only for my hard-working employees, but for the supposed "patriotism" so closely identified at the time with the so-called "war effort," thoroughly disenchanted me not only in regard to that "war effort" but also in regard to the whole economic/political structure which was behind it. At the time we were shut down we were finally producing at a profit which promised eventually to be sufficient to meet all our financial obligations and to deliver the required piston pins to the war effort as required. As the result of the Government's shut-down action, however, virtually all work in process was lost to that supposedly patriotic war effort. Thus, my first experience with downward mobility was a completely involuntary one.

Bankruptcy having set me free from the rigorous schedule I had been keeping for years, my wife, Connie, and I began to explore alternative life

---

7. By then my father had retired, and I was sole proprietor.

styles. Among the individuals and groups we then became acquainted with, Arthur Morgan and the Religious Society of Friends (Quakers) attracted us most. I had met Arthur Morgan once in Washington, D.C. while I was still in business, and we felt ourselves to be kindred spirits. So, after I was stripped of all my assets (my income at one time had shown a book value of $50,000 a year in 1943 dollars) our young family (including one 18-month-old boy by then) accepted an invitation from the Morgans to visit them in Yellow Springs, Ohio.

Our stay there was to be short because a draft board was calling me back to Bridgeport for hearings. The pacifist and other associations we had cultivated in the meantime, plus my then-rapidly-developing personal values in relation to "the war effort," had led me to feel that I simply could not in good conscience accept the conscription which was in store. Apart from the natural reluctance which I assume all of us have to submit to a situation where others are trying to kill you and you them, and apart from my then disenchantment with the war effort in general, I felt most clear about refusing to be conscripted, for any reason. I was especially opposed to agreeing to obey every superior officer whether against my personal conscience or not. So, when I refused induction I was sent to the "Federal Correctional Facility" (i.e., federal prison) in Danbury, Connecticut. Thus did my downward mobility continue.

The war ended while I was in prison, so I was incarcerated for only eight months, out on "third-time parole." But during that time I had many precious hours to read, to write, to meditate, and to think. I was convinced that I had done the right thing in refusing to be conscripted, but felt most clearly the challenge, as the founder of Quakerism, George Fox, put it, "to take away the *occasion* of all wars." How, I asked, can society be changed so as to avoid war and other evils of our day?

This challenge has stayed with me for the past nearly five decades, and has manifested itself in the concern referred to in the title of this chapter: How can we ensure that the power which we instinctively feel urged to pursue, as one of life's basic, upward-mobility urges, can be both pursued and implemented in humane and equitable ways?

After getting out of prison in 1945 our family returned to Yellow Springs, and lived there for the next five years. There I took up again my interest in Arthur Morgan's work, which centered on rebuilding small communities. Arthur Morgan was largely a self-educated man. His civil engineering firm had built the seven dams around Dayton, Ohio, even though he hadn't had a college education. He had educated himself so broadly that he was asked to take on the presidency of Antioch College in

1921. In the early thirties he had suggested the TVA (Tennessee Valley Authority) idea to then President Roosevelt, and had become its first director. Out of all these experiences he had become persuaded that the health of American society depended on its grass roots small communities. So, after leaving an active role in Antioch and in the TVA, he founded Community Service Inc., a non-profit corporation set up to do what this volume largely advocates: namely, to revitalize grass roots community life; not only in America, but all over the world.

In the course of working for Community Service Inc. on bibliographies dealing with grass-roots community-building, I learned of a number of cooperative communities which had developed for the purpose of "taking away the occasion for war," and which were in the tradition of the early American dream, but which I hadn't known about until then. Community Service was already sponsoring a Small Communities Conference each summer. So I suggested sponsoring a Cooperative Communities Conference immediately following the other. This we did, and out of it developed what became the Fellowship of Intentional Communities, since renamed the Fellowship *for* Intentional Communities. For me personally, it was a delight to find that the early American dream was still alive! In fact, Yellow Springs at the time was itself a kind of laboratory for experimenting with ideal community life. A number of Antioch graduates had settled there, and others, like us, had come specifically to join the effort.

Nevertheless, in 1951 we left Yellow Springs (by then a family of five) to tour intentional communities and other pioneering educational projects in the eastern United States. After about three years of visiting and participating in a number of them, we lived for the next ten years (from 1954 to 1964) in one about 30 miles west of Philadelphia, called *Tanguy Homesteads*. While living there I became president of Fellowship of Intentional Communities, but we found it difficult to generate interest in "the movement" among people already living in communities. Members of actual, working communities tended to get completely absorbed in internal problems, mostly because building truly equitable communities is a very demanding task! And the final blow to the community movement as it was from about 1945 to 1960 came when the newly elected U.S. President, John Kennedy, sucked a great deal of idealistic energy into the nation-state scene by saying, "Ask not what your country can do for you; ask what you can do for your country."

Living ten years in a cooperative community of thirty families, where all decisions were made by unanimity, was a great experience for the entire family. The ten years ended in 1964 when, as our offspring were leaving the nest, we moved to Berkeley, California just as the Berkeley Free Speech Movement and other student protests were getting under way.[8] I had come to realize some of the limitations of living in a close-knit intentional community, and I felt I could no longer ignore the need for social change at the global level. "The Athens of the West," as Berkeley was then called by some, seemed to offer what I needed and what our family needed. As for my needs, the student unrest there presented a rare opportunity to enter that larger arena. To make a very long story short, the next fifteen years were spent in Berkeley.

* * * * * * * * *

Soon after our tour of various experimental communities and educational projects, I had begun teaching. By the time we arrived in Berkeley I had taught all levels of mathematics from 7th through 12th grade in public school, had taught in a Quaker day-school, taught and served as Dean of Boys in a Quaker boarding school, and taught mathematics, logic, physics, and philosophy of science at Lincoln University for three years. So, I felt ready to return to the adult education interests I had pursued at Yellow Springs. I never taught at the University of California, Berkeley, but I participated in the Faculty Peace Committee and got quite involved in political questions relating to the socially responsible role of a university in society. The implications of that statement go far beyond the scope of this volume, but I will give a hint of what I mean by this.

By the mid 1960s the sense of social crisis that had been growing in me for a number of years was then focused on what I called "the civilization level." In addition to the other influences on me mentioned above, I now must add Arnold Toynbee's writings, especially his *Study Of History*; and most especially his notion of *optimum* challenge (which offers the opportunity for healthy growth) as against too little challenge (which leads to stagnation) and too much challenge (which leads to moral confusion and ultimate collapse). I had come to see civilization (in the *civilizing* sense) as the process of developing safeguards against the misuse of the *power* which technology necessarily develops, and, ideally, as the process of developing such safeguards at a *pace* which "keeps pace" with the moral dilemmas which the political and economic power of technology necessarily generates. And I had come to see the development of *knowledge* as both (1) the basic and indispensable catalyst for building such technical power, and (2) the indispensable means of developing the necessary civilization *safeguards* against the *misuse* of that power.

---

8. It was about this time that I received the letter I quoted at the beginning of this chapter.

Add to this my persistent interest in wholesome community life, and the result was predictable: I became persuaded that a large part of the cause of our social problems was to be found somewhere in the knowledge centers as they then existed (and still exist), and that the solution to these social problems depended on developing *alternative* intellectual communities which were deeply committed to social responsibility.

One result of this conclusion was my effort to find some kernel of such a responsible intellectual community in Berkeley. I gave a talk on Pacifica Radio, called *The Knowledge Explosion,* about the same time Alvin Toffler was thinking along the same lines. The talk was well received; so I was encouraged. I organized a meeting of key faculty people in various UC Berkeley departments to discuss the possibility of advocating a moratorium on scientific research, *but only until society is politically mature enough to cope with its results in a humane and equitable way.* The meeting broke up when one participant accused another of carrying on the most irresponsible kind of research.

In effect, I was suggesting that the universities of the world (especially the major research universities like UC Berkeley) were generating knowledge-power (which the military industrial complexes of the world then turned into "bottom line" industrial and military power) at a *pace* far beyond the pace at which *safeguards* against its *mis*use were being developed. At first I found considerable interest among certain members of the Berkeley faculty. But, as it became apparent that slowing this "pace" would require research scientists to accept a kind of "downward mobility," that interest waned rapidly. Again, PhDs prepare people for specialties, and give them little training in applying their skills to other fields. In short, I found that *upward* mobility had been so ingrained into the university research establishment that any thought of *downward* mobility, socially required or not, was all but unthinkable.

This experience, plus others resulting from attempts to get researchers to consider their work from the point of view of social responsibility, left me quite discouraged with scientists at "our great universities." So I turned to writing. I wrote a pamphlet entitled *The University, Greatest Menace, Greatest Hope.* I also developed a multi-media series called *To Save A Civilization,* which was in three two-hour parts, and was shown at several locations around the San Francisco Bay Area in the late 60s. I also organized several "residence seminar houses" around the Berkeley campus specifically for the purpose of confronting social issues.

But there was very little evidence that any of these efforts was taking me closer to my goal. In short, my efforts at becoming a part of a socially responsible intellectual community were not succeeding. *But my political education was proceeding by leaps and bounds!*

After we had been in Berkeley several years the US Internal Revenue Service began to pursue me in earnest for my refusal, since about 1946, to file a US tax return. After getting out of prison I had written to the State Department suggesting that there must be some misunderstanding about my "obligations" toward the US Government. I told them that I was sent to prison because of this misunderstanding and would like to get the matter cleared up so that we could avoid further confrontations. In order to reach a resolution of our differences, I had asked the State Department to justify the US Government's claims of "obligation," in whatever form, whether for military service or for payment of taxes. Two years of such correspondence produced, as one might expect, no agreement. So I ended by saying that I would obey those laws I could in good conscience obey, but that I couldn't be counted on for the rest.

One of the laws I couldn't in good conscience obey was that demanding of me financial support for what I had come to feel was a government too inequitable and inhumane for my conscience to accept. So, from about 1946, I have refused to file income-tax returns or to give the IRS any information which would imply acceptance of their authority over me. After several meetings with IRS agents in the late 60s they eventually seized our Berkeley house and sold it at auction. Each time I met with IRS agents I told them that I would be happy to pay what they asked if they could persuade me it was the socially responsible thing to do; but they would never speak to that question. I do, however, believe that putting the issue that way eventually convinced a number of them of my sincerity. Another convincing factor may have been my refusal to even give them information which would reduce the amount of their claim, such as that regarding expenses serving to reduce the "taxable" amount.

The end result was not as financially devastating as one might expect. The agent who finally had charge of my case was a decent human being. He was evidently one of those persuaded of my sincerity. As evidence of this I will record a touching incident that occurred just before the auctioning-off took place.

A group of supporters had worked with us to organize a demonstration outside the Richmond, California Post Office where the sealed-bid auction was to take place. I paid a visit to the local Postmaster for the purpose of reaching an understanding with him about areas in which we would stand and march, and those in which we would not; and I composed a statement to be handed out. Then I phoned the IRS agent,

Mr. Morrison, told him what we were planning, and asked if he wanted to know some details of our demonstration and to see what would be handed out. His response was brief and to the point: "I'll be right over."

He was obviously eager to hear what I had to say. So, I gave him all the information about the forthcoming demonstration, and copies of the literature. But it was only as he was leaving that he revealed how much this meeting had meant to him. As he stepped out the door onto the porch he turned back to me and said something like the following: "Mr. Andersen, I really appreciate your asking me over. You didn't have to do that. You didn't have to do that. I'll never forget it." Then he turned and left. Whether it was Mr. Morrison's doing or not I may never know, but the historic fact is that the local IRS didn't do all they could have legally done, and we were able to regain our house with minimal financial loss, and without making any "deal" with the US Government.

What happened was this. Mr. Morrison and I had previously discussed the bidding procedure. As I recall, I was asked if I wanted the IRS to act in my interest by submitting a bid for an amount it considered to be fair market value. The presumption was that the more the IRS got from the sale the more would be applied toward the roughly $50,000 they were claiming from me. In any case, I made it clear to Mr. Morrison that I didn't want the IRS to submit any bid on our behalf, and I put this in writing. I had already discovered through research that we could legally "redeem" the house from the highest bidder at the price s/he paid for it at the auction; so, hoping for no bids other than a $100 bid a friend was submitting,[9] I hoped to redeem the house for somewhat less than market value. Mr. Morrison said that he would honor my request, and he did.

We had our demonstration in front of the Richmond Post Office. Just before the envelopes containing the closed bids were to be opened a journalist inquired of the IRS officials about how many bids had been submitted. According to his report, only one! So, we assumed it was the token $100 bid our friend had submitted. However, at the actual opening a few minutes later there were two envelopes, the second from a contractor, for $1,500. Thus, we were able to redeem the house from him for the $1,500 he paid for it. And the IRS hasn't bothered me since.

Why, one might ask, did Mr. Morrison and the IRS accept a mere $1,500 in place of the $50,000 they were seeking? As implied above, the partial answer, I believe, is that Mr. Morrison persuaded his colleagues of my sincerity. But I suspect that a major reason was this: they realized

---

9. We had urged others, both in personal contacts and through publicity, not to submit bids.

that the credits I would have been legally entitled to if I had cooperated with them in filing a return might well have reduced very substantially the amount actually "owed". Thus, all in all, they may have been reluctant to push for the amount actually claimed, and may even have recruited the last minute bid of $1,500 from the contractor, feeling that though they really couldn't justify settling for $100, $1,500 might be defended, all things considered. But all this is pure speculation on my part.

Does this mean that the IRS has a conscience? I doubt it. But I am persuaded that IRS agents do, and that at least some of them have considerable flexibility in enforcement if they are convinced of the sincerity of the person they are dealing with or if they judge it to be in their overall interests (negative publicity being one consideration).

But our IRS problems and related ones put a tremendous strain on our marriage relationship. The result was that Connie and I found that our common ground, though great, and great enough to provide a good home for three offspring over a period of over thirty years, was not great enough to encompass what each felt called to do at the time. The separation, though painful, was amicable, as was the ultimate divorce when I came to the point of remarrying.

My Sights Turn Global

During my residence in Berkeley, as noted, I became increasingly per-suaded of the view mentioned above: that the crises we face are at the civilization and global level. So, the focus of my interests gradually turned "from local to global." Increasingly I became aware of social-change activities on that global level. For instance, I became very interested in a series of United Nations Special Conferences, beginning with the UN Special Conference on the Environment in Stockholm, Sweden in 1972. Several others followed: one each on The Population Explosion, The World Food Crisis, Women's Rights, and, finally, summing them all up, the UN Special Conference on Habitat and Human Settlements, in Vancouver, B.C., Canada in the summer of 1976. The theory behind the title given to this Vancouver Conference was that all major crises manifest themselves in human settlements.

I arrived in Vancouver a couple of weeks ahead of opening day to find a very inspiring group of several hundred young people working hard to renovate several huge, old airplane hangars at the edge of Vancouver. This was to be the site of the concurrent NGO (Non-Governmental Organization) Forum, and the Canadian Government had given a sizable amount of money to cover basic expenses. It was a huge undertaking. I got deeply involved, made a small presentation, and participated actively in framing the final official NGO statement, which opened as follows:

> In accordance with our first statement we are of the opinion that the various aspects of human settlements' problems, such as housing, basic services, energy, land use, participation, financing, etc. cannot be dealt with and resolved in an isolated and individual manner. We consider that these problems can only be solved by a global and integral approach which has to go to the heart of the matter and transform the economic, social, and political *structures* which caused them, both at the national and international levels. In other words, we need not only a New International Economic Order, but simultaneously and not less urgently we need new and just *internal* economic orders.

The experience of participating in this NGO Conference in Vancouver was one of the highlights of my life. It was a very brief experience, but it was one of global community with intelligent kindred spirits. My personal experiences in the Great Depression made it possible for me to appreciate (at least somewhat) the plight of the hundreds of millions of victims of existing inequitable and inhumane structures throughout the world. My personal experiences with grass roots community life, of both the "intentional" and conventional kind (such as in Yellow Springs), made it possible to identify with the problems of the thousands of small communities in which the bulk of the people in the Third World still live.

My personal search for answers to global crises made me highly appreciative of such intense communication with so many who had come to Vancouver motivated by a similar search. But, most of all, I was intrigued by the possibilities presented by the existence of hundreds of Non Governmental Organizations (NGOs) associated with the United Nations, and thus evidently concerned about global issues without being tied to the vested interests which limit what the member states of the UN can do. If, I thought, this Vancouver Conference is an example of what such NGOs could do in the way of generating vitally needed dialogue, and if the statement they issued was an example of the depth of their commitment, then this was indeed a "community" of kindred spirits!

My hopes for the potential in NGOs were soon to be shattered. After the Vancouver Conference was over the organizers seemed exhausted. In any case, they simply dispersed into their various long-neglected pursuits. They had come from many parts of the world, some at great sacrifice. But little provision had been made for keeping in touch or for continuing the dialogue. I tried to organize some meetings to discuss follow-up, but there were so many stimulating activities on the program right up to the last minute that nothing came of my efforts. I stayed around Vancouver after the Conference to explore the possibility of follow-up in Vancouver itself, but no plans had been made for it. The gears of the established political and economic structures began grinding again as soon as the last scheduled event was completed. In fact, the site was to be dismantled; what remained was little more than a dream, a dream of a temporary revitalization of the early American dream on a global scale.

But, there were to be other United Nations "Special" gatherings. The next one I attended was the 1978 UN Special Session on Disarmament, held in New York City. I attended as an NGO delegate, sponsored by the Quaker UN Office in New York. This was my first close-up experience with the UN on its home turf. I was hoping for another global-community experience such as I had had in Vancouver. But this was not the wide open spaces of Vancouver's west edge. This was crowded New York City, and there was little provision for NGO meetings. In fact, there was no concurrent NGO Conference in the Vancouver sense. All activities centered around the official UN meetings, with NGO activities and delegates quite scattered. I and others made several efforts to organize NGO delegates, but found that the NGOs in their own permanent offices around UN Plaza were not much interested in joint activities. Each had its own programs. Some had had misunderstandings with each other in the past. Almost all NGO offices in New York were US based. And all NGOs from all countries have their status at the UN only so long as their home governments approve of their activities. So, most NGOs show great reluctance to jeopardize the privileges they have built up over the years -- such as being able to go out on the floor of the General Assembly, sit in on some committee meetings, hobnob in the delegates' lounge, and generally participate in the social life at the UN.

One highlight of this UN Special Session was worth it all for me personally. It was June 12th, 1978; NGO day. This was the day NGOs were to have their say in the UN General Assembly. Most of the delegates found they had more important things to do, and those who did come seemed easily distracted. There *were* unprecedented NGO speeches from the rostrum, and this was a *first*, but it was clear that at that time (today the situation is somewhat different) the official delegates from UN member states were giving only a token and perfunctory nod to the NGO delegates to whom they had reluctantly and temporarily turned over their chamber rostrum.

As implied above, for me personally this day was to constitute one of the most significant turning points in my entire life! I was listening from the balcony, and so also was a woman who was to become my future life's companion, Dorothy Dungan Norvell. After the session we had dinner with some of the other NGO delegates in the UN cafeteria. She was originally from the US Midwest and had attended Antioch College while I was in Yellow Springs in the 40s. Even though neither of us recalled meeting there, we found we had many mutual friends. At the time of our meeting our homes were a continent apart, because she lived in Halifax, Nova Scotia. But we found we had so much in common, beginning with our living in Yellow Springs and being affiliated with Quakers, that everything seemed to fall into place over the next several months. It was a second marriage for both of us, and neither had dreamed of experiencing such a congenial and happy relationship.

We lived for a short time in Berkeley, but we soon moved to Ukiah, California, a small town of about 15,000 about 110 miles north of the Bay Area. For me it was a return to small-community living after getting the sought-after global perspective. We did attend together one more UN Special Session in 1980, this one on global economic issues. But our social-action posture was now focused, though with a global perspective, on a local community of kindred spirits, many of whom had moved to Ukiah for many of the same reasons we did. For each of us it was "downward mobility" as far as high-tech urban living is concerned. It was in that semi-rural setting that I was able to turn in earnest to the "dissertation" I wasn't permitted to submit twenty years before.[10]

That volume gives a more complete explanation for my present life style than space permits in this essay. But I do want to give a hint of what lies behind my particular slant on downward mobility, such as it is. I say "such as it is" because I have never committed myself to downward mobility as such; only as I was forced into it (such as in imposed bankruptcy or imprisonment), as seemed necessary for reasons of social responsibility, or to grope for a more profound perspective on this amazing life. For instance, as noted above, I have never deliberately reduced my income in order to fall outside the tax-filing or tax-owed bracket. I have simply lived my life, engaged in employment, and sought upward mobility (according to my values) insofar as my conscience would allow and my life-drive impelled me. In order to convey to readers the rationale behind this particular slant on downward mobility, I feel I must present some of my views on the nature and source of economic power.

In what follows, therefore, it may seem as if I am switching to the "teaching" mode. But I hope readers will think of the change in style as just a switch to another form of the *reporting* mode. In the immediately

---

10. I refer, of course, to my *Liberating the EARLY American Dream*.

previous pages I have mostly been reporting certain experiences in my life along with my responsive actions and commitments. For most of what follows I will be reporting to you some of the basic beliefs which serve as guides to the actions I take and the commitments I make.

The Nature and Source of Economic Power

As suggested in the opening paragraph of this chapter, we all need a certain amount of the *power* necessary to pursue our purposes: as a minimum, that needed to meet our basic needs for survival. And our various urges and desires serve as cosmic encouragement to actively *pursue* certain purposes, and to generate the *power* necessary to pursue them effectively. But our consciences constantly remind us that others are also thus encouraged. *Thus, the challenge posed in this essay: how do we both pursue and use power "in humane and equitable ways"?* In my efforts to answer that question I've found it helpful to explore the nature of power and its ultimate source. In what follows, that analysis will be limited to a discussion of the nature and source of *economic* power.

Access to Nature's Resources is clearly a necessary condition for generating economic power in human affairs. I think of it this way: we pursue our purposes by employing Nature and Nature's laws. More specifically, we bring about *changes in* "the face of Nature," whether these changes take the form of picking berries off a bush, of forming a shelter so crude it barely rises above the natural landscape, or of constructing huge factories for manufacturing cars by means of robots. In each case, nothing is accomplished without some degree of "access to Nature's Resources."

In the case of either a shelter or a factory, the minimum access needed is a section of the earth's surface on which to put the one or the other. And when certain locations are sought by more than one of us, we are morally challenged to devise ways to "humanely and equitably" share them. But, thus far in human history the dominant practice has been for the most aggressive and acquisitive among us to simply invade a desirable territory and charge the rest of us rent (sometimes in the form of taxes) for using it.

Space is another of Nature's Resources indispensable to developing power to pursue our purposes: space above the earth's surface (into which our buildings and transport vehicles soar ever higher) and space below (out of which we mine ever deeper for precious ores, oils, and gasses). In our cities, buildings compete with each other for surface and space like trees in a forest. And it is in our ever-more-surface-and-space-limited cities that the moral challenge to *share* surface and space "in humane and equitable ways" soars to its greatest heights. As already noted, at present these natural resources are **not** being humanely and equitably shared. And therein lies a large part of the explanation for "the rich getting richer and the poor getting poorer."

In addition to access to Nature's space and earth-surface, no human power can be generated and no human purposes pursued without access to Nature's *substantive* materials: air, water, fertile soil, trees for wood, clay for bricks, sand and calcium for concrete, ores for yielding precious metals, uranium for mixed motives, and fossil fuels in the form of coal, oil, and gasses. Thus, we are morally challenged to devise ways to assure also that access to Nature's *substantive* Resources is humanely and equitably shared. And, again, it is clear that such is not the case in today's world, and that the most aggressive and acquisitive continue to claim monopoly access. To be sure, their monopoly is less and less by way of *overt* seizure; rather, it is by perfectly "legal" means as prescribed by economic and political *structures* which have been largely established and maintained by the most aggressive and acquisitive themselves, and thus are grossly *in*equitable and *in*humane.

In short, what I am suggesting is that the basic *material power* in this world is in the form of access to Nature's Resources, both in their "natural," *un*modified state and in the **modified** form of factories and urban infrastructures which have been built over the generations on and with these **unmodified** Resources. And I am implying, further, that to the extent that the most aggressive and acquisitive achieve a virtual *monopoly* of such access they can hold hostage the rest of the earth's population, both human and non-human, in a form of economic slavery.

This is why I believe that if the right to a fair share of our common heritage of access to Nature's Resources were ever to be acknowledged by the governments of the world we would see a major reversal in the trend of the rich getting richer and the poor poorer. The first step would seem to be to distinguish between (1) that part of productive capital which is the result of a person's personal efforts and (2) that part which is rightly considered our common heritage because no human ever made it or inherited it from someone who did. If the common-heritage part were held in trust, leased out at market value, and the income distributed equitably among the earth's inhabitants, then each person would have a basic income as a right. Such a basic income would provide each person with economic leverage with which to bargain for a *fair* wage in any employment designed to supplement it.[11]

In the meantime, I suggest, the oppressed can become *partially* liberated by gradually shifting their economic concerns from (A) "getting a job" working with Nature's Resources under someone *else's* control to (B) getting ever more access to Natural Resources which they themselves control, whether in the form of land, of productive tools and machines, of factories (in cooperation with others), or of that form of capital which is convertible into any of these (i.e., money which has been honestly earned and frugally saved) and which (until one has accumulated enough to purchase one's own "access") can yield rental income (called "interest") from those who do have access to Nature's Resources and who need such capital for operation and expansion.

Thus, if this analysis is correct, those who continue to depend on labor alone for income will find themselves increasingly competing with a growing number of others for a decreasing number of those jobs which only pay enough to barely survive. On the other hand, those who achieve even a modicum of ownership and control of Nature's Resources will increasingly share in the exhilaration of partnership with Nature directly, rather than only indirectly by way of "a job" in which that relationship is under the control of someone else.

Knowledge about Nature's Laws is the second of the "necessary conditions" noted above for developing *power* in human affairs, whether economic or otherwise. A large part of such knowledge has been discovered by persons in previous generations, for most of whom the basic motive was simply to understand how Nature "works." And insofar as they were successful they simply shared it freely. In most societies a certain amount of such knowledge is made generally available to anyone who will take the time and invest the effort to avail themselves of it. But, again, those who have been ground into poverty by the most aggressive and acquisitive often can't afford to let their children take full advantage of the formal education available. For one thing, their children are often needed to help generate family income.

On the other hand, children of the most aggressive and acquisitive not only inherit an inequitable share of Nature's Resources of land surface and the land's substantive resources, but they also get far greater access to *knowledge* about Nature's laws. Clearly, this resultant near-monopoly in "knowledge-power," added to the near-monopoly in Nature's Resources, tends to make the gap between the most aggressive and

---

11. See Chapter XIV in my *Liberating the EARLY American Dream.*

acquisitive, on the one hand, and the "marginalized," on the other hand, ever wider, especially as a society gets increasingly technological and the *power* which such technology yields to an elite few mounts dramatically.

Thus, it seems to me, there are two devastating consequences which flow from the present state of affairs in the knowledge industries of the world: (1) the research taking place at these universities serves directly the near-monopolistic interests of the most aggressive and acquisitive, and thus tends to make them ever richer as the marginalized get ever poorer; and (2) the various kinds of *power* fed by knowledge-power are impinging on modern life at a *pace* far greater than the pace at which safeguards against its misuse can be developed.

Art and Skill in Applying Nature's Laws is another of the necessary conditions for generating economic power. This condition is traditionally met by engineers, machinists, architects, and other craftspeople. Knowledge about Nature's laws is of little use unless someone is skilled in applying them in working with Nature. Therefore, those who have such skills also have a role to play in bringing about the more humane and equitable use of power. They can refuse their services to morally questionable pursuits while offering them to socially responsible ones.

Freelance craftspersons have *some* control over who benefits from their services. Those who work for a large firm have very little control, A firm which does contract work can exercise some moral judgment in turning down some jobs and accepting others. But products made for the impersonal marketplace end up with the highest bidder regardless of the moral qualities of the use to which they will be put. And the farther that marketplace extends geographically and culturally the less the control. Thus, the present moves from local to global markets will diminish still more the extent to which those who participate in those markets can exercise social responsibility.

Art and Skill in Trading has an increasing impact on the development and use of economic power. As an increasing number of goods are sold to traders in the role of "middlemen" between producer and consumer they will have increasing power to determine who produces what for whom. Even now, the traders of the world, especially in the financial markets, exercise tremendous power for good or ill. At present, their power is mostly used "for ill." There are two basic reasons for this: (1) their decisions are almost exclusively determined by what purchases and sales will yield the greatest profit, with almost no consideration given to moral factors, and (2) their vested interest lies in speeding up the *pace* of trading and exchange as much as possible; and we have noted the consequences which an out-of-control pace is already having on quality of life.

Trading in international currencies is an increasingly major activity in the financial markets. As the fortunes of whole economies rise and fall, the values of their currencies in the global marketplace follow, and therewith profits and losses for those who hold them. Such trading can feed back to influence confidence in the government issuing it, and thus in its economy and the well being of the people who depend on it. I see no good solution to the hazards for innocent people in this state of affairs other by bringing about the basic changes in economic and political structures suggested in this chapter.

Art and Skill in Working with Others constitutes the fifth of the "necessary conditions" which I perceive as needed for developing the power to pursue one's purposes. There is very little anyone can do without the cooperation of others. Here, also, however, those who have a monopolistic advantage in securing access to Nature's Resources and to knowledge about Nature's laws have a major cultural advantage in learning how to work with others who are in positions of power. The art and skill of working with others is, of course, a great advantage at any power level, but when the already powerful join with others like themselves the sum-total power generated is far greater than can be generated by the joining of those who are basically disempowered.

The Role of Economic and Political Structure in generating economic and political power is the most fundamental of all. Of the two, political structure is the more fundamental because it determines what is enforced. It is for this reason that I have placed so much stress on structural change in these areas. As noted, suggested changes in political structure are beyond the scope of this chapter[12]. But I will say here that it must be based on true federation, from local to global, of genuine communities, where people know each other personally and are committed to a high level of justice toward each other.

I have also concluded that the cost of governing should be met according to a very simple principle. A person should be charged for the cost of governing to the extent -- and only to the extent -- that s/he behaves in ways that require governing. It follows from this that businesses, especially hazardous ones, should generally be charged much more heavily than individuals. Large corporations, especially multinationals, should carry the bulk of the burden. In applying this principle the costs passed on to consumers of goods produced and distributed by socially and environ-

---

12. This matter is a major focus in my forthcoming book, *Toward Sustainable Justice, Local to Global.*

mentally hazardous businesses would be high. But those passed on by socially and ecologically benign businesses would be minimal. There would be no tax on income as such, or on property or any other kind of wealth, except as those holding it required governing. For instance, since power tends to corrupt, some accumulations of power in the form of wealth may have to be governed.

There would, as noted, be lease charges for using parts of our common heritage, but these would not (contrary to what is advocated by current followers of Henry George) be applied to financing governing. As noted above, the income from such leasing would be distributed to the residents of the world as a right.

Fairness in such distribution would be determined by governments, from local to global, based in communities of persons committed to justice and familiar enough with each other to reach consensus among their various senses of justice.

This would be very difficult to accomplish within the existing U.S. political structure. In that political marketplace the competition is for getting a majority of the votes, where any majority will do, even that of the most self-serving. So, the appeal from politicians tends to be voting according to self-interest rather than to "justice for all." The result is that political power and its accompanying economic power goes to those who, out of *their* self interests in power can afford to hire the most skillful manipulators of such votes. Such manipulation becomes easier the farther we move away from genuine community toward an impersonal mass society such as characterizes our present so-called "world community" of territorial states. Again, a major moral weakness in the U.S. Constitution is its favoring such a mass society over one characterized by a federation of genuine, caring communities. And it can be shown that this constitution was designed by its founders to do just that.[13]

Is The Goal "Realistic"?

Throughout this chapter I have concluded that the goal of achieving more humane and equitable economic and political structures depends on individual and group commitment to justice as revealed by sense of justice and as urged upon us "for conscience sake." The ordinary person can be appealed to in this way, because they don't question the credibility of their consciences or senses of justice.

---

13. See especially Chapters XIII and XXI of my *Liberating the EARLY American Dream.* See, also, *Manufacturing Consent, the Political Economy of the Mass Media,* by Edward S. Herman and Noam Chomsky, Pantheon Books, NY, 1988.

But this chapter is designed to also appeal to intellectuals in the knowledge industries of the world, especially those researchers who constantly feed knowledge-power to the upwardly mobile corporate elite of the military industrial complexes. Many of these researchers, and those influenced by them, have built their specialty careers on the assumption that the universe they inhabit is nothing but a great clock-like machine which operates by immutable laws. In that paradigm, so solidly entrenched for the past three centuries, since Newton, in the very foundation of all their professional, scientific thinking, if not in their practical lives, all conscious entities, including themselves, can only be seen as "epiphenomena" with no future beyond their present, doomed-to-deteriorate machine-like bodies. Thus, according to this paradigm, the sense of free choice which we "epiphenomena" have must be an illusion, and the voice of conscience and sense of justice merely the result of "social conditioning."

Yet we all have our personal experiences with sense of justice. It is a *sense* which emerges early in the life of a child. Anyone who works with young children hears the telling phrase over and over again: "That's not fair"! To be sure, what *constitutes* fairness is influenced by "social conditioning" as well as personal experience, but the recipient of all such influences -- that elemental sense of justice --is prior. If it were not prior there would be nothing to influence. Thus, true justice *requires* that all relevant and ever-changing factors be considered in determining what truly is just in each particular situation with particular persons and communities. It is only when all such factors are considered, such as in the deliberations of a jury, that a determination of true justice can be arrived at. Therefore, the mere fact that sense of justice and conscience is influenced by social circumstances in no way discredits them; rather, it is an essential feature of each of them. To imply otherwise shows a lack of appreciation for their true nature and function.

Even though this mechanistic paradigm has no credibility today among modern physicists, as long as it is not replaced by a credible alternative it remains the one which dominates most knowledge-industry specialists. For many it still provides a way to rationalize away personal conscience.

In fact, one modern physicist has suggested an alternative paradigm which posits a central, even determining, role for "consciousness" while still escaping personal responsibility. He does so by positing a quantum-physics variation of the long-standing Advaita metaphysic in which our individual identities, and thus consciences, are viewed as illusory, temporary parts of a single, universal "Brahman" who makes all decisions.[14]

There is, however, an alternative paradigm emerging: *the systems paradigm.* It has developed gradually over the past half century. It is manifested in the ecology and environmental movements because one of the "systems" it provides for is the ecosystem. Biological organisms can themselves be considered systems. In fact, this emerging paradigm might be named the biological paradigm if it were not for the fact that not all systems are biological ones.

In 1975 a philosophically minded physicist named Fritjof Capra wrote a book which gave scientific credibility to the systems paradigm. It was called *The Tao of Physics,* and it was followed by another, *The Turning Point,* in 1982. A recently produced feature-length film, called *Mind Walk,* is based on the latter book. It and the books show how "systems theory" and the resulting systems paradigm can be used to address both laboratory and common sense facts far better than the old mechanistic paradigm. The latter is still useful in designing and building houses and many other things in the macro world, but the new *systems paradigm* has far more universal application.

One species of "system" determines the development and reproduction of trees, another of dog bodies, another of human bodies, another, supposedly, of the eco*system* as a whole. Systems transcend classical mechanisms via the flexibility revealed in scientific laws by quantum physics. Since the development of this revolutionary science, the most fundamental laws of physics are no longer seen as strictly "deterministic." This means that a *great many* future patterns of events are *potentially* possible as followers of current events. Put another way, past events haven't "determined" present events, and present events won't "determine" future events.

Quantum physics provides for *triggering* at the level of *in*determinate electrons and other micro entities into any of a great variety of manifestations from the potential state to the actualized state, where they become parts of event sequences, each one having been only one of a great variety of *potential* sequences before being triggered into actuality. Such triggering becomes possible because at the "potential" level of such micro activity there are no physical objects as we know them. They exist there only *potentially.* The particular physical form each potential entity (such an electron in wave-form as distinct from particle form) will take when triggered into physical actualization will depend on the needs of a

---

14. *The Self-Aware Universe, how consciousness creates the material world,* by Amit Goswami, G.P. Putnam, NY, 1993

system. If a "system" encounters nothing unusual in its operation the manifestations which will take place will be, presumably, those which have the highest probability. But unusual circumstances might "trigger" unlikely manifestations as a way of rescuing a system from a malfunction which would otherwise occur. There are, of course, limits to such rescuing operations, but the systems paradigm provides for such rescuing operations in ways which the mechanistic paradigm did not and does not.

The human brain can be considered a "system" where such triggering takes place. The brain functions in certain predictable ways and in certain unpredictable ways. Presumably, the electron-like particles in my brain which "trigger" the sequence of events resulting in my fingers moving over the keys of my console have first been "triggered" *into* physical manifestation as particles *from* a potential-only, probability state. The systems paradigm provides no explanation for what "causes" the triggering. It merely implies that this combination of triggering takes place on the occasion of our choices. Apparently, the "system" in accordance with which my brain operates is somehow "programmed" to be sensitive to my conscious choices from among options which occur to me. The result is that my fingers move in ways designed to implement my choices.

The mechanistic paradigm would not allow for such triggering activity. And I'm not sure the systems paradigm would. The reason is that the systems paradigm doesn't seem to have any place for genuine conscious choice. It can't have, because it doesn't seem to have any place for those conscious persons which you and I know ourselves to be by direct self-awareness! Thus, there is no place for all those conscious experiences of pleasure, pain, grief, hope, fear, excitement, compassion, love, hate, -- nor for those commitments, and actions which make up meaningful life as you, my reader, and I know it. In the systems paradigm you and I as self-conscious beings still seem to emerge as "epiphenomena"!

It is interesting to note, for instance, that after Sonya, the physicist in the *Mind Walk* movie, has presented the systems paradigm the poet in the group makes the following telling statement:

"So, tell me, Sonya, where are all of us in there, the real people, with their qualities, their longings, their weaknesses? Where are you in there, Sonya? I feel just as much reduced being called a system as a clock."

Is this part of the dialogue meant to imply that Capra is also questioning the adequacy of the systems paradigm?

In any case, if we are to have a paradigm which gives the kind of credibility we noted the need for at the beginning of this final section, credibility for *conscience*, and for *sense of justice*, then we must transcend not only the mechanistic paradigm but the systems paradigm as well. In what follows I will suggest such a transcending paradigm. But first I will introduce some important preparatory concepts.

The new insights into the nature of the physical world provided by quantum physics suggests that what we perceive via our very selective senses as solid physical objects turn out, under close inspection, to be *overwhelmingly* empty space. Imagining oneself moving around in it, it would be hard to find anything "solid" at all. In fact, even the "solid" particles, like an electron particle, turns out to be a mere "probability wave" when not being "observed." So, the first new concept we need is that of the entire physical universe as a combination of (1) *actual* experiences of manifestations in physical form -- such as of an electron particle -- and (2) *potential* manifestations -- such as a potential electron particle, where .the likelihood of each of the various potential manifestations can be expressed mathematically as probability waves.

Add to this new perspective the fact that the only way we know any of this is by way of our conscious experiences as sentient beings; that is, as the conscious persons you and I know ourselves to be by immediate self awareness and it becomes easier to bridge the gap between intangible *persons* and the increasingly intangible and wave-like physical world. In short, the reality we know most directly and immediately is the reality of personhood -- most directly as oneself but also as others persons whom we communicate with, are friendly with, feel compassion for, and love!

One more new concept; that of a *carrier wave*. Every radio or TV station is assigned a carrier wave of a specified frequency on which to send its communications. Those doing so by varying the amplitude are called AM stations. FM stations do so by varying frequency. But whether AM or FM, each station must send its communications on a "carrier wave."

Now visualize the entire physical universe as a kind of carrier wave, sent to us by some cosmic entity as a very special kind of communication. Think of it as fundamentally in wave form, as partially revealed by quantum physics, but with some parts temporarily manifested in various physical forms such as we build physical structures with and on. Think of this carrier-wave-like universe as a communication inviting us to use it as a vehicle on which to send our communications to each other, and think of communication among conscious beings of various degrees of conscious awareness cosmically and here on earth as the *meaning* of life!

Obviously, a cosmic entity capable of sending such a carrier-wave communication is far beyond our imagination. Perhaps its source is not so much a single being as a cosmic community of beings. In any case, such being(s) must be experiencing an extremely high level of conscious awareness. And the sensitivity implicit in such awareness must be especially heightened in sending us the kind of communications we get by way of sense of justice and conscience. Consider the level of sensitivity a parent needs in giving moral guidance to a child while still allowing the child considerable freedom. How much more sensitivity is implicit in the moral guidance communicated by way of sense of justice and conscience to billions of human beings on this planet alone!

For the final, all-inclusive, cosmic visualization, visualize all reality as comprised of (1) conscious beings -- of great variety in conscious awareness -- and (2) their communications to each other. Thus, the duality which Rene Descartes and others tried to reconcile are so reconciled. The basic duality inherent in meaningful and purposeful social life as we know it consists in conscious beings, on the one hand (#1 above), and, on the other, their communications to each other. Without such duality there could be no meaningful relationships among sentient beings. So, we need not be concerned about. We can rejoice in it!

Our participation as humans is made possible because of the carrier-wave communication sent for our use by more consciously aware beings. We are encouraged to engage in "upward mobility" to our hearts content provided we remain within the moral bounds indicated by sense of justice and urged by conscience. In this paradigm our physical bodies are sent to us as part of the cosmic carrier-wave communication, along with all the various systems allowed for in the systems paradigm. Thus, the paradigm I am suggesting includes, while transcending, both the mechanistic paradigm and the systems paradigm. *I call it the persons-in-community paradigm.*

We achieve our identities *as persons* by way of the choices, especially the commitments, we make. It is our commitments which give us our basic identity, because commitments are a special kind of choice. Commitments extend into the future. They are themselves generators of systems. We count on each other's commitment systems in making our personal choices and commitments in much the same way we count on other systems we identify in life, some being much more reliable than others.

It is by way of *common* commitments that social *structures* are built. And humane and equitable structures are built with *common* commitments to justice as a minimum, thus making possible relationships based on friendship, compassion, and other kinds of beautiful "communication."

We note that the very possibility of choices and commitments depends on there being that crucial, triggering flexibility in the brain parts of our bodies. Without this triggering flexibility, brain changes, and resulting triggered bodily movements which we take so much for granted, couldn't happen. Yet, without a large amount of immutability in scientific laws and systems of various kinds we wouldn't be able to count on them in implementing our commitments. We need both rigidity and flexibility.

There is, of course, a price to pay for the reliability of this combination. The price is in terms of accidents, sometimes tragic, as the result of the working of natural and human laws, systems, and human choices which are not completely predictable. But this is the price which we sentient beings must pay for the privilege of participating in the cosmic drama which is unfolding.

Having removed the theoretical barrier to considering our consciences and our senses of justice as genuine moral messengers, we can take a fresh look at what they tell us about cosmic support for justice. As for our senses of justice, it seems to me they do provide evidence of such cosmic support. Even stronger evidence is implicit in our felt consciences as they urge us to live *according to* sense of justice in our lives. With such strong evidence of cosmic support for justice, it wouldn't make cosmic moral sense to let those suffering gross injustice in this life -- especially the ones suffering from "accidents" derived from the cosmic order itself, -- to go uncompensated in some future life. Nor would a just cosmic Being (or Beings) invite fellow conscious beings to the kind of exciting life which we know this life can be at times only to cut off conscious awareness completely at the death of our bodies.

In closing, I can honestly say that in living with this persons-in-community paradigm for several decades I have had it sufficiently confirmed in my experience and by scientific evidence to be persuaded of its credibility, of the credibility of both my sense of justice and of any pangs of conscience I feel alerting me to it, and of commitment to justice on the part of whatever is the cosmic source of all of the above. So, I close by urging those who are aware of the collapse of the mechanistic paradigm, but have not yet found a credible alternative, to consider the person-in-community paradigm suggested here.

Finally, I suggest that the most fundamental way to test the hypothesis that there *is* cosmic support for justice is to accept with reverent appreciation any felt cosmic support for upward mobility while being committed to undertake downward mobility "for conscience sake." I have found that confirmation of the person-in-community paradigm has increased according to the depth of such a commitment in my life. And implicit in that paradigm is a prediction of the same result for anyone else.

EPILOGUE

As I write this Epilogue I imagine myself communicating with two groups of people -- those of you who have read the book and those of you who always read the end of a book before deciding whether to read the rest of it.

Perhaps all of you would be interested in the responses of a few people who read an earlier draft.

The first reader of the manuscript who had not met any of the authors was Linda McKillip Barnes, then a school bus driver in Arizona. We felt we'd been understood when she wrote, "What a wonderful book -- a real eye opener. Just think of the impact on our whole world if each one of us who has too much were to conscientiously work at our own versions of downward mobility."

Margaret Whittle, who is active in environmental concerns in Australia and who read this book while travelling in North America, wrote, "My job takes me all over the southwest of the state from Perth to Albany and I work with environmentally aware people who are making big strides in working towards sustainable lifestyles." She asked for news of the book's publication because, as she put it, "You have a market here already."

Oliver Loud, a science professor emeritus of Antioch College, Yellow Springs, Ohio, suggested that there is an important point which we, the authors, had not made explicit. "One must be free so that the threat of economic reprisal does not diminish one's political courage. Those who testify in your anthology are perhaps beyond consciousness of any such deterrent as economic reprisal, because of the strength of their convictions from their earliest years as concerned citizens." That is true for some of us. I think especially of Juanita Nelson who has told us that as a teenager she sat in every car of a segregated train during the late 1930's, more than

20 years before the civil rights sit-ins of the 60's, and who has led a life of political courage ever since.

Simple living helps to create the freedom to act with integrity, but it is not a complete answer. Having income from one's fair share of the common heritage of nature's resources, as urged in Al Andersen's chapter, would be another important factor in giving everyone an economic base from which to act with political courage.

Oliver Loud went on to say, "As you surely intended, the book's effectiveness is enhanced by the variety of circumstances and choices represented in the 'true life stories'. Another source of the book's effectiveness is the way in which living more simply served simultaneously such objectives as living more richly *and* denying one's support to abhorrent public policies *and* lessening one's adverse impact as a consumer on the biosphere *and* diminishing one's complicity with pervasive evil *and*, for good measure, increasing one's investment in positive efforts to win diverse increments of social justice."

We, the writers, realize that, of course, we haven't answered all the questions nor solved all the problems of the three immense challenges I spoke of in the Prologue: to save our planet, to live peaceably. and to be fair. We're working on it. We presume that you are, too. We hope that these accounts of our experiences help you in *your* efforts.

Dorothy Andersen

RELATED BOOKS

The following are books about simple living and books about the state of the world which caused some of the authors of this book to conclude that simple living in the industrialized countries is part of the solution to the problems of injustice, war, and destruction of the environment in the world.

Alfred F. Andersen, *Liberating the Early American Dream, A Way to Transcend Capitalism and Communism Nonviolently*; Rutgers University, New Brunswick, NJ, Transaction Books, 1985 (available from the author)

Wendell Berry
  What Are People For, San Francisco, North Point Press, 1990
  The Unsettling of America, New York, Avon, 1978

Lester Brown, and others of Worldwatch Institute, *State of the World*, annual reports 1984 to 93; N.Y., W. W. Norton

Virginia Coover, et al, *Resource Manual for a Living Revolution*; Philadelphia, New Society Publishers, 1977

J. Morrison Davidson, *Concerning Four Precursors of Henry George*; Millwood, NY, Kennikat Press, 1971

Paul Ekins, ed.; *The Living Economy*; London, Routledge & Kegan, 1986; A TOES (The Other Economic Summit) book

Duane Elgin, *Voluntary Simplicity*; N.Y., Morrow Publishing Company, 1981

Melissa Everett, *Breaking Ranks*; Santa Cruz, CA, New Society Publishers, 1988

202   Downward Mobility for Conscience Sake

Richard A Falk, *Toward A Just World Order;* Boulder, CO, Westview Press, 1982

Richard J. Foster, *Freedom of Simplicity;* New York, Harper & Row, 1981

Amit Goswami, *The Self-Aware Universe . . .How Consciousness Creates the Material World;* G.P. Putnam & Sons, NY, 1993

Henry George, *Progress and Poverty;* New York, Robert Schalkenbach Foundation, 1979

Susan George, *How the Other Half Dies;* New York, Penguin Books, 1976

Maurice Goldsmith, ed, *Science and Social Responsibility;* London, Whitefriars Press Ltd., 1975; 23 contributors, mostly English

James P. Grant, *The State of the World's Children,* annual report of UNICEF United Nations Children's Fund, U.K., Oxford University Press, 1989-93

Charles Gray, *Toward a Nonviolent Economics,* Eugene, OR, 1989. (available from author)

Hazel Henderson, *Politics of the Solar Age: Alternatives to Economics;* Indianapolis, Indiana, Knowledge Systems, 1988

William Ernest Hocking, *Science and the Idea of God;* Chapel Hill, U. of N.C. Press, 1944

Joseph Holland and Peter Henriot, *Social Analysis* revised edition; Washington, DC, Center of Concern, 1983

Rajni Kathari, *Footsteps Into The Future;* N.Y., Macmillan Publishing Co., 1976

Louis Kelso, *Two Factor Theory;* N.Y., Random House, 1967

Clark Kerr, *The Uses of the University;* Cambridge, MA, Harvard U. Press, 1963

Doris Longacre, *Living More With Less;* Herald Press, 1980

Mildred J. Loomis, *Alternative Americas;* New York, Universe Books, 1982

Susan Meeker-Lowery, *Economics as If the Earth Really Mattered;* Philadelphia, New Society Publishers, 1988

Rigoberta Menchu, *I, Rigoberta Menchu: An Indian Woman in Guatemala*, Introduction by Elizabeth Burgos-Debray; Routledge, Chapman and Hall, 1984

Lewis Mumford, *Technics and Civilization;* N. Y., Harcourt, Brace & World Inc., 1934

Anne Near, *A Dubious Journey*, Oakland, CA, Hereford Press, 1993

Marc Nerfin, ed. *IFDA Dossier*, bi-monthly periodical; 4 place du marche, 1260 Nyon, Switzerland, International Foundation for Development Alternatives

Schumacher, E.F., *Small is Beautiful;* N.Y., Harper & Row, 1975

Scott and Helen Nearing
Living the Good Life: How to Live Sanely and Simply in a Troubled World; New York, Schocken Books, 1971.
Continuing the Good Life: Half a Century of Homesteading; New York, Schocken Books, 1979.

Juanita Nelson, *A Matter of Freedom and Other Writings*, Peace and Gladness Press, P.O. Box 11478, San Francisco, CA 94101, 1988

Michael Parenti, *Inventing Reality: Politics and the Mass Media;* New York, St. Martin Press, 1985

Judith Plant, Editor, *Healing the Wounds: The Promise of Ecofeminism;* Philadelphia, New Society Publishers, 1989

James Robertson, *Future Wealth: a New Economics for the 21st Century;* N.Y., The Bootstrap Press, 1990

Theodore Roszak, *The Making of a Counter Culture;* New York, Doubleday & Co., 1969.

Mark Satin
New Age Politics; New York, Dell Publications, 1979.
New Options for America, Fresno State University Press, CA, 1991

E. F. Schumacher, *Small is Beautiful: Economics As If People Mattered;* N.Y., Harper and Row, 1975

Simple Living Collective, *Taking Charge;* New York, Bantam Books, 1977

Hedrick Smith, *The Power Game;* N.Y., Random House, 1988.

Thoreau, Henry David, *Walden, Civil Disobedience;* N.Y., Harper &

Row, 1958

Tightwad Gazette, RR1, Box 3570, Leeds, ME 04263

Ernest Volkman and Blaine Baggett, *Secret Intelligence*; N.Y., Doubleday, 1989

Paul Wachtel, *The Poverty of Affluence: A Psychological Portrait of the American Way of Life*; Philadelphia, New Society Publishers, 1988

Howard Zinn, *A People's History of the United States*; N.Y., Harper and Row, 1981

Addresses of the Authors

Dorothy Andersen
3120 N. Romera Road, #39
Tucson, AZ 85705

Al Andersen
3120 N. Romera Road, #39
Tucson, AZ 85705

Judi Buchman and Richa
448 Pleasant St. S.E.
Grand Rapids, MI 49503

Ken and Peg Champney
Box 427
Yellow Springs, OH 45387

Kathy Epling
Box 111
Piercy, CA 95467

Charles Gray
888 Almaden
Eugene, OR 97402

Jo-ann Jaeckel
Box 464
Ukiah, CA 95482

Anne Near
809 W. Clay Street
Ukiah, CA 95482

Juanita Nelson
The Bean Patch
Keets Road
Deerfield, MA 01342

Barbara Terry
750 Clear Lake Ave.
Lakeport, CA 95453

Additional copies of *Downwardly Mobile for Conscience Sake* can be ordered from Tom Paine Institute, 3120 N. Romero Rd. #39, Tucson, AZ 85705.

Clip here . . . .

Please send _____copies of *Downwardly Mobile for Conscience Sake* to

_____

(Name)

_____

(Street and number)

_____

(City, State, and Zip code)

_____copies @ 10 each_____

Shipping @ $1.50, first book, and .50 each addiitonal_____

Total _____

Make check or money order payable to Tom Paine Institute.

. . . .

Please send _____copies of *Downwardly Mobile for Conscience Sake* to

_____

(Name)

_____

(Street and number)

_____

(City, State, and Zip code)

_____copies @ $10 each_____

Shipping @ $1.50, first book, and .50 each additional_____

Total _____

Make check or money order payable to Tom Paine Institute.